D1141304

ELIZABETHAN AND OTHER ESSAYS

SIR SIDNEY LEE

From a portrait by Professor William Rothenstein

ELIZABETHAN AND OTHER ESSAYS

BY

SIR SIDNEY LEE

SELECTED AND EDITED

BY

FREDERICK S. BOAS, M.A., LL.D.
PRESIDENT OF THE ELIZABETHAN LITERARY SOCIETY

AMS PRESS
NEW YORK

This reprint has been authorized by
the Clarendon Press Oxford
Reprinted from the edition of 1929, Oxford
First AMS EDITION published 1970
Manufactured in the United States of America

International Standard Book Number: 0-404-03928-6
Library of Congress Number: 78-133811

AMS PRESS INC.
NEW YORK, N.Y. 10003

TO THE
ELIZABETHAN LITERARY SOCIETY
OF WHICH
SIR SIDNEY LEE
WAS PRESIDENT
1889–1926

PREFACE

IT has been thought desirable by Sir Sidney Lee's literary executors, Sir Frederick Macmillan and Mr. P. A. Barnett, that a selection of his Lectures and Essays should be published. They have done me the honour of asking me to prepare such a volume and see it through the press. Lee's editorial connexion for nearly thirty years with *The Dictionary of National Biography*, and his concentration during the last period of his life upon his monumental *Biography* of King Edward VII, have tended to divert attention from his literary and academic work. The latter circumstance also helps to account for the fact that no literary manuscripts suitable for publication were found among his papers after his death.

Three volumes of lectures and papers by Lee appeared during his lifetime, *Great Englishmen of the Sixteenth Century*, lectures delivered in America (1904); *Shakespeare and the Modern Stage, with other Essays*, mainly reprinted from periodicals (1906); *The French Renaissance in England*, lectures delivered at Oxford (1910). But there remain uncollected a number of addresses and essays, from 1907 to 1922, including some that are out of print and others that are not easily accessible. From these I have made a selection for the present volume, with the omission of some passages that were only of temporary application, with the addition of a few bracketed notes, and with some silent changes in punctuation. I have arranged the contents in three sections, but, as the Introduction attempts to show, they have an underlying unity.

I have to thank all those who have facilitated my work. The late Sir John Murray permitted the reprint of 'The

Place of English Literature in the Modern University', and of 'Ovid and Shakespeare's Sonnets' from the *Quarterly Review* centenary number, of which he presented a copy. The Council of the Modern Humanities Research Association permitted the reprint of the Inaugural Address on 'Modern Language Research'; the Executive Committee of the English Association did likewise with the pamphlets on 'The Perspective of Biography' and 'The Impersonal Aspect of Shakespeare's Art'; and the Council of the British Academy with the lecture on 'Shakespeare and the Italian Renaissance'. The Syndics of the Cambridge University Press permitted the reprint of the Leslie Stephen lecture on 'Principles of Biography' and presented a copy; so also did Messrs. Charles Scribner's Sons of New York with the four articles on 'The Call of the West' in their Magazine. Messrs. Constable permitted the reprint of the article on 'Tasso and Shakespeare's England' from the *Anglo-Italian Review*; and the editor of *The Times* that of the articles on 'Shakespeare and the Inquisition', and the reproduction of the facsimile of a page from the censored Valladolid Second Folio.

The frontispiece is from a portrait of Lee, drawn in the last months of his life, by Professor William Rothenstein, Principal of the Royal College of Art. I have to thank Professor Rothenstein for permission to reproduce this drawing, which was presented by friends of Lee to East London College. The Principal of the College, Mr. J. L. Hatton, has kindly placed at the disposal of the Delegates of the Press a photograph (reproduced facing p. 84) presented to him by Lee for inclusion in a private volume relating to the College commemoration of the Shakespeare Tercentenary in 1916.

Throughout the preparation of this volume I have had the advantage of the advice of Mr. P. A. Barnett, to which I owe much; valuable suggestions have also been made by Sir Charles Firth who, in particular, drew my attention to 'The Call of the West' articles, which had never been reprinted in this country; my wife has contributed to a work of *pietas* by compiling the Index.

Finally, thanks are due to the Delegates of the Clarendon Press for undertaking the publication of these Lectures and Essays. It was for them that Lee accomplished one of his most notable labours, the great series of Shakespearian facsimiles and the census of the extant copies of the First Folio. It was as a Balliol undergraduate that he began his literary career, and it was at the installation of one of his Balliol contemporaries, Lord Curzon, as Chancellor of the University, that he was made an honorary Doctor of Literature. It is fitting that this volume should bear the Oxford imprint.

F. S. B.

WIMBLEDON.

October 1929.

CONTENTS

List of Illustrations xii

Introduction xiii

I

PRESIDENTIAL AND ACADEMIC ADDRESSES

The Place of English Literature in the Modern
University 1

Modern Language Research 19

Principles of Biography 31

The Perspective of Biography 58

II

STUDIES IN SHAKESPEARE AND THE RENAISSANCE

The Impersonal Aspect of Shakespeare's Art . 85

Ovid and Shakespeare's Sonnets 116

Shakespeare and the Italian Renaissance . . 140

Tasso and Shakespeare's England . . . 169

Shakespeare and the Inquisition: a Spanish Second
Folio 184

III

THE CALL OF THE WEST: AMERICA AND ELIZABETHAN ENGLAND

The Example of Spain 199

The Teaching of the Huguenots . . . 232

The American Indian in Elizabethan England . 263

The Path to Jamestown 302

Index 339

LIST OF ILLUSTRATIONS

Sir Sidney Lee. From a portrait drawn in 1926 by Professor William Rothenstein, in the Library of East London College (University of London)

Frontispiece

Sir Sidney Lee. From a photograph included in a Shakespeare Tercentenary Commemoration Volume, 1916 . . . . *facing p.* 84

Facsimile of a censored page of *King Henry VIII* in a copy of the Shakespeare Second Folio in the English College at Valladolid. From *The Times,* 10 April, 1922 . . . . *facing p.* 192

INTRODUCTION

THE opening section of this volume contains four lectures delivered between 1911 and 1918 which illustrate Sir Sidney Lee's attitude and approach to the two subjects which formed his life-long interest, and which for him were never wholly separated, Literature and Biography. His earliest essays, published in *The Gentleman's Magazine* (February and October, 1880) while he was a Balliol undergraduate, 'The Original of Shylock' and 'A New Study of *Love's Labour's Lost*', were concerned with the biographical background of Shakespearian investigation. His appointment in 1883 as sub-editor of *The Dictionary of National Biography* (of which he became successively joint, and sole, editor) accentuated, at a critical point in his career, the biographical side of his activities, though his own articles were chiefly on Elizabethan literary figures, including that on Shakespeare in the 51st volume. This was expanded into his *Life of William Shakespeare* in 1898, and was rewritten and much enlarged in 1915. So also his article on Queen Victoria in the first supplement to the *D. N. B.* (1901) was expanded into a *Life* (1902); and that on King Edward VII (1912) was the basis of the *Biography* in two volumes, of which the first appeared in 1925, and the second after his death.

But neither Lee's preoccupation with biography nor his bibliographical labours on the Clarendon Press facsimiles of the Shakespearian First Folio, the Poems and *Pericles* (1902–6), diminished his interest in the study of the general aspects of English literature, especially in its relations to classical and continental literature. In his Introduction to a new and rearranged edition (1904) of Arber's *Elizabethan Sonnets* he emphasized in strong fashion the debt of these Sonnets to foreign models. In *The French Renaissance in England* (1910) he illustrated from another and wider point of view the features in

Elizabethan literature for which the sources had to be sought across the Channel.

In an address on 'The Study of English Literature' given at Toynbee Hall in 1893 he had shown how eager he was to popularize this subject. When the English Association was founded in 1906 he welcomed it whole-heartedly and acted as Chairman of its first general meeting on 12 January 1907.

'The Association', he stated, 'hopes to provide some means of direct intercourse—some machinery for the exchange of views—among all who have faith in the power of English literature to humanize life and learning. From the elementary school to the university, we are anxious that the obligation should be recognized to treat the proper writing of English, the proper speaking of English, the proper appreciation and respect for English literature, as not less but more important acquirements than any other that can come of educational training.'

This statement shows that Lee's interest comprised not only the study of literature, but the training in expression, both written and spoken. An opportunity of advancing all these was offered when comparatively late in life he entered the academic sphere on his appointment to a University of London Chair of English Language and Literature at East London College. His inaugural lecture, delivered on 2 October 1913, opens this volume. It is a comprehensive survey, proving that Lee's width of outlook had not been limited by his specialist labours, of 'The Place of English Literature in the Modern University'. He deals in turn with criticism, the history of literature, philology, and composition, and ends with a plea for 'a large and well-ordered store-house of books' as 'the laboratory of the English student'. A passage in his *apologia* for 'criticism' or 'exegesis' goes to the heart of his conception of what the academic study of literature should be:

'Literary criticism is in the university no light-hearted expression of the personal likes and dislikes of professor or student. It applies scholarly, even scientific, principles of inquiry to the intellectual and emotional phenomena within its sphere. It aims at determining the true force and value of literary matter and manner. . . .

'The reading of books in a literary School must be no lazy sauntering along a level or a downhill path. It should be a bracing exercise. It is a wrestling with ideas greater than any we can create for ourselves; it is a striving to get into close touch with thought and fancy, which are above our capacity to invent.'[1]

Lee also laid stress, as would be expected, on the importance of 'comparative criticism', and declared that 'some study of foreign literature' should 'form an integral part of a sound critical analysis of English literary achievement'. This theme is further developed in his Presidential Address which inaugurated, on 19 October 1918, the Modern Language Research Association, now known as the Modern Humanities Research Association. Lee shared acutely the fear felt by many in the closing days of the war, that the pressure of material needs after the mighty convulsion would lead to a monopoly of individual and national energies by scientific research 'to the exclusion or the disparagement of research in humanistic studies'. He was therefore glad to give a benediction to a new society concerned with research in the humanistic field, and specially aiming at international co-operation, thus 'smoothing the path of that League of Nations', which was still only in the air in October 1918. His concrete suggestions are still of interest, but they are less important than the spirit which inspires the Address. It may be taken as typical of the many inaugural, ceremonial, or commemorative addresses for which Lee was probably more in request than any other contemporary scholar. Among them, to give a few instances, were the addresses at the unveiling of the Shakespeare Memorial in Southwark Cathedral on 4 November 1912; at the opening of the Shakespeare Exhibition at the Grafton Galleries in aid of the Red Cross, 19 January 1917; and as a 'prologue' to the jubilee year celebration of the Sunday Shakespeare Society on 20 January 1924. To the preparation of these

[1] pp. 6–7.

c

occasional discourses Lee gave the same conscientious care
as to weightier enterprises.

Holding a special place among such discourses are the
Leslie Stephen lecture on 'Principles of Biography' (1911)
and the English Association Presidential Address on 'The
Perspective of Biography' (1918). In them Lee sets forth
his convictions on the subject with which 'the main
business of my life has brought me into practical touch'.
Both discourses rest on the same fundamental ideas, and
(as Lee acknowledged) contain some repetition. But it is
an advantage, as I think, to be able to read them here side
by side, for they approach their theme from differing
angles, and they vary considerably in their illustrations.
In Lee's eyes biography existed to satisfy 'the commemorative instinct'; its aim is to hand down 'the history of
individual men and women, to transmit enduringly their
character and exploits'.[1] And in the two lectures he is
primarily concerned with the tendencies and conditions
that 'hamper or promote the production of sound and
useful biography'. The epithets are characteristic. Truth
and utility, in its higher sense, which does not imply
edification, were to be the biographer's objects; artistic
portraiture and literary style were to be subordinated to
these. Otherwise we may get not 'efficient biography'
but a 'character', not a 'life' but 'a nebulous impressionist
study'.[2]

Probably Lee would have classed as 'characters' the
brilliantly drawn portraits by one of the most eminent of
his successors as Leslie Stephen lecturer, Mr. Lytton
Strachey; and the dazzling Gallic arabesques of Monsieur
André Maurois, who also at Cambridge, as Clark lecturer
in Trinity College, has recently spoken on 'Aspects of
Biography'. Lee instanced a life of Shelley by 'an eminent
man of letters of our own day', evidently Edward Dowden,
as an example of 'the whitewashing method'. I leave it
to readers of the two lectures in the present volume to
deduce from them what would have been his verdict on

[1] p. 34.   [2] p. 63.

Monsieur Maurois's *Ariel, ou la vie de Shelley*, where the
poet becomes the hero of a typical *roman* of the Boulevards;
or Mr. W. E. Peck's *Shelley: his Life and Work*, which shows
him as 'the man of the street' and includes a list of the
cheques drawn by him. And what would he who wrote
that 'Death is a part of life and no man is fit subject for
biography till he is dead'[1] have thought of the premature
flood of memoirs by those of whom he spoke in 1918 as
'the statesmen and commanders who are controlling the
nations and the world's destinies'?[2]

Such are some of the points that the lectures suggest
to-day. But even those who may prefer a less sober-
suited conception of the biographer's art or who may think
that Lee in the light of recent research does less than
justice to the personality of Boswell,[3] and somewhat over-
estimates the competence of Lockhart in his treatment
of Scott's correspondence,[4] must recognize the permanent
interest and value of this confession of faith by the chief
architect of *The Dictionary of National Biography*.

The English Association lecture, 'The Impersonal Aspect
of Shakespeare's Art' (1909) forms a natural bridge to the
second section of this volume, which contains some of
Lee's addresses and articles on distinctively Shakespearian
and Renaissance themes. In this lecture he handles what
is a biographical, or autobiographical, problem—the
question whether Shakespeare reveals himself in his plays.
'Do we', he asks, 'learn from them his private opinions on
religion, on politics, and the other matters which, more
or less, occupy every thinking man's attention?'[5] To that
question he returns an almost unqualified negative. And
he is particularly concerned in attacking what he calls
'the fundamental basis of the personal theory':

'It mainly rests on an alleged correspondence between the dominant mood or tone of a play taken as a whole, and the dominant
mood or tone of Shakespeare's private sentiment or experience at

[1] p. 36.   [2] p. 82.   [3] p. 52.   [4] p. 55.   [5] p. 89.

the time of writing. Put broadly we are asked to believe that some great sorrow, some overwhelmingly tragic incident in his own career, impelled Shakespeare to tragedy, while joyousness of mind and happy episodes impelled him to comedy and romance.'[1]

The 'personal theory' in this form had been most explicitly set forth in Edward Dowden's study of *Shakspere's Mind and Art*. He naturally saw in Lee's pamphlet a challenge which he took up in an article in the *Contemporary Review* (November 1909) 'Is Shakespeare self-revealed?' In a controversy where so much depends on the interpretation of terms complete victory cannot well lie with either side, but Lee in the main (as it seems to me) bore off the honours.

As is well known, he sought also (in my opinion, unsuccessfully) to minimize the amount of self-revelation in the Sonnets. This attitude to some extent colours the *Quarterly Review* article on 'Ovid and Shakespeare's Sonnets' (1909). There runs through it the suggestion that many of the sentiments are not the poet's own but echoes of his Latin model. Thus Lee will admit no personal significance in Shakespeare's boast that his verse will immortalize his friend. 'The Sonnets' classical and conventional claim to eternity has been misread as an original tenet of Shakespeare's poetic creed.'[2] But whatever view may be taken on this problem the essay is important as the most signal proof of Lee's abiding interest, amidst his more modern preoccupations, in classical literature, original or translated, of which the section on Plutarch in his Leslie Stephen lecture is another illustration.[3] And his pages catch an unusual glow from the grandeur of the theme, as he expounds Shakespeare's interpretation (with Golding as a medium) of Ovid's neo-Pythagorean conception of Time's 'endless rotatory process', and deduces therefrom the indefeasible claim of the Sonnets 'to rank with the richest fruits of the pagan Renaissance'.[4]

Of that pagan Renaissance Italy was the head-quarters,

[1] p. 101.   [2] p. 124.   [3] pp. 46–8.   [4] p. 138.

and in his British Academy lecture, 'Shakespeare and the Italian Renaissance' (1915), Lee analyses the humanism of Florence, and its sister cities, into its cardinal elements, 'the idealization and worship of beauty', and the liberation of reason, with their varied manifestations in poetry, art, philosophy, scientific inquiry, and geographical exploration. He indicates the channels through which this 'new faith in beauty and reason' filtered by way of France from Italy to England, where it found disciples in Sidney, Spenser, and above all in Shakespeare, 'the greatest of humanists in the broad sense which the term justly bears in the history of the Italian Renaissance'.[1] A pendant to the Academy lecture may be found in the paper on 'Tasso and Shakespeare's England' (1918) written when Allenby's recent deliverance of Jerusalem had recalled the noble Italian epic on the First Crusade and its echoes in this country. On the other hand, in 'Shakespeare and the Inquisition' (1922), we are given a glimpse, in the mutilation by the Holy Office of a copy of the Second Folio at Valladolid, of the working of the forces hostile to the liberating influences of the Renaissance.

But the persecuting intolerance of the Inquisition was far from blinding Lee to the greatness of Spain's achievement in the sixteenth century. In the third section of this volume are reprinted for the first time four papers which appeared in 1907 in *Scribner's Magazine*, under the general title, 'The Call of the West: America and Elizabethan England'. The sub-title is too narrow, for the papers cover the activities in North and South America, of England, France, and Spain till the beginning of the Stuart period. And in the first paper, 'The Example of Spain', Lee pays a fervent tribute to Castilian enterprise and valour in the western hemisphere, and insists on 'Spain's priority as explorer, as scientific navigator, as conqueror, as settler'.[2] It was Spain that set the precedent to other European nations of colonial organization, and they were attracted

[1] p. 156.   [2] p. 199.

by the 'pregnant and pervasive force' of her example. France was the first to follow in her wake, though, as is set forth in the paper, 'The Teaching of the Huguenots', she struck out original ideas of her own. To the French, and especially to the Huguenots flying from persecution, the New World appeared as the 'unfettered land of freedom',[1] and in the native communities they looked to find the innocence of the primeval golden age. *The Tempest*, according to the view set forth in the paper on 'The American Indian in Elizabethan England', provided in the picture of Caliban and otherwise an ironical comment on such visions. The sight of such 'natives' as were brought home by some of the adventurers and exhibited as 'monsters' did not encourage idealistic fancies, and Shakespeare is found twitting Montaigne.[2] But there had been nothing in the experiences of Englishmen on the western mainland during the sixteenth century to foster a spirit of optimism. Their ventures had ended in failure. 'No living English colonist occupied a foot of land in America when Queen Elizabeth died.'[3] Such, in the concluding paper, 'The Path to Jamestown', is Lee's tragic summing up of the results of the heroic ventures of Frobisher, Gilbert, Raleigh, and their fellows. It was not till the reign of the first Stuart, in 1607, that at Jamestown the earliest permanent English settlement was made, and the transatlantic 'plantations' were begun.

It may be thought that Lee is too insistent on the gloomier sides of English overseas activities in the sixteenth century. And his narrative in 'The Call of the West' is coloured by his persistent search for the imitative elements in Tudor England, whether in the field of thought or of action. 'The Elizabethan', as he puts it, 'was a mighty assimilator of foreign ideas.'[4] Since he wrote in 1907, it has been proved that as early as 1516–17 an English expedition was organized to go in quest of the 'new found lands'. It soon came to grief through mutiny, but John Rastell, the printer and dramatist, who was one of the 'venturers',

[1] p. 232. [2] pp. 292–4. [3] p. 319. [4] p. 199.

has left a record of its failure and of the hopes with which it set out in his play, *The Interlude of the Four Elements*:[1]

> Within this twenty yeer—
> Westwarde be founde new landes
> That we neuer harde tell of before this
> By wrytyng nor other meanys.
>
> .   .   .   .   .
>
> O, what a thynge had be than,
> Yf that they that be englyshe men
> Myght haue ben the furst of all
> That there shulde haue take possessyon,
> And made furst buyldynge and habytacion,
> A memory perpetuall.
> And also what an honorable thynge,
> Both to the realme and the kinge,
> To haue had his domynyon extendynge
> There into so farre a grounde.

Lee's generalizations therefore need to be qualified. But, taken as a whole, 'The Call of the West' renders in broad and effective sweep the splendid epic of European adventure and endurance in the New World which was the counterpart of its mighty achievements in poetry, drama, and the pictorial arts.

In the light of what has been said about the contents of this volume, it may perhaps help to set Lee as a scholar and man of letters in truer perspective. His position in his closing years was not without an element of paradox. To the general reading public he was the leading Shakespearian authority. He was Chairman of the Trustees of Shakespeare's Birthplace. In American and continental eyes he was the *doyen* of English scholars. There was keen disappointment in the United States when he could not take part in the Anglo-American Conference of Professors of English at Columbia University, New York, in 1923. But there had begun to grow up in this country a school of

[1] See A. W. Reed, *Early Tudor Drama*, pp. 11–12 (1926). This is the play, of which the authorship was then not known, to which Lee refers (p. 212) as 'a rudimentary English drama'.

Shakespearian investigation with other methods and ideas than his. Among the subjects of special interest to them were the details of Elizabethan stage-history, the organization of the professional companies, the technical arrangements and equipment of the Elizabethan theatres; above all, the problems of the transmission of the text of the plays, including the relations of the printed versions to the original manuscripts, 'prompt' and censored copies, questions of spelling and punctuation. I do not, of course, suggest that Lee had not considerable interest in such matters, but he had not specialized in them intensively. Both by instinct and training he was distrustful of conjecture and hypothesis, and he did not feel the fascination of methods which, whatever their ultimate results, have opened a new chapter in Shakespearian textual criticism. In commenting on a passage expounding the theory of 'dramatic' punctuation he wrote ironically, 'It is then in Shakespeare's "stops" that we must seek for the final proof of his dramatic genius'. Thus some of his younger contemporaries were alienated, and tended to depreciate or ignore his services to Elizabethan scholarship.

Every generation must go its own way, but if Lee's work is to be judged aright it must be looked upon as that of one who was primarily not a stage-historian nor a textual critic but a humanist. It was thus that he was drawn to Shakespeare as 'the greatest of humanists', the mightiest representative of that Renaissance age which looked back to Plato and Plutarch, to Cicero and Ovid, and forward through its explorers and scientific discoverers to worlds as yet unrealized, and new triumphs of the spirit of man. The writings here collected throw light on his beliefs and ideals. They have 'the virility and perspicuity', which he found in the work of his master, Leslie Stephen. I am convinced that, when all discount has been made, his own work, so single-minded and large of purpose, will remain a conspicuous landmark in English literary scholarship.

THE PLACE OF ENGLISH LITERATURE
IN THE MODERN UNIVERSITY[1]

I

THE study of English language and literature is a newcomer in the curriculum of advanced education. Only in the latter part of last century was it accorded recognition by English universities. Advanced education in England long developed on lines which wholly ignored the native language. The language and literature of Greece and Rome, with a modest admixture of logic and mathematics, filled the whole curriculum of our universities. It was within the memory of living men that this narrow field saw expansion. By slow degrees, and in the face of formidable opposition, the natural sciences, modern history, modern languages, and finally English language and literature, were admitted to the academic arena.

The widening of the university curriculum beyond the confines of classics and mathematics is mainly the work of the young universities of London and of the provinces. In the absence of a rigid tradition the new academic institutions have readily responded to the demands of the nation's intellectual and material development. The new universities multiply a hundredfold the opportunities of advanced education. It is natural that they should broaden the scope of study. The highest ideal of a modern university is catholicity in the range of its curriculum. Provision should be made for students of all intellectual affinities and aspirations. There should be room for the pursuit of all substantive branches of knowledge side by side. Each branch should beware

[1] An Inaugural Lecture delivered at East London College, University of London, on 2 October 1913. [The introductory section on 'the function of a Professor' and some of the notes have been omitted.]

of the precedent of ascendancy which the classics set in the past. Any ambition to play the rôle of Aaron's serpent should be repressed. No subject can be spared. The various branches should form collectively a happy family.

The more advanced students in a university rightly specialize in single subjects; the many who are less advanced pursue in London University four subjects together. Each topic of study has to serve two purposes. On the one hand, it should, in its completeness, prove of value and interest to the student as a practically independent and self-sufficing unit. On the other hand, it has, in a partial manifestation, to show itself a useful member of a mixed society. Like its companions, English study must be able, to the general advantage, both to march with other studies and to walk alone.

With, I hope, the modesty befitting a newcomer I propose to consider what may fairly be expected of English study alike as an ally of other studies (for the general student) and as an isolated pursuit (for the specialist). He who delivers an inaugural address should not make too rigid a confession of faith or speak too confidently of his coming labours. The workaday world pays little heed to mere counsels of perfection. Experience may well compel correction, modification, perhaps reconstruction of the anticipatory views of a new settler. 'Let not him that girdeth on his harness boast himself as he that putteth it off.'

II

The philosophic aim, I take it, of advanced education in its widest aspect, is to rouse in the student an active and lasting enthusiasm for things of the mind, and to foster disciplined habits of thought. The final hope will be to excite in him a desire and capacity for well-considered research. At the same time the student has a right to expect instruction which shall contribute to the material welfare of his future life. It is quixotic to ignore the practical motives of advanced education, although it may be disadvantageous to parade them unduly. With a frankness which is not to be rashly emulated, Bacon remarked that close study is pursued 'most times for lucre and a profession, and seldom sincerely to give a true account of our gift of reason for the benefit and use of man'. There is need, at any rate, of a co-ordination of the practical with the ideal. Advanced education cannot afford to ignore either side of the shield. English study will have to satisfy the normal duality of outlook. Whatever intellectual or spiritual contribution it make, either to the general training of advanced students who are not confining their energies to it, or to the special training of those who concentrate on it all or most part of their undergraduate activity, it should give some kind of aid in the pursuit of a vocation.

The main theme of English study is English literature. English language must always remain a subsidiary branch of the study. Literature is the mistress of the household, language the chief handmaiden. Philology has immense claims to the student's attention; it can exert an immense fascination; but by the nature of things it is subject in English study to the superior control of literature. Verbal structure is secondary to mental substance.

It is needless to cite definitions of literature. We all know it to be the storehouse of the best thought and feeling, set forth in the most lucid, harmonious, and pleasure-giving forms, of which words are capable. Milton called a book 'the precious life-blood of a master spirit'. The eloquent phrase sufficiently suggests what literature is and distinguishes it from what it is not. The word 'literature' is often loosely applied to any writing which is committed to print. But true literature has to satisfy a more exacting test. In matter and manner it has to stir an intellectual or an emotional interest, an admiration and a delight transcending any impression produced by the record of a literal experience. Literature is no mere reporting of human affairs. Life is its raw material. But the raw material of life is steeped in a flood of thought and imagination before great literature comes into being. Literature makes a three-fold appeal—to the mind, to the heart, and to the ear, and it should generate a sensation of elevated pleasure.

Literature is of varied texture, of varied forms, of varied values. Like the firmament it finds place for stars of many magnitudes. Shakespeare's work is the greatest contribution to English literature. But an infinite mass of writing, inferior to his, lies within the limits of English study, which should be comprehensive. We are bound to descend from the summit of the mountain and explore the slopes until we reach that border-line near the base which severs significant literature from insignificant. There is no real difficulty in distinguishing worthless literature from that which for our purposes has some measure of worth. Critics may differ as to the precise place that an author should hold in the scale of fame. But there comes a time in the career of every book when a final decision is reached as to its general merit. The student will not wisely ignore any book which has been admitted by recognized authority within the charmed circle.

Current writing which awaits the final verdict does not claim the attention of the lecture room. The student may be well advised if in his leisure he attempt to appraise current writing by the standard of the old literature which has stood Time's test. Current writing is for the most part ephemeral writing, and pretends to nothing beyond providing amusement, recreation, or mere instruction. Literature of that restricted aim has no lawful place in the literary course of a university.

III

When in the last century the study of English was struggling for recognition in the curriculum at Oxford, resistance was based on a series of pleas which still deserve passing attention. First it was argued that the reading of English literature by English students called for no such mental effort as was justly required of an instrument of education. Latin and Greek construing and composition were gymnastic exercises of the mind for which English study offered no opportunity. In the second place it was argued that the appreciation and proper comprehension of English literature depended solely on taste or feeling, that an endeavour to teach taste or feeling was as futile as to try to teach personal beauty, and that to 'examine' in taste or feeling was like seeking to weigh in avoirdupois scales the colour of the hair or eye. The innuendo here was that no subject in which it was difficult to 'examine' was fit to be taught. In the third place it was represented that the professor of English literature had nothing to offer his students save criticism of literature or gossip about literary men, and neither could rise far above the level of idle chatter. In a word the study of literature, according to this depreciatory estimate, was imbued with a dilettantism which was foreign and fatal to the academic atmosphere. These arguments, which for a time carried weight at Oxford and elsewhere, are worthy of attention as plausible misconceptions. It may be useful to trick them out in their true colours.

The study of English inevitably divides itself into four main branches—(1) criticism, (2) history, (3) philology, and (4) composition or practical experiment in the art of expression on the part of the student. All the branches need concurrent treatment, though the student may be led by his idiosyncrasy to pay greater attention to one than to another. No Oxford critic is likely to charge philology or history with vagueness or frivolity. Students' experiments in composition have been known to betray such qualities, but these defects, as I hope to prove, are remediable accidents. It is, in any case, at criticism that the sceptic points the finger of scorn most confidently. I accept the challenge, for criticism is at the root of the whole matter. The ultimate good derivable from the academic·study of English literature will largely depend on the professor's practical interpretation of that chameleon-like term.

I will examine the kinship of literature with history, philology, and the practice of composition in the order in which I name those topics. But I will first invite your attention to the vexed character of criticism in the present context. In my belief the problem revolving about the precise meaning of the word is rather less perplexing than it looks at first sight. 'Exegesis,' a Greek word which literally means 'the leading out of a thing that which is in it', is a satisfactory synonym for literary criticism in the academic sense. Its signification is quite plain. Exegesis embraces all means of throwing light on the text of a piece of writing and of drawing forth its full meaning; it examines the form; it seeks to unravel the mode of composition; it traces the inspiration to its sources; it shows the strength or weakness of the author's thought and feeling. Literary criticism is in the university no light-hearted expression of the personal likes and dislikes of professor or student. It applies scholarly, even scientific, principles of inquiry to the intellectual and emotional phenomena within its ᴐhere. It aims at determining the true force and value . literary matter and manner.

This is not the occasion to descend to details. But it will be understood that to test the genuineness of an author's text, to discover the materials on which he worked, to analyse the dominant features of the style, is no elegant trifling. A student will usually find it of service to acquaint himself with the contemporary estimate of an author, and with any surviving comments by the author on his own work. Thus he may the better attune his mind to the author's purpose. Finally, the student will be required to describe the impression which the work leaves on his own intelligence. Room must always be left in the fabric of literary study for the play of the student's individual taste and judgement.

If all be done efficiently, there will be no rambling incoherence at any stage. The critical training will be at all points systematic. The reading of books in a literary school must be no lazy sauntering along a level or a downhill path. It should be a bracing exercise. It is a wrestling with ideas greater than any we can create for ourselves; it is a striving to get into close touch with thought and fancy which are above our capacity to invent.

There is an auxiliary department of literary criticism which can never be safely ignored, at any rate by special students. It is criticism which commonly bears the distinctive epithet of 'comparative'. Comparative criticism is the testing of one nation's literature by a comparison of it with that of other nations. Literature is a living organism gathering sustenance from all quarters. No great national literature has ever subsisted without some foreign nutrition. English literature owes almost as deep a debt to classical literature as Roman poetry owed to Greek. But the classics are only one of the many foreign sources of English poetry and prose. 'A people', wrote Walter Pater, 'without intellectual commerce with other peoples has never done anything conspicuous in literature.' The foreign element is always there. It should be defined and weighed. Some study of foreign literature should therefore form an integral part of a sound critical analysis of English literary achievement. English literature cannot be viewed in a just perspective until the comparative study has brought some foreign literature within the range of the student's vision. Elizabethan literature, for example, has an unassailable line of foreign descent and kinship, and disregard of the pedigree involves a risk of ignoring the processes at work in its composition and of distorting the critical judgement. Absolute originality of idea or of form is rarer in great literature than is commonly imagined. Inventiveness in literature is a power of infinite gradations, which the comparative method of study will alone enable us to adjust nicely.[1] A piece of great literature is usually a mighty chain of which the links are forged in many workshops.

The history of literature, the second division of our study, needs no elaborate definition. In literary history we seek the external circumstances—political, social, economic—in which literature is produced. Literary history co-ordinates, either chronologically or according to the special branch of effort, the lives of authors; it dates events with precision and deduces facts from original authorities. We learn the circumstances attending the publication of great books, and the personal relations in which the writers stood in life to one another and to the world at large. A mere collection of dates, facts, and names has been known to do duty for literary history. Dates, facts, and names form a non-nutritious diet for students of literature, whose memory should not be suffered to work mechanically, but should be fertilized by genuine mental effort. Literary history ought to be no skeleton, no charnel house of dry bones. It should be a thing of flesh and blood, a living guide to the aspiration and practical endeavour of the author and a moving picture of his environment.

Philology deals with words which are the raw materials of literature. Language is in many ways the most magical of all man's attributes. The wonders of wireless telegraphy pale into insignificance before the miraculous working of the tongue and pen. Philology well deserves all the labour that has been bestowed upon it, and the student of literature who fails to realize its importance will never be wholly efficient. Philology has all the characteristics of an exact science, and has the same disciplinary value. Language is always growing; it is always

---

[1] It is more important to determine what a great author makes of his borrowings or his adaptations of foreign ideas than to set forth in all its minutiae that which he has borrowed or adapted. But we must know in some detail what an author absorbs from others before we can estimate his eminence finally; not otherwise shall we stand on firm critical ground.

shedding old words and inflexions, and putting forth new expressions. Words constantly change their meaning. Some which are held by one age to be inelegant or indelicate or pedantic are welcomed by another age to the best verbal company. Great literature is for ever offering new material for philological inquiry. One of the benefits which great authors render their fellow countrymen is the invention of new words to express new thoughts, or, it may be, old thoughts to which language has not hitherto done justice. There is no stagnation in a living tongue, and a due comprehension of a great people's literature through the centuries presumes a thorough understanding of the language in all its stages. The student has to master all the processes of decay and growth from the earliest till the latest period. The earliest stages will be less familiar than the latter and will absorb much of his attention. But no stage will he safely overlook. Philology embraces every aspect of language. Under its aegis stands the study of phonetics —the science of pronunciation—which is rapidly growing in scholarly favour. Pronunciation is a potent force in the formation and transformation of words. Philology and phonetics are both pursuits ancillary to literature, but there will be small hope for the efficiency of literary study if the philological branch be treated lightly.

IV

The last branch of literary study, to which I direct your attention, is the practice of literary composition by the student. From a national point of view this branch might seem to transcend in importance the other three. It will not be pursued successfully if the others be neglected; it can hardly be pursued at all if the first branch, literary criticism, be treated perfunctorily.

I would lay down the axiom that no one writes well who has not read well, that no one writes good English who has not read good English with appreciation and intelligence. Consider historically what it is that has prompted good writing in the past. The command of a definite thought and the ambition to divulge it to others have rarely proved in themselves quite sufficient motive forces. In one or other degree assimilation of pre-existing literature is a main element in all effective literary composition. Whether a writer be great or small, he will be seen on due inquiry to assimilate much that others have written, before he produce anything memorable. In the evolution of literary expression there is no process that can be confidently described as spontaneous generation. *Ex nihilo nihil fit* is a maxim applicable to the composition of literature as to that of all else.

Originality in literature usually means the saying—in a more convincing, more impressive, more beautiful way—of something nearly resembling what has been said before. Acquired or inherited knowledge is provided with a new setting; it receives a new application, a new significance. But processes of assimilation have been first at work.

This conclusion is not merely true of men of ordinary and mediocre capacity; it applies to men of highest genius. Shakespeare's work is an exemplification of it. Endless modes of pre-existing thought and style wrought on his mind before his supreme power revealed itself. In the effort of humbler persons who, having no claim to genius, cherish the praiseworthy ambition to write their own language perspicuously and with propriety, a more or less deliberate cultivation of the assimilative faculty is primarily essential to a profitable issue. The testimony of a recent eminent man of letters, Robert Louis Stevenson, clears the point of doubt. Other witnesses of the same calibre might be cited: but Stevenson's detailed description of the manner in which he became a writer is especially pertinent to my present argument.

'Whenever I read a book or a passage that particularly pleased me, in which a thing was said or an effect rendered with propriety, in which there was either some conspicuous force or some happy distinction in the style, I must sit down at once and set myself to ape that quality. I was unsuccessful and I knew it; and tried again, and was again unsuccessful and always unsuccessful; but at least in these vain bouts I got some practice in rhythm, in harmony, in construction and the co-ordination of parts. . . . I have thus played the sedulous ape to Hazlitt, to Lamb, to Wordsworth, to Sir Thomas Browne, to Defoe, to Hawthorne, to Montaigne, to Baudelaire, and to Obermann. That, like it or not, is the way to learn to write; whether I have profited or not, that is the way. It was so Keats learned, and there was never a finer temperament for literature than Keats's; it was so, if we could trace it out, that all men have learned.' [1]

Dryden's counsel on the same subject offers useful corroboration: 'The proprieties and delicacies of English are known to few. It is impossible even for a good wit to understand and practice them without the help of a liberal education, long reading, and digesting of those few good authors we have amongst us.' [2]

Stevenson's way we must all follow. By assimilation, of course, I do not mean plagiarism or, to use a shorter term, 'cribbing,' which is a reprehensible practice. We should read good books with our full attention. We should form a habit of drinking in the matter and manner of our author—without excess of conscious effort, without overstraining the attention. Our minds should become steeped intuitively and instinctively in our study. Some mechanical rules may be of service. Passages that move our special admiration may be committed to memory or to a commonplace book. The reading of literature aloud aids one immensely in appreciating the qualities of its structure. We should take especial note of

---

[1] Stevenson's *Memories and Portraits: A College Magazine.*

[2] To these aids to good writing Dryden adds, as no less important, 'the knowledge of men and manners, the freedom of habitudes and conversation with the best company of both sexes'. Valuable, too, is Dryden's final word of advice to the student who would excel in composition that he should neglect no opportunities of 'wearing off the rust which he contracted while he was laying in a stock of learning'.—'Preface to Sylvae: or, the Second Part of Poetical Miscellanies' (1685) in *Critical Essays*, ed. Ker, i. 253.

the way in which paragraphs are built up by practised pens. The common rules of grammar and syntax should be respected. But if our hopes of good writing are to be realized, all the mechanism should become part of our nature. In the result we ought to discover in ourselves a power of expression, a command of vocabulary which will be coloured by our reading, although there should be no slavish reproduction of any man's style or words. Probably we shall never write so well as any of our models. But we may look forward to acquiring, in the light of our reading, a facility, a grace, a clearness which will be beyond our grasp if we remain in ignorance of the written work of great authors.

A study of literature which does not endow the student with the desire and the ability to write well, misses great part of its true aim. Fine writing, the use of slang, tautology, are some of the pitfalls against which the student always has to be vigilant. But in the light of great literature he ought quickly to realize that the merit of writing is proportioned to its simplicity, directness, good taste, sincerity. An orderly arrangement of thought should keep pace with an easy flow of words. The student should pray with Milton that his words 'like so many nimble and airy servitors will trip about him at command, and in well-ordered files, as he would wish, will fall aptly into their own places'.[1] I hope for the best, although I do not underrate the difficulties. Never, at any rate, ought a conscientious student to have ground for reproaching his teacher of literature at the end of the course in such words as these of Shakespeare:

> My tongue's use is to me no more
> Than an unstringed viol or a harp,

---

[1] Milton, *Apology for Smectymnuus*. In Shakespeare's *Henry VIII* (ii. iv. 111–13) a cognate idea finds expression:

> Your words,
> Domestics to you, serve your will as 't please
> Yourself pronounce their office.

Or like a cunning instrument cas'd up,
Or, being open, put into his hands
That knows no touch to tune the harmony.[1]

Of students who justly echoed such a rebuke it might
well be said in Milton's phrase:

The hungry sheep *looked* up, and *were* not fed.[2]

When we sum up the general value of English study
in advanced education, we may be inclined to set the
highest value on its power of encouraging good writing.
Whatever one's walk in life or one's special interest,
whether we become men of science or engage in commerce or in work of administration, the power of writing
well will always increase one's efficiency and contribute to
one's success. Complaint is commonly made that, owing
to defects in our educational system, a command of
clear and pointed language is more narrowly distributed
in England than in other countries. Lord Haldane, the
late Secretary of State for War, declared not long ago
that few officers in the army were able to write an intelligible dispatch. Men of science, eminent in their
profession, have been accused within very recent years of
inability to set forth their results effectively. I have
heard critics of our present educational method—the
critics are numerous and voluble—assert that school-
masters in high position do not always write English
which can be understood. I do not know how far these
censures are justified; but I know how a promising attempt may be made to remedy such defects wherever
they are proved to exist. Let every student, whatever
other work he may be doing, devote some part of his time
to an intelligent study of great English literature. Thus
only may he realize the capacity of language to express
thought with grace and clearness.

[1] *Richard II*, i. iii. 161 *seq.*
[2] *Lycidas*, line 125 : 'The hungry sheep look up and are not fed.'

V

There are many other advantages no less substantial, although not so easy to bring home to the world at large, which the general student will derive from the partial application of his time to literary study. More than 200 years ago, in 1708, a first tentative effort was made to recognize poetry at Oxford as an academic subject, by the foundation of a chair of poetry. The unprecedented step was justified on the ground that 'the reading of the old poets contributes not only to give keenness and polish to the natural endowment of young men, but also to the advancement of severer learning whether sacred or human'.[1] That is a text still worth emblazoning in places of education. It might be added by way of gloss that the student of English literature comes into direct intercourse with great minds. 'The reading of books,' said an older author than the one I have just cited, 'what is it but conversing with the wisest men of all ages and all countries, who thereby communicate to us their most deliberate thoughts, choicest notions, and best inventions, couched in good expression, and digested in exact method?'[2] These words also deserve general currency. To come into touch with the 'most deliberate thoughts, choicest notions, and best inventions' of great thinkers is inevitably to quicken enthusiasm, to encourage high purpose, to broaden interest and experience.

All great literatures—Greek, Latin, French, German, Italian, Spanish—hold in solution the spirit of liberal culture such as universities exist to disseminate. Foreign literatures are composed of the same constituent elements as those with which we credit English literature. But English literature is our own literature. It may be said, without undue self-assertion, to enjoy at the

[1] Cf. Prof. J. W. Mackail's *Henry Birkhead and the foundation of the Oxford Chair of Poetry*, 1908, p. 9.

[2] Isaac Barrow, *Sermons*: 'Of Industry in our Particular Calling as Scholars.'

moment a patent of precedence in the world at large. In France, Germany, Russia, and Italy, English literature is studied with almost as much zeal as the indigenous literature. It is reckoned in those foreign lands a liberalizing agent. It is difficult to dispute, in presence of the universal estimate, that English literature at an English university should fill a foremost place in the hierarchy of literary studies.

By the special students of English in an English university, these conclusions will be accepted without demur. The special student will pursue each of the four branches of the study—criticism, history, philology, and composition—with a greater concentration than the students who are not specializing in English. Their reading will be wider, their scholarship should be more profound, and as writers they should wield a more supple pen. It is to be hoped that some special students, after they have taken their first degree, will engage in original research which may add to the stock of knowledge and advance the cause of learning. They will find stimulating examples abroad. Foreign students of English in foreign universities have prepared many monographs embodying discoveries of value. The field is not all explored. There is room for fresh labourers. No college will completely fulfil its function if it fails to foster some postgraduate research. The professor should endeavour to point out such learning as is already available, but the best proof of his success will lie in the endeavour of some of his students to better his instruction and to make paths for themselves in unknown territory.

VI

The laboratory of the English student is the library, and no English school can flourish without a large and well-ordered storehouse of books. The fit equipment of an English school costs very much less than the fit equipment of a scientific and certainly of an engineering school. But it costs something. The student must have ready to his hand the best texts of every author who has made any memorable contribution of whatever value or dimensions to the nation's literary achievement. The texts are of primary importance. Cheap reprints, however welcome in certain conditions, will not serve the full need of the scholar. He must make direct acquaintance with the written word in the form in which, as far as it can be ascertained, it came from the pen of the author. The student must be on his guard against the inevitable frailties of the printer who hastily reproduces the text for the undiscerning market.

The scholarly text is the first and foremost source of literary knowledge. No sound progress is possible without it. Most of the old authors have now been carefully edited on scholarly lines, and they circulate in paper and print worthy of their eminence. It is to the standard editions of repute that the student should have constant access in the college library. At the same time the student should in addition have at his command there a well-chosen store of wise and pertinent comment, and all treatises of philology and literary history and biography, which lend genuine help to interpretation. Not all annotation of literature satisfies that qualifying clause. There are editions of great authors in which the author's words meander like a trickling stream through a boundless and barren desert of editorial comment. The test of a good commentary lies in its terseness and relevance. Its value is usually in inverse ratio to the bulk.

In the case of special students, lists of books bearing on their own subject will prove valuable implements of work. The scholar constantly needs to know what others are doing in his own department of study, not merely all over the country but all over the world. In any topic which, like our topic, attracts widespread industry, we should have ready access to critical bibliographies well up to date.

A college library, if sufficient money is expended on it, can be made to meet most of the student's needs.

But as his ambition advances and his range of outlook widens, it may be needful for him to seek admission to a larger treasury of books than any local institution can conveniently house. The national library at the British Museum will alone satisfy the requirements of any who engage in original and independent research. But an English library, planned on the comparatively modest lines which I have laid down, is a preliminary condition of the successful conduct of any English School.

At the same time the student of English must not place all his reliance on the college library, or even on the national library. From an early date in his career he should seek to form a library of his own. Naturally one's own collection of books must be proportioned to one's means. From the lives of those who have been imbued by nature with a passion for literature, and have distinguished themselves in future careers, I could quote many heroic instances of physical sufferings cheerfully encountered in youth in the endeavour to acquire books.[1]

No comparable sacrifice is asked of any one in these days of cheap reprints. The cheap reprints of great literature which abound at the moment may not satisfy the highest demands of scholarly study, but they are useful auxiliaries because they give the young student whose pecuniary resources are small the opportunity of

[1] William Cobbett's account of his first experience as a bookbuyer is typical of many in a like situation in youth. Cobbett writes: 'When only eleven years old, with three pence in my pocket—my whole fortune—I perceived at Richmond, in a bookseller's window, a little book, marked "Price Threepence"—Swift's "Tale of a Tub". Its odd title excited my curiosity; I bought it in place of my supper. So impatient was I to examine it that I got over into a field at the upper corner of Kew Gardens, and sat down to read, on the shady side of a haystack. The book was so different from anything I had read before—it was something so new to my mind that, though I could not at all understand some parts of it, still it delighted me beyond measure, and produced what I have always considered a sort of birth of intellect. I read on till it was dark, without any thought of supper or bed.' Cobbett's *Advice to Young Men*, 1830.

acquiring for himself the records of great thought, great ideas, great emotion.

I will not decry the practice of borrowing books provided the borrower return them punctually and in good condition. Every student is bound to borrow a great many expensive books or to read them in the college or in a public library. But the borrowing of books has little spiritual advantage compared with the buying of books for oneself. The sense of ownership of books is an ennobling pleasure. There is no sordid alloy in that acquisitive instinct.

VII

In conclusion, let me pass from any purely academic view of English literature. A larger point of view justly claims the last word. Will not a knowledge of great literature, and such a habit of reading it as calls into play the higher faculties, make for something more valuable even than first-class honours in examinations, and the prizes which those honours bring? The effectual study of literature can hardly fail to make for the happiness of the student's life in all its future stages. It has been said—a little extravagantly—that reading can get the better of most physical sufferings, all indeed save the pangs of hunger. Literary sympathy and enthusiasm will certainly give consolation in times of sorrow and add zest to the enjoyment of good fortune. I do not claim that academic training is essential to the creation of a love of right reading. But I hold that academic training, if it be wisely devised, can stimulate the healthy growth of that beneficent taste, may even create it in those in whom it has not been implanted by nature and is discouraged by environment. I hope that in the succession of students who graduate from this college there will be many who, having studied English literature here, will spread far and wide in the outer world the glad tidings of literature's saving grace.

MODERN LANGUAGE RESEARCH[1]

I

WE shall all be agreed that the ideal state is one in which the efficient pursuit of knowledge is held in general esteem, in a general esteem incomparably greater than that accorded the pursuit of wealth, or sport, or military glory. Plato insisted that Kings should always be chosen from the ranks of philosophers, from men of the loftiest learning and wisdom. Bacon argued that in a perfect commonwealth human energy should be mainly organized to the end of searching after 'the knowledge of causes and the secret motions of things'. No state, Bacon insisted, could reckon with any confidence on genuine or lasting greatness or happiness unless, within its boundaries, learning was constantly growing broader and deeper.

The day, we believe, is at hand when a country's proved capacity for research, for conquering and improving new fields of human knowledge, will be reckoned a better guarantee of national welfare than naval or military prowess. In the eye of Bacon and of those who think with him learning is essentially a philanthropic, a civilizing, humanizing, socializing force in the world's affairs. No sane judgement can allow the honourable title of learning to accumulations of knowledge which can lend themselves to the encouragement of deeds of dishonour and inhumanity, and to the poisonous sophistication of truth and morality.

It is of good promise that a state comparatively young in years but of notable magnitude in all else should be first in the field in giving practical recognition to the

[1] The inaugural Presidential Address delivered on 19 October 1918 to the Modern Language Research Association (now the Modern Humanities Research Association). [Reprinted here in abbreviated form.]

principles which both Plato and Bacon championed,—principles which will, I am confident, soon press for recognition everywhere. In the United States of America the advancement of learning of the true humanizing pattern (as the Carnegie, Rockefeller, and many large, but smaller, foundations testify) is tending to become a national ambition.

In this country there are as yet no such imposing foundations in aid of research as have lately come to birth in America. At the same time no good purpose is served by painting our past in too dark colours, by ignoring or underrating, as is sometimes done by half-informed Jeremiahs, our own contributions to the advanced knowledge of philology or any other subject. When we examine the advances in various branches of learning, in natural science, for example, either in the past or in the present, we have no reason to be ashamed of our record. So honourable a record is the best guarantee that with the complete and efficient organization which is at present lacking we need not in the near future continue under obligations.

In paying closer and wider attention to the historic development of our own language, we shall be reinforcing, confirming a robust tradition which is of old standing, although in course of time it has ebbed as well as flowed. Anglo-Saxon research began during Queen Elizabeth's reign while Shakespeare was a child. The University of Cambridge then first took up the study with patriotic ardour. Oxford entered the field of Anglo-Saxon research in the seventeenth century. The libraries of both Universities early acquired rich collections of early English manuscripts, and much palaeographical and critical energy was applied to their elucidation. Truth compels me to state that an immigrant from Germany gave the movement some help in those distant days. In the result 'Saxon' learning, as it was called, flourished in England at the opening of the eighteenth century, and the 'Saxon' scholars of that time included prophetically a woman, Elizabeth Elstob, who was hailed in literary circles as 'the celebrated Saxon nymph'. Miss Elstob's memory should not be without honour to-day.

But in spite of strenuous effort in most branches of English philology in early eighteenth-century Oxford, the end of the century saw some decline of interest. It was then that foreign scholars first figured prominently on the scene.

At the end of the eighteenth century foreign students seem first to have applied themselves to early English and other philology with a zeal and ability which, we must in fairness admit, carried philological scholarship beyond the point which it had hitherto reached here. Rask of Copenhagen—a Dane, not a German—and Jacob Grimm (a German, ultimately professor at Berlin) gave a new impetus to research in the history of our own as well as of other languages.

The most eminent English investigators of the early nineteenth century derived help from German tuition and example. But it is a ludicrous error, of a kind which the Germans have been prone to encourage, to credit the Germans with a *monopoly* in philological research, in our own or other languages through the nineteenth century. The torch was kept burning in this country during the first half of the century, and in the opening of the second half an immense impetus was given to the study by a very characteristic Englishman, Dr. Furnivall, through his foundation of the Early English Text Society, which he followed up by forming the Chaucer and the Wyclif Societies. At the same time, as Secretary of the Philological Society, Dr. Furnivall had a main hand in setting afloat the *New English Dictionary*, as ample and as creditable a monument of philological research as anything ever made in Germany.

This Association also purposes to promote and expand literary research no less assiduously than philological research. It hopes to deal with the history of English and foreign literature and with the disciplined criticism of

English and foreign literature in which biography and exegesis play their parts. Research in English literature owes comparatively little to foreign activity. Like philology English literary history and criticism began their serious careers in the eighteenth century, and although important contributions have been made in Germany to the history and criticism of the early periods, the study of the later and the more fertile periods of English literature has been, during the past century and a half, advanced by ourselves or by men of our own race. Thomas Warton's *History of English Poetry*, which was published between 1774 and 1781, began a chain of notable native achievements in literary history, of which Courthope's History and Saintsbury's many encyclopaedic ventures may be regarded as lately added links. I think in this connexion I may without immodesty mention the *Dictionary of National Biography*.

At the same time, in spite of the valuable work which has been done here of late in philology, criticism, and literary history, there are wide regions in all these branches awaiting more thorough exploration. We want more scholarly effort in this country of the sort which is identified with the name of one of our Vice-Presidents, Dr. Paget Toynbee, whose researches into Dante offer an inspiring example of devotion. There should be a larger public interesting itself in such erudition.

From signs I have observed I judge that the cause of organized and endowed research in natural science is making to-day surer progress than the cause of research in literary science. One of the reasons that have weighed with me in supporting the formation of this Society is that the prospect of organizing research in the departments of the arts, in the roll of which modern languages and literatures must inevitably hold a foremost place, are less rosy at the moment than the prospects of the sciences. The cry for developing scientific research is, we are glad to think, growing too insistent to be ignored in the coming period of Reconstruction. But we must guard ourselves against the dangers lurking in any monopolization of the intellectual energy of a people, in any monopoly of its educational resources by scientific research to the exclusion or the disparagement of research in humanistic studies, the studies which lie outside the range of the physical sciences. One cannot live by bread alone. The empire of the mind has many provinces, and while fully acknowledging the need of cultivating more intensively than ever the scientific provinces of that empire, I think this Association will deserve well of the nation if it succeed in quickening public interest in the desirability of submitting to a like intensive treatment a literary province of the empire of mind, a literary province which is quite as important as any other in the circle of the arts. The endowment of literary and philological research will never be so expensive as the endowment of scientific research, and the intellectual efficiency of the nation in its highest aspects will be incompletely or one-sidedly developed if the literary side of advanced study be overlooked or denied a fairly proportioned share of practical recognition.

II

There is another point of view which gives research in foreign languages and literature—and especially in foreign literature—a peculiar and a very emphatic political importance, an importance which, great as it is at the moment, is likely hereafter to increase. To a larger extent abroad than at home, the men of letters of a nation are reckoned national heroes and benefactors, and for the scholarship of one country to throw new light by dint of research on the literature of another is welcomed by the enlightened opinion of that other country as an act of fraternal homage which helps to promote good understanding between the two peoples at large. If this Association, therefore, stimulate literary research in foreign literature it will, I claim, be deepening and broadening the fraternal bases of humanity, and will be smoothing the path of that League of Nations which is to consecrate the coming peace.

I may perhaps illustrate this general point by a special instance. I think it is the conviction of us all that our entente with France gives the happiest assurance of the future well-being not of the two countries alone but of the civilized globe. We shall all be agreed, too, that no effort on our part to perpetuate that auspicious entente should be spared. In glancing at the history of that entente and at the stages through which it reached fruition, I think it no extravagance to reckon among the favouring breezes the recent development in France of research in our own literature.

It is to be admitted that the French reading public has shown a lively interest in many of our great authors, notably in our novelists, for some two centuries. Shakespeare during the same period has had somewhat chequered fortunes in French opinion. I am not sure that the mere circulation of popular foreign literature in native translations has very much effect on international political relations. But within quite recent times, within scarcely more than the last thirty years, English literature has experienced at the hands of French scholars a new and previously unknown attention. English literature has been promoted to the rank of a learned study, and research of a progressive intensity by French savants has shed new light on many passages of our literary history. Numerous scholarly and erudite monographs from French pens bear witness to the excellent quality of French research in its exploration of our own literature. It would be invidious to cite examples from the growing mass of successful achievement in this direction, but I may perhaps mention in passing the work of Angellier on Burns, of Legouis on Wordsworth, of Berger on Blake, of Feuillerat on Lyly and the early organization of the Elizabethan theatre. Nor could I willingly omit the great collection of books embodying the profound yet fascinating learning of M. Jusserand, long the French ambassador in Washington—a friend of my own, I am proud to add, of more than thirty years' standing.

To this new French movement I venture to attribute something at any rate of the change in political and social sentiment between the two nations. English literary research requires frequent visits to this country on the part of those who undertake it. It requires a perfect command of our language and an understanding of our temperament. The Frenchmen who have engaged, are engaging, or will engage, in such pursuit may never be very numerous, but I believe each one of them inevitably becomes the centre of a small circle from which radiates international goodwill. The greater their number, the better the prospect of the two peoples' happiness. This Association will, I trust, take to heart the French example and among its many aims will strive, *en revanche*, to foster research by English students in French literature, where there is still room, I venture to suggest, for much repaying effort.

This process of interchange in research is capable of very varied application. Italian literature, to which ours is deeply indebted, is wealthy enough to furnish English scholars with more opportunities of research than have yet been used. Thus our present alliance with Italy might be aided. Our literary loans from Scandinavian language and literature are sufficiently large to justify some of our students seeking fresh themes of research there. Many old nations, small in area and population, which glory in their national languages and literatures, are about to regain their long-lost independence and national liberties. There would be a mutual advantage if some of our students investigated the languages and literatures of Poland, Bohemia, Serbia, and Armenia, and if students of those nationalities applied themselves to the advanced study of our language and literature. I am aware that some are already thus engaged. Any assistance that this Association can render them and those who follow in their footsteps will, I feel sure, be most readily rendered. It will, I imagine, be one of the aspirations of this Association to encourage and facilitate every permutation of research of the kind.

Then there is the correlated comparative study of literatures, the precise measuring of the debt which one country's ideas, thought, and fancy owe to another country's. This branch of literary study is again capable of vast expansion and wellnigh infinite development. Its importance and interest deserve a far fuller recognition than has yet been given it. Valuable contributions have been made in France, America, Germany, and this country, but it is easy to suggest fresh directions in which comparative literary research may be pursued with profit.

Ideas and literary forms are, like words, always travelling in more or less mysterious ways from one literature to another, and the close observation of the processes is as exhilarating as any branch of learning. Here again is work which makes for international goodwill. The efficient study of comparative literature which illustrates and explains the never resting interchange of thought and fancy is likely to prove that the English-speaking world and its European allies are 'for intellectual and spiritual purposes' already well qualified to become 'one great confederation bound to a joint action and working to a common result'.

III

In this country research has never been exclusively pursued by those practically engaged in education, and our Association looks for support to many who are not in any way connected with Colleges or Schools. In the subjects with which we are specially concerned, English philology, phonology, literary history, criticism, and biography, the active researchers include Thorpe, Ellis, Furnivall, Courthope, Leslie Stephen, and several of a younger generation who cannot be reckoned among professional instructors of youth. In Germany and America, and indeed in France and Italy, it is much rarer than with us to find learning advanced by men, so to speak, of the world. We may rest assured that the English tradition of non-academic research will continue with undiminished benefit to the cause of knowledge.

At the same time it is of good omen that the teaching profession in its higher branches should be liberally represented on our roll of members. To my mind, the systematic promotion of national research and the systematic improvement in methods of research, and the widening of the ranks of researchers, can only come if the Universities and all places of advanced study acknowledge the obligation of enlisting in their teaching services men and women capable of adding by their own personal effort to the existing store of knowledge. I do not attach importance to the view that faculty for research impairs or is inconsistent with teaching efficiency. It may be possible, I know, to cite evidence in support of such a contention, but I believe that a broad examination of the facts will justify an opposite conclusion. I have heard it said that to employ an expert in research in teaching is like employing a razor to cut wood. There are, of course, proprieties to be observed. One would not reasonably expect a Gibbon or a Macaulay to instruct pass students in rudiments of history. You would not expect an eminent expert to devote eight hours a day all the working year round in oral instruction or the correction of exercises. There will, too, always be successful teachers in the lower branches of the educational system who will not and cannot engage in research. But in the higher branches the whole spirit of education will be quickened and will be genuinely progressive from generation to generation only if an aptitude for research is recognized as a qualification for the highest appointments. The conditions of such employment ought, too, to leave the professor or teacher adequate opportunity of continuously advancing in the seclusion of his laboratory or library the bounds of his knowledge for the good of himself and others.

Another point is worth a word. History tells us that professors inspired by a passion and a power for research stimulate in a unique fashion the zeal and efficiency of the best kind of student. It is well known how in the past the reputation of very erudite teachers drew to their lecture-rooms students from all quarters, who in due time went out into the world to spread the knowledge of their professor's work, and by their own efforts to carry that work many stages forward. Such students invariably preserve affectionate memories of their professor's guidance and counsel, and the system fosters harmony throughout the spheres of learning. Indeed, where the fame of a researching professor works as a magnet attracting foreign students, the system very signally contributes to international good fellowship.

I hope this Association may do something to give new strength to the beneficent influence exerted by researching professors on the educational hierarchy. This Association might usefully set up an advisory bureau to which students from all parts of the world might turn for advice when they are seeking the professorial aid best fitted to develop their special proclivities in research.

I think this Association should so organize itself from the outset as to be an effective instrument of propaganda.

Bacon showed by a practical example that the first preliminary to a substantial extension of research in any and every branch of knowledge was to survey what had been done and report on what remained to be done. He advised what he called 'a public designation concerning such parts of knowledge as may appear not to have been already sufficiently laboured and undertaken'. I think co-operative and co-ordinated effort in such a direction should be organized at an early date by this Association, as far as modern languages and literatures are concerned. The field of collective, critical bibliography in these departments of learning is, in my opinion, in urgent need of up-to-date development. The hour seems ripening for a vigorous attempt to supply the deficiency. The foundations of the *New English Dictionary* were laid as long ago as 1858. Those of the *Dictionary of National Biography* were laid in 1882. Both those enterprises are testimonies to the ingenuity and energy of Victorian scholarship. The time seems almost to have come round when some equally imposing venture of cognate aim should be launched under the auspices of our own Georgian age. An exhaustive historical and critical bibliography of modern languages and literatures conceived in the spirit of Bacon's *Advancement of Learning*, with the deficiencies and insufficiencies duly noted, might well carry forward whatever is good in the Victorian tradition. Such an undertaking, while its preparation would furnish students with excellent practical opportunities of right training, would stimulate useful research hereafter and make its foundations sound. Many years and many hands would be needed, but this Association would well justify itself if it gave such a project a prominent place in its programme.

Let my last words, like my first, echo the wisdom of the greatest of English prophets and champions of research, Francis Bacon. In his great plea for the advancement of learning, Bacon laid down three general fundamental conditions which, in his view, could alone ensure the success of sustained researching endeavour.

A chief condition was what Bacon called 'conjunction of labour' (by which he meant fraternal co-operation in the way of personal intercourse and correspondence) 'whereby', he said, 'the frailty of man may be supplied' (i. e. corrected or insured against).

Next there must be, in Bacon's view, 'soundness of direction', by which he meant there should be opportunities for training students in sound method, in method which 'preventeth error'.

The third Baconian condition is that research should

be adequately rewarded; 'only thus,' Bacon said, with his penetrating common sense, could 'endeavour be multiplied.'

This Association intends, I cannot doubt, to do all it can to satisfy all three conditions.

PRINCIPLES OF BIOGRAPHY [1]

I

I APPRECIATE very highly the honour which the electors have done me in conferring on me the office of Leslie Stephen Lecturer in this University. A word of respectful admiration seems due to the liberality of the electors in bestowing this dignity for the second time in succession on a graduate of the sister University.

I propose to deal broadly with a very familiar ambition—the ambition to record in written words, on the printed page, the career of a man or woman. My design is to consider in the first place the essential quality of the theme which justly merits biographic effort, and in the second place to discuss the methods of presentment which are likely to serve the true purpose of biography to best effect. Some paths which the biographer should avoid will also call for notice. I hope to suggest causes of success or failure in the practice of biography.

II

It is outside my scope to deal in any detail with the biography of particular persons. But I think I may without impropriety venture at the outset on a few words about the man in whose memory this lectureship has been founded, and whose name it bears. I am conscious that I lack many of the qualifications which my two predecessors in this honourable office [2] enjoyed. But I believe I may without immodesty claim one advantage in this post, which neither of them shared with me. Leslie Stephen was the master under whom I served my literary apprenticeship, and it was as his pupil that I grew to be his colleague and friend. He

[1] The Leslie Stephen Lecture, delivered in the Senate House, Cambridge, on 13 May 1911.
[2] [Professors A. C. Bradley and W. P. Ker].

gave me my earliest lessons in the writing of biography, and in speaking of its principles I am guided by his teaching. I am expressing views coloured by the experience for which he trained me.

There still happily survive members of this University and literary friends in London who knew Leslie Stephen in days far earlier than those of my first acquaintance with him. Compared with the companions of his youth or early middle age I have small right to speak of him. My association with him only concerned the last twenty-one years of his life. Yet I may plead that outside the ranks of his family I owe him debts of knowledge and encouragement which have not, I think, been excelled.

Stephen belonged to a notable generation, a generation the heroes of which seem to have been cast in a larger mould than those of my own. Stephen was the affectionate disciple of Darwin, the admiring acquaintance of Tennyson, the frequent but rather critical companion of Froude, the close friend of Henry Sidgwick, of George Meredith, of James Russell Lowell. He was personally known to Browning, Ruskin, Fitzgerald, and Carlyle. With such men as these he would be the first to disclaim equality, but he belonged to their orbit.

It was Stephen's habit to depreciate himself, and to underestimate the regard in which others held him. His qualities did not make for wide popularity. He did not seek what Tennyson calls 'the blare and blaze of fame'. Yet he established a reputation which his greatest coevals acknowledged—a reputation which came of the virility and perspicuity of his work in ethics, in literary criticism, and, above all, in biography.

Justly may the University claim some share in his fame. To Cambridge Stephen owed mainly the greatest blessing of life—health, as well as a large stock of his intellectual equipment. In Stephen's case Cambridge made of a weakly boy an athletic man. His training as an undergraduate turned him into an athlete in body no less than in mind. Not that his physical health was ever obtrusively robust, but the physical exercise of his undergraduate days, in which he engaged with a wholly spontaneous zeal, clearly helped him to measure a span of life exceeding the psalmist's three score years and ten. Even more notable is the influence which this place exerted on his intellectual temper. The ideal of dry common sense, which dominated thought here in his youthful days, was his guiding star through life. He was always impatient of rhetoric, of sentimentality, of floridity in life or literature. His virtues as man and writer were somewhat of the Spartan kind. It was his life here in youth and early middle age that chiefly bred the terseness, the frankness, the dialectical adroitness which give his literary work its savour. Although he severed his connexion with his University before he was forty, and though to some extent his sympathies with Cambridge afterwards decayed, its beneficent influences were never obliterated in him.

To the world at large as years advanced he seemed reserved and melancholy. I have heard him groan for hours together over the verbosity and blindness of biographers. But his seasons of depression, save in sickness, were passing moods. No man found richer solace than he in the early friendships which he formed in his University. His enthusiasm for his college while undergraduate, fellow, and tutor, always kept alive happy memories, which helped to assuage sorrow, as I can testify from some evenings spent with him, when heavy domestic grief bowed down his spirit. 'I love the sleepy river,' he said in his last days, 'not even the Alpine scenery is dearer to me.'

Often a gladiator wielding unsparingly the sword of plain speech against orthodox beliefs, he dealt his strokes fairly and squarely, and few of his adversaries cherished lasting resentment. Wary of enthusiasm and impatient of insincerity or incompetence, he admired without reserve all greatness in deed or thought. Every honest endeavour won his sympathy. His tenderness of heart was without any uncharitable leaven. There was always abundance of affectionate interest in those with whom he worked. Notably in his case is the style of the author the character of the man. 'I think', wrote Robert Louis Stevenson, 'it is always wholesome to read Leslie Stephen.' The dictum is in too minor a key to sound the whole truth, but it is the unpretending sort of language which Stephen would have appreciated about himself, especially from such a quarter.

III

Biography exists to satisfy a natural instinct in man— the commemorative instinct—the universal desire to keep alive the memories of those who by character and exploits have distinguished themselves from the mass of mankind. Art, pictorial, plastic, monumental art, competes with biography in preserving memories of buried humanity. But Jacques Amyot, the great prose writer of the French Renaissance—Amyot who, by his French translation of the works of Plutarch, first made the Greek master of biography an influence on modern thought and conduct— wrote these wise words on the relative values of biography and art as means of commemorating men's characters and achievements: 'There is neither picture, nor image of marble, nor arch of triumph, nor pillar, nor sumptuous sepulchre, can match the durableness of an eloquent biography, furnished with the qualities which it ought to have.' 'Furnished with the qualities which it ought to have'—there is the problem which we are met to face. Biography is not so imposing to the general eye as pyramids and mausoleums, statues and columns, portraits and memorial foundations, but it is the *safest* way, as Thomas Fuller wrote, to protect a memory from oblivion. Plutarch, Tacitus, and Suetonius' biographical memorials of distinguished men have worn better than the more substantial tributes of art to their heroes' fame.

The aim of biography is, in general terms, to hand down to a future age the history of individual men or women, to transmit enduringly their character and exploits. Character and exploits are for biographical purposes inseparable. Character which does not translate itself into exploit is for the biographer a mere phantasm. The exploit may range from mere talk, as in the case of Johnson, to empire-building and military conquest, as in the case of Julius Caesar or Napoleon. But character and exploit jointly constitute biographic personality. Biography aims at satisfying the commemorative instinct by exercise of its power to transmit personality.

The biographic aim implies two constant and obvious conditions. Firstly, the subject-matter, the character and achievement out of which the biography is to be woven, must be capable of moving the interest of posterity. Secondly, the manner or style of the record should be of a texture which is calculated to endure, to outlive the fashion or taste of the hour. In other words, biography depends for its successful accomplishment on the two elements of fit matter and fit manner, of fit theme and fit treatment.

Good treatment will not compensate for a bad theme, nor will a good theme compensate for bad treatment. Theme and treatment must both answer equally a call of permanent distinction. There are cases in which a good subject is found in combination with a bad form. That indeed is no uncommon experience. In the result, the commemorative instinct remains unsatisfied and biography fails to perform its function. The converse association of a bad theme with good treatment, of bad matter with good manner, is rarer, and may kindle some literary interest, although not an interest of biographic concern. For the life of a nonentity or a mediocrity, however skilfully contrived, conflicts with primary biographic principles. Unless subject-matter and style be both of a commensurate sufficiency, biography lacks 'the qualities which it ought to have', the qualities which ensure permanence, the qualities which satisfy the commemorative instinct.

What constitutes fitness in a biographic theme? The question raises puzzling issues. The commemorative instinct which biography has to satisfy scarcely seems to obey in its habitual working any one clear immutable law. The Italian poet Ariosto imagined, with some allegorical vagueness, that at the end of every man's thread of life there hung a medal stamped with his name, and that, as Death severed life's thread with its fatal shears, Time seized the medal and dropped it into the river of Lethe. Yet a few, a very few, of the stamped medals were caught as they fell towards the waters of oblivion by swans, who carried off the medals and deposited them in a temple or museum of immortality. Ariosto's swans are biographers: by what motive are they impelled to rescue any medals of personality from the flood of forgetfulness into which they let the mass sink?

Perhaps the old Greek definition of the fit theme of tragedy may be usefully adapted to the fit theme of biography. A fit biographic theme is, in the Aristotelian phrase, a career which is 'serious, complete, and of a certain magnitude'. An unfit biographic theme is a career of trivial aim, incomplete, without magnitude, of or below mediocrity. The second clause in this definition, which prescribes the need of completeness, offers no ambiguity. It excludes from the scope of biography careers of living men, careers which are incomplete, because death witholds the finishing touch. Death is a part of life, and no man is fit subject for biography till he is dead. Living men have been made themes of biography. But the choice defies the cardinal condition of completeness. There is usually abroad an idle curiosity about prominent persons during their lifetime. It is not the business of biography to appease mere inquisitiveness. Its primary business is to be complete. The living theme can at best be a torso, a fragment. There clings to it, too, a savour either of the scandal or of the unbalanced laudation which living men rarely escape. Politicians, while they are yet active on the political stage, are often panegyrized or vilified by biographical partisans. The efficient commemorative instinct, which sets little store by such panegyric or vilification, craves, before all things, the completeness which death alone assures. No man's memory can be accounted great until it has outlived his life.

At the same time there is danger in postponing indefinitely biographic commemoration in cases where it is rightly due. There are insuperable obstacles to writing the lives of men long after their relatives and associates have passed away. Even the life of Shakespeare has suffered through the long interval which separates the date of his death from the first efforts of his biographers, and there are some of Shakespeare's literary contemporaries, whose biographic commemoration has been postponed to so distant a date after their career has closed that the attempt to satisfy the just call of the commemorative instinct has altogether failed.

But the theme of biography must be far more than 'complete'. It must be, in addition, both 'serious' and 'of a certain magnitude'. By seriousness we may understand the quality which stirs and firmly holds the attention of the earnest-minded.

What constitutes the needful 'magnitude' in a biographic theme? It is difficult to set up a fixed standard whereby to measure the dimensions of a human action. But by way of tentative suggestion or hypothesis, the volume of a human action may be said to vary, from the biographer's point of view, with the number of times that it has been accomplished or is capable of accomplishment.

The magnitude of human action is necessarily of many degrees; the scale ascends and descends. The production by Shakespeare of his thirty-seven plays is an action of the first magnitude, because the achievement is unique. The victory of Wellington at Waterloo is an action of great but of lesser magnitude, because deeds of like calibre have been achieved by other military commanders, and are doubtless capable, if the need arise, of accomplishment again. As we descend the scale of achievement, we reach by slow gradations the level of action which forms the terminal limit of the biographic province. Actions, however beneficent or honourable, which are accomplished or are capable of accomplishment by many thousands of persons are actions of mediocrity, and lack the dimension which justifies the biographer's notice.

The fact that a man is a devoted husband and father, an efficient schoolmaster, an exemplary parish priest, gives him in itself no claim to biographic commemoration, because his actions, although meritorious, are practically indistinguishable from those of thousands of his fellows. It follows further that official dignities, except of the rarest and most dignified kind, give *in themselves* no claim to biographic commemoration. That a man should become a peer, a member of parliament, a lord mayor, even a professor, and attend to his duties, are actions or experiences that have been accomplished or are capable of accomplishment by too large a number of persons to render them in themselves of appreciable magnitude. At the same time office may well give a man an opportunity of distinction which he might otherwise be without; official responsibility may well lift his career to the requisite level of eminence.

In appraising the magnitude—the biographic capacity or content—of a career, one must needs guard against certain false notions—εἴδωλα or idols in Baconian terminology—which prevail widely and tend to distort the judgement. Domestic partiality, social contiguity, fortuitous clamour of the crowd—such things frequently cause mediocrity to masquerade as magnitude. The biographer has to forswear the measuring rods of the family hearth, of the hospitable board, of journalistic advertisement. A kinsman or a kinswoman, an intimate companion, is easily moved by private affection to credit undiscriminatingly a man or woman's activity with the dimensions that justify biographic commemoration. A newspaper records day by day the activities of some seeker after notoriety, until his name grows more familiar to his generation than that of Shakespeare or Nelson. Evanescent repute may very easily, through journalistic iteration, be mistaken for that which will excite the commemorative instinct hereafter.

In estimating the magnitude of human action, there is need of some workable measure or gauge which shall operate independently of mere contemporary opinion. Contemporary fame is often withheld as arbitrarily as it is bestowed. Posthumous fame at times comes into being with strange suddenness, without any contemporary heralding at all. How suggestive to the student of biography is the fact that the name and work of Gregor Mendel, the Austrian monk and biological inquirer, who died nearly thirty years ago 'unwept, unhonoured, and unsung', should fill ten columns of the new edition of the *Encyclopaedia Britannica*,[1] a space in excess of that devoted to any one of the numerous heroes of science who enjoyed repute in their own lifetime. Current fame is no sure evidence of biographic fitness. The tumult and the shouting die and they may leave nothing behind which satisfies the biographic tests of completeness, seriousness, and magnitude.

IV

The biographer having found his fit theme is faced with the problem of its treatment. His aim is to transmit personality, to satisfy the commemorative instinct. He may learn something of the lawful processes from a preliminary study of the processes which are unlawful. The main path which he should follow may gain in clear definition if he be warned at the outset against certain neighbouring paths which are easily capable of leading him astray. Biography must resolutely preserve its independence of three imposing themes of study, which are often seen to compete for its control. True biography is no handmaid of ethical instruction. Its purpose is not that of history. It does not exist to serve biological or anthropological science. Any assistance that biography renders these three

[1] [The eleventh edition, 1910–1. Later editions have appeared since that date].

great interests—ethical, historical, and scientific—should be accidental; such aid is neither essential nor obligatory. Biography rules a domain of its own; it is autonomous—an attribute with which it is not always credited.

It was an amiable tenet in the orthodox creed of an ancient biographic school, that the career destined for biographic treatment should directly teach morality, should be conspicuously virtuous. The biography should, before all else, 'show virtue her own feature', or at any rate hymn her worth. Gentle Izaak Walton, like many biographers who wrote before and after him, regarded biography as 'an honour due to the virtuous dead, and a lesson in magnanimity to those who shall succeed them'. In Walton's demure judgement, dead men who are morally unworthy lie outside the scope of biography. It speaks well for the goodness of the world that good men have occupied more biographic pens than bad men, and that biographers have always cherished a charitable preference for benefactors over malefactors. But therein lies no proof that the merits of biography depend on its powers of edification.

It is with very large qualifications that Walton's ethical presumption can pass current. Sinners excite the commemorative instinct as well as saints. The careers of both Napoleon I and Napoleon III satisfy all conditions of the biographic theme, in spite of their spacious infringements of moral law. Suetonius defied no biographic principle when he treated of Roman emperors, many of whom were monsters of infamy. Biography is a truthful picture of life, of life's tangled skein, good and ill together. Biography prejudices its chances of success when it is consciously designed as an ethical guide of life.

Candour, which shall be innocent of ethical fervour or even of ethical intention, is a cardinal principle of right biographic method. It is often the biographer's anxious duty to present great achievements in near alliance with moral failings. Coleridge was a great poet and an illuminating thinker. But he was deficient in the moral sense, and justified himself for his offences by 'amazing wrigglings and self-reproaches and astonishing pouring forth of unctuous twaddling'. Byron, Porson, Nelson, Parnell, and many more for whom the commemorative instinct assuredly demands biographic commemoration combined great exploits with notorious defiance of virtue.

The ethical fallacy of biography has sanctioned two evasive methods of handling such perplexing phases of life—a method of suppression and a method of extenuation. The method of suppression has found distinguished advocates. Tennyson asked 'what business has the public to want to know about Byron's wildnesses ? He has given them fine work and they ought to be satisfied'. Here indeed we are advised, either to dispense with all biography of Byron, or only to accept a biography of him from which his 'wildnesses' are excluded. The cravings of the commemorative instinct which Byron's career has already excited render both these counsels futile.

The alternative method of extenuation has been adopted by an eminent man of letters of our own day in treating of an illustrious poetic contemporary of Byron— of Shelley. Writing Shelley's life under the admiring eyes of surviving relatives, the biographer has made other people responsible for most of Shelley's flagrant errors of conduct and has credited the poet's personality with an unfailing beneficence. In view of the biographer's true goal it is difficult to speak of the whitewashing method more indulgently than of the method of suppression. The biographer is a narrator, not a moralist, and candour is the salt of his narrative. He accepts alike what clearly tells in a man's favour and what clearly tells against him. Neither omission nor partisan vindication will satisfy the primary needs of the art.

At the same time the biographer is likely to miss his aim of transmitting personality truthfully if he give more space or emphasis to a man's lapses from virtue than is proportioned to their effects on his achievement. Although he may not fill the preacher's pulpit, a touch of sympathy with human frailty, of charity for wrongdoing, will the better fit him for his task.

There is a French proverb: *Tôt ou tard, tout se sait*— 'Sooner or later everything comes to light'. There is another French proverb: *Tout comprendre, c'est tout pardonner*—'To understand all is to pardon all'.

Both apophthegms make appeal to the biographer, and the second is quite as relevant to his work as the first. Lives written in a hostile spirit may not be wholly untruthful. But they tend to emphasize unpleasing features and thereby give a wrongful impression. Scurrility is not candour. To pander to a love of scandal is a greater sin in a biographer than in anybody else. Lord Campbell wrote lives of lawyers, which satisfy many of the conditions of biography. But their depreciatory tone, which prompted the epigram that biography lends a new sting to death, suggests malignity and distorts the true perspective. The competent biographer may fail from want of sympathy even when his skill is not in question. Like the portrait painter who is fascinated by forbidding aspects in a sitter's countenance, he may, even without conscious intention, produce a caricature instead of a portrait.

All gradations of moral infirmity, from serious crime to mere deviation from accepted codes of good manners, will from time to time claim the biographer's notice and call for presentation in due perspective. Downright offences are not his only sources of embarrassment. Perhaps more often is he confronted with inconsistencies of conduct or opinion, with sudden changes of beliefs, religious or political, which are currently suspected of dishonesty. Defective sympathy or partisan hostility is here as harmful as any resolve to point a moral. 'That conversion', says the moralist, 'will always be suspected which concurs with interest.' The suspicion is inevitable, but is conversion invariably dishonest ? May not increase of knowledge or a greater concentration of thought on the questions at issue induce a natural and an honest process of development ? Was Wordsworth a lost leader who left the revolutionary

companions of his early years for the orthodox Tories just
to receive a handful of silver and a bit of ribbon to stick in
his coat ? Was Disraeli's early abandonment of a radical
programme the act of a self-seeking adventurer ? Was
Gladstone's unexpected adoption of the policy of Irish
Home Rule prompted by impulses of reckless ambition,
by the hope of stealing meanly a march on political rivals ?
The biographer must hold the scales even. He must look
before and after, and close his ears to party resentments of
the hour. He must abide by the just and generous principles which move a critical friend's judgement. Wherever
he honestly can, a friend allows the benefit of the doubt;
he extenuates nothing, nor sets down aught in malice.
Brutus claimed that the record of Caesar's life in the
Capitol presented the dictator's 'glories wherein he was
worthy' by the side of the dictator's 'offences wherein he
was unworthy'. Neither were the merits under-estimated
nor were the defects over-emphasized. Brutus's simple
words suggest the nicely adjusted scales in which the
moral blemishes of great men should be weighed by the
biographer. The aim of biography is not the moral
edification which may flow from the survey of either vice
or virtue; it is the truthful transmission of personality.

V

The pursuit by the biographer of the historian's aims
may prove as disastrous as any competition with the
austere aims of the moralist. The historical method is as
harmful to biography as the method of moral edification.
History encroaches on the biographer's province to the
prejudice of his art. Bacon, in his survey of learning,
carefully distinguished the 'history of times' (that is,
annals or chronicles) or the 'history of action' (that is,
histories in the accepted sense) from 'lives'. Bacon warns
us that history sets forth the pomp of public business;
while biography reveals the true and inward sources of
action, tells of private no less than of public conduct, and

pays as much attention to the slender wires as to the great weights that hang from them.

The distinction between history and biography lies so much on the surface that a confusion between them is barely justifiable. History may be compared to mechanics, the science which determines the power of bodies in the mass. Biography may be compared to chemistry, the science which analyses substances and resolves them into their constituent elements. The historian has to describe the aggregate movement of men and the manner in which that aggregate movement fashions political or social events and institutions. The historian has only to take into account those aspects of men's lives which affect the movements of the crowd that co-operates with them. The biographer's concern with the crowd is quite subsidiary and secondary. From the mass of mankind he draws apart those units who are in a decisive degree distinguishable from their neighbours. He submits them to minute examination, and his record of observation becomes a mirror of their exploits and character from the cradle to the grave. The historian looks at mankind through a field-glass. The biographer puts individual men under a magnifying glass.

It goes without saying that the biographer must frequently appeal for aid to the historian. An intelligent knowledge of the historical environment—of the contemporary trend of the aggregate movement of men—is indispensable to the biographer, if he would portray in fitting perspective all the operations of his unit. One cannot detach a sovereign or a statesman from the political world in which he has his being. The circumstance of politics is the scenery of the statesman's biography. But it is the art of the biographer sternly to subordinate his scenery to his actors. He must never crowd his stage with upholstery and scenic apparatus that can only distract the spectators' attention from the proper interest of the piece. If you attempt the life of Mary Queen of Scots, you miss your aim when you obscure the human interest and personal adventure, in which her career abounds, by grafting upon it an exhaustive exposition of the intricate relations of Scottish Presbyterians with Roman Catholics, or of Queen Elizabeth's tortuous foreign policy. These things are the bricks and mortar of history. Fragments of them may be needed as props in outlying portions of the biographical edifice, but even then they must be kept largely out of sight.

On these grounds I am afraid that that mass of laborious works which bears the title of 'the life and times' of this or that celebrated person, calls for censure. These weighty volumes can be classed neither with right history nor with right biography. Most of them must be reckoned fruit of a misdirected zeal. One would not wish to speak disrespectfully of the self-denying toil which has raised a mountain of stones on however sprawling a plan to a great man's memory. But when one surveys that swollen cairn *The Life of John Milton narrated in connexion with the political, ecclesiastical and literary history of his time* which occupied a great part of David Masson's long and distinguished career, I accept in spite of the varied uses of the majestic volumes that plaintive judgement of Carlyle: 'Masson has hung on his Milton peg all the politics, which Milton, poor fellow, had never much to do with except to print a pamphlet or two.' Masson has hung on 'his Milton peg' not only 'all the politics which Milton, poor fellow, had never much to do with' but also all the ecclesiastical and literary history with which Milton had even less concern. Biography is not a peg for anything save the character and exploits of a man whose career answers the tests of biographic fitness.

I should hardly be bold enough to speak of the relations of biography and science, and of the peril to biographic method of bringing the two studies into too close a conjunction, had not the late Sir Francis Galton and several living correspondents urged on me, in my capacity of editor of *The Dictionary of National Biography*, the general advantage of adapting the biographic method of the

Dictionary to the needs of the scientific investigation of heredity and eugenics.

Biography, it has been argued, should serve as hand-maid to this new and absorbing department of biology and anthropology. The biographer should collect, after due scrutiny, those details of genealogy, habit, and physiological characteristics which may help the student of genetics to determine human types, to diagnose 'variations from type', to distinguish acquired from inherited characteristics, and to arrive by such roads at a finite conception of human individuality. If biography, without deviating from its true purpose or method, can aid the scientific inquiry into the origin and development of ability or genius, all is well. But, if biographic effort is to be swayed by conditions of genetical study, if it is to inquire minutely and statistically into the distant ramifications of every great man's pedigree, with the result that undistinguished grandfathers, grandmothers, fathers, mothers, even second cousins, shall receive almost as close attention as the great man himself, then dangers may be apprehended. Whether the secret of genius will ever be solved is for the future to determine. The biographer has no call to pursue speculation on the fascinating theme.

VI

Like all branches of modern literature, biography was efficiently practised by Greece and Rome, and it is to classical tuition that the modern art is deeply indebted. It was Amyot's great French translation of Plutarch which introduced the biography of disciplined purpose to the modern world, with lasting benefit to life and literature.

Plutarch's method is in one respect peculiar to himself. He endeavours to emphasize points of character and conduct in one man by instituting a formal comparison of them with traits of similar type in another man. He writes what he calls 'parallel lives' of some twenty great Greeks and Romans. Having written of Alexander the Great, he gives an account of Caesar; having written of

Demosthenes, he gives an account of Cicero. In every instance he adds to his pair of lives a chapter of comparisons and contrasts. The parallel method enhances the vividness of the portraiture, but it is not the feature of his work which gives it its permanent influence. His individual themes, and his detached treatment of them, deserve chief scrutiny.

Plutarch's subjects are all leaders in politics or war. Heroes of literature and art lie outside his sphere. From the modern point of view the range is arbitrarily limited. But his limitation of theme does not prejudice the value of his example. His guiding principles of treatment are of universal application. He collects authorities in ample store. His materials included not only written books and documents, but also experience and knowledge gathered in converse with well-informed persons. He bases his narrative on contemporary evidence wherever it is accessible, but he is watchful of the lies and fables of hearsay accretions. Where two conflicting versions of one incident are at hand, he selects the one which is in closer harmony with his hero's manners and nature.

But wide as is Plutarch's field of research, he is discriminating in his choice of detail. He knows the value of perspective. He did not, he tells us, declare all things at large. At times he wrote briefly of the noblest and most notorious achievements. He preferred to concentrate his attention upon what to the unseeing eye looked insignificant—upon 'a light occasion, a word or some sport'. 'Therein,' he adds, 'men's nature, dispositions, and manners appear more plainly than the famous battles won, wherein are slain 10,000 men.'

Personality was Plutarch's quarry. It was therefore needful for him to bring into due prominence the singularity of each human theme. His studies inevitably acquainted him with many unhappy or ungracious features in great men's lives, which asked admission to his canvas. The frailties were neither suppressed nor extenuated. Yet a sense of what he called 'reverent shame' deterred him from enlarging on men's frailties beyond the needs of his art. He was a just biographer who was not distracted from his proper aim by ethical fervour or by partisanship. Nor were the purposes of history or science within his scope.

None of Plutarch's biographic principles can be ignored with impunity. Very efficiently does his example warn the biographer against two faults to which biography of more modern date has shown itself peculiarly prone—the fault of misty sentimentality or vague rhapsodizing and the fault of tediousness. The value of rhapsodical or sentimental biography is commonly over-estimated when it is credited with any method at all. In a few instances an eloquent piece of literature is the outcome. But it is literature which belongs to another category than that of biography. Boccaccio's rhapsodical account of Dante is a favourable specimen of its class. We learn there much of the effect of love on youthful hearts. There is a fiery denunciation of the city of Florence for her guilt in banishing her greatest citizen. But Boccaccio's impassioned rhetoric leaves the story of Dante's life untold.

The rhapsodical or sentimental mode of biography will always have its votaries. It often makes a powerful appeal to the hearts of the ingenuous kindred of a departed relative. But the vapour of sentimentality is usually fatal to biographic light. I have already suggested how liable domestic partiality is to err in the choice of the biographic theme. It is no less harmful in ordinary conditions to biographic treatment or method. Very rarely will domestic sentiment recognize the limitations of the biographic art, or obey the cry for candour and perspective. Whether the theme be fit or no, the pen which is guided by domestic enthusiasm will, as a rule, flow to satiety with sentimental vagueness and inaccuracy. The advantage of intimate knowledge which might seem to come of a kinsman's personal propinquity to the biographic hero counts, save in a few notable instances for very little or for nothing. The domestic pen is too often innocent of literary experience.

The faculty of selection and arrangement is wanting, or is at any rate lost in the stream of cloudy panegyric. There are tendencies to emphasize the immaterial and to ignore the material. The sentimental image has to be protected at all hazards. How often has one found in biographies of distinguished men, which are compiled under the domestic eye or by the domestic hand, that youthful struggles with sordid poverty or suffering, that irregular experiences of budding manhood are ignored or half told from a misguided fear of disturbing sentimental bias. I may not reveal the secrets of my own prison-house. But I could recall many a surprising example of domestic anxiety to gloss over or misrepresent truthful and pertinent details in careers of immediate ancestors, because domestic illusion, which is often bred of the blindest conventions of propriety, scents an unedifying savour in facts which are quite harmless but quite necessary.

Domestic sentimentality has been known to exert pressure on the biographer who stands outside the domestic circle. He at times lacks the nerve to resist all its assaults. The peril is indeed ubiquitous. It is perhaps some consolation that Shakespeare's life was written after all his descendants were dead; for who knows, had they been alive, that such a detail as that his father was a village shopkeeper and went bankrupt would have been dismissed to oblivion by an invertebrate and conciliatory biographer, at the call of an ill-balanced domestic pride.

VII

Leslie Stephen said of a recent biography—which enjoyed some vogue—that it was 'too long and too idolatrous'. Those epithets 'too long and too idolatrous' indicate the two worst faults in biographic method, which Plutarch's teaching condemns. Of the biographic vice of idolatry, which springs largely from domestic partiality, I have already spoken enough. The vice of undue length is equally widespread and its prevalence stands in little need of illustration. It is a failing against which Plutarch's example warns us even more loudly than against idolatry. Yet it flourishes luxuriantly in spite of the master's warning. The lineal measurement of biography has no single, fixed scale. There is a threefold graduation answering in the first place to the importance of the career, in the second place to the gross amount of available material, and in the third place to the intrinsic value or biographic pertinence of the surviving records. The correspondence or the journals or the reports of conversation out of which the biographic web is to be woven vary immensely in biographic service. Lack of the raw material would make it impossible to write a life of Shakespeare of the same length as Lord Morley's *Life of Gladstone*. But brevity may be enjoined, in the case of men of the first eminence, not solely on the ground that the raw material is scanty. Even where the raw material be abundant, it may be deficient in the quality which illumines personality and may prove useless for biographic purposes. Among men of action especially, the faculty of self-expression in letters and papers is often crude and ill-developed. Diaries are filled with formalities of daily experience, with excerpts from travellers' guidebooks, or with commonplace reflections. The intrinsic interest for the biographer amounts to little more than proof of the writer's inability to transmit his individuality through his pen. Here drastic summarizing is alone permissible. In citing diaries the half or much less than half is very frequently more valuable than the whole. Rigid selection and lavish rejection of available records are processes which the biographer has often to practise in the sternest temper.

It may be needful for the biographer to examine mountainous masses of manuscript, but he must sift their contents in the light of true biographic principles. The balance has to be kept even between what precedes and what follows. No digression is permissible from the straight path of the hero's personality. The mode of work, which was adopted by one of the most skilful artists in black and white of our time, Phil May, may well offer the biographer suggestion here. Phil May in his drawings presented character with admirable fidelity. In the finished result the fewest possible lines were present. But the preliminary draft was, I understand, crowded with lines, the majority of which were erased by the artist before his work left his hand. Let the biographer note down every detail in fulness and at length. But before offering his labour to the world, let him excise every detail that does not make for graphic portrayal of character and exploit. No mere impressionist sketch satisfies the conditions of adequate biography. But personality is not transmitted on the biographic canvas through overcrowded detail. More than ever at the present day is there imperative need of winnowing biographic information, of dismissing the voluminous chaff while conserving the grain. The growing habit of ephemeral publicity, the methods of reporting the minutiae of prominent people's daily life, not merely by aid of the printing-press, but by the new mechanical inventions of photograph, phonograph, and even cinematograph, all accumulate raw biographic material in giant heaps at an unprecedented rate. The biographer's labours will hereafter be immensely increased; but they will be labours lost, unless principles of discrimination be rigorously applied.

VIII

A discriminating brevity is a law of the right biographic method—a brevity graduated by considerations on the one hand of the genuine importance of the theme or career, and on the other of the genuine value and interest of the available material. Instances of biographic failure, owing to infringements of this law of brevity, are legion, and one or other recent examples will leap to the minds of every one who subscribes to a circulating library. But every law is liable in uncovenanted conditions to a temporary suspense. To every rule there are exceptions, which prove its normal justness. The longest biography in the English language

is also the best. Boswell's *Life of Johnson* is indeed reckoned
the best specimen of biography that has yet been
written in any tongue. Critics agree that life on a desert
island would be tolerable with Boswell's biographic work
for companion. That verdict may be a metaphorical
flight. But it has not been risked in comment on any
other biography, and only in comment on two other books
in English, the English Bible and Shakespeare.

To what is attributable Boswell's unique triumph, in
spite of its challenge of the law of biographic brevity?
The triumph is primarily due to an unexampled con-
fluence of two very unusual phenomena. A biographic
theme of unprecedented breadth and energy found biographic treatment of an abnormally microscopic intensity.
The outcome is what men of science might well call a
'sport'.

There is no precise parallel to the episode of which
Boswell's biography was bred. Dr. Johnson, a being of
rare intellectual and moral manliness, draws to himself,
when well advanced in years, the loyal and unquestioning
adoration of a rarely inquisitive young man, whose chief
virtues are those of the faithful hound. Boswell's personality, save in his aspect of biographer, deserves small
respect. Self-indulgent, libidinous, drunken, vain, he
develops in relation to Johnson a parasitical temper which
makes him glorious. Boswell pursues Johnson for twenty
years like his shadow, and takes note of all that fell from
the great man's lips, the tones of his voice, the expressions
of his countenance. It is fortunate for us that he should
have done much which self-respecting persons would scorn
to do. The salt of Boswell's biography is his literal reports
of Johnson's conversation, reports in the spirit of the
interviewer, which run to enormous length and account
for the colossal dimensions of the book.

No other biographer has sought or obtained the like
opportunity of interviewing his hero and reporting his
conversation. It is doubtful if any hero save Johnson could
have come through the ordeal satisfactorily. It is falla-

cious to suggest that a mediocrity would, if submitted to the pertinacious scrutiny of a Boswell, give occasion for a biographic *tour de force* comparable with Johnson's life. There was a singular union of two exceptional human forces which, despite dissimilarity, proved to be mutually complementary. That miracle is responsible for the supreme effect. Until such a conjunction be repeated, Boswell's work will stand alone, quite out of the sphere of normal biography.

Boswell's book defies all traditional biographic scale; its flood of reported talk is biographic license, not law. Yet it is the paradoxical truth that Boswell's work illustrates to perfection many features of first importance to right biographic method. In spite of its unconscionable length and diffuseness, Boswell's biography always keeps with admirable tenacity to the fundamental purpose of transmitting personality. Every page makes its contribution to this single end. There are no digressions, no superfluities, no distracting issues. All the meticulous detail makes for a unity on which Plutarch could hardly improve.

In the second place, Boswell is the supreme champion of the great principle of biographic frankness; his native candour robs his tendency to idolatry of its familiar mischiefs. He declines to suppress anything that helps his reader to realize Johnson's personality. He bluntly refused Miss Hannah More's request 'to mitigate some of the asperities of our most revered and departed friend'. He would 'not cut off the doctor's claws nor make his tiger a cat to please anybody'. He was so faithful to the biographic law of candour that the frequent snubs which the doctor administered to the writer himself find a due place in the record.

Boswell's presentation of himself in the biography offers a third piece of valuable instruction to the biographer. It was not in Boswell's nature to efface himself. Yet it cannot be said of him, as of some other biographers, that he brings himself on the stage at the expense of his subject.

There are biographies which fail helplessly because the writer is always thinking as much, or perhaps more, of himself than of his theme. He is seeking to share in the honours of publicity. Boswell does not efface himself, but he envelops himself in the spirit of his theme; he stands in its shadow and never in its light.

Lastly, Boswell was an industrious collector of information. It may be objected that for the fifty-four years of Johnson's life which preceded Boswell's introduction to him, something more than Boswell knew has come to light since he wrote. It may be admitted that Boswell neglected a few sources of information from petty personal grudges against those who controlled them. The cry has indeed been lately raised, that some pigmy contemporary biographers of Johnson reveal a few phases of the doctor's character which Boswell either wilfully or unwittingly overlooked or minimized. Spots have been detected in the sun, but the sun's rays are undimmed. Boswell's achievement glows with a steadier and more expansive radiance than any other star in the biographic firmament.

There is yet another biography in the English language which transgresses the law of brevity without marring its effect, nay, with enhancement of its effect. There is a second exception to the principle of brevity which fails to impugn the normal rule, if on grounds quite different from those which Boswell pleads with security. Lockhart's *Life of Scott* is the second best biography in the language, Boswell's biography being the first. But Lockhart's merit is mainly due to the excellence and the abundance of the raw material provided for him in Scott's ample journals and correspondence. He was spared Boswell's toil of reporter and collector of information; almost all was ready to his hands, and he had merely to apply to his vast store those faculties of selection and arrangement which came of his literary efficiency and experience. It is very rare for a man of Sir Walter Scott's supreme genius, whose career and character, too, are free of dark places or mysteries prompting suppression or extenuation, to leave to a competent biographer an immense mass of fit biographic records penned by his own hand. So happy an event seems as unlikely to recur as a second meeting of a Johnson with a Boswell. Lockhart's challenge of the law of brevity is justified, and the justification barely touches normal experience.

IX

Encyclopaedic or collective biography is a special branch of biography which has not been infrequently practised, both in classical and modern times. To collective biography, in the form of national biography, Leslie Stephen dedicated immense energy, and to it I, in succession to him, have devoted almost all my adult life. The methods of collective or national biography clearly differ from those of individual biography in literary design and in the opportunity which is offered of literary embellishment. But there are points at which the method of the two biographic kinds converge. Collective or national biography, which brings a long series of lives within the confines of a single literary scheme, presses the obligations of brevity and conciseness to limits which individual or independent biography is not required to respect. Facts and dates loom larger in collective or national biography than in other biographic forms. The object of national as of all collective biography is Priestley's object in scientific exposition— 'to comprise as much knowledge as possible in the smallest compass'. Indulgence in rhetoric, voluble enthusiasm, emotion, loquacious sentiment, is for the national biographer the deadliest of sins. Yet his method will be of small avail if he be unable to arrange his bare facts and dates so as to indicate graphically the precise character of the personality and of the achievement with which he is dealing—if he fail to suggest the peculiar interest of the personality and the achievement by some happy epithet or brief touch of criticism. There are instances in which a miniature memoir thus graced has given a reader a sense of satisfaction almost as great as any that a largely planned biography can give—the feeling, namely, that to him is imparted all the information for which his commemorative instinct craves.

The methods of national biography are Spartan methods heartlessly enforced by an editor's vigilance. It might perhaps be doubted if any of the Spartan methods of collective biography could be adopted with advantage by independent biographers who are free of the collective biographer's shackles.

Yet the virtue of liberty may be overvalued. The collective biographer submits from the outset to a strict discipline. Without underrating the dissimilarity of the conditions in which the independent biographer works, one may often impute to him without injustice a lack of any such training as is required of his humbler brother-craftsmen. In the absence of disciplinary control, an untrained biographer has been known to fling before his readers a confused mass of irrelevant and inaccurate information, to load his page with unimpressive sentiment, with the result that the hero's really eminent achievements and distinctive characteristics are buried under the dust and ashes of special pleading, commonplace gossip, and helpless eulogy. Occasionally, at any rate, nothing would be lost by an exchange of a shapeless and woolly effigy from the unchartered workshop of a free and independent biographer, for a skeleton of facts and dates from the collective biographer's law-ridden factory.

X

None the less, from the purely literary point of view, a contribution to collective biography however useful and efficient cannot rank with a thoroughly workmanlike effort in individual biography. It is individual biography which gives unrestricted opportunities of literary skill. Where the theme is fit, the independent biographer has scope for the exercise of almost every literary gift.

Varied qualities are demanded of the successful biographer. He must have the patience to sift dust heaps of

written or printed papers. He must have the insight to
interpret what he has sifted, and the capacity to give form
to the essence of his findings. A Frenchman has said that
the features of Alexander ought only to be preserved by
the chisel of Apelles. The admonition implies that magnitude in a career demands corresponding eminence in the
biographer. No doubt the ideal partnership is there indicated. But like all counsels of perfection, this ideal union
shrinks from realization. Did the precept prevail, the field
of biography would be very circumscribed and few biographers would find employment. It is more workaday
counsel to bid the biographer avoid unfit themes and to
treat fit themes with scrupulous accuracy, with perfect
frankness, with discriminating sympathy, and with resolute
brevity. Not otherwise is one of ordinary clay likely to
minister worthily to the commemorative instinct of his
fellow men and to transmit to an after-age a memorable
personality.

THE PERSPECTIVE OF BIOGRAPHY [1]

I

THIS is not the first time that I have spoken or written of biography: the main business of my life has brought me into practical touch with the theme. I cannot refrain from drawing deductions from a prolonged personal experience, but I am not intending to-day any autobiographical excursion or confession. I am proposing especially to examine various moral and intellectual tendencies and certain chronological conditions which in my view either hamper or promote the production of sound and useful biography. I fear that I cannot avoid repeating some things that I have said before, but I am endeavouring to traverse some ground which I have not gone over before.[2]

It is an accidental coincidence that I have chosen a subject some aspects of which my appointed successor in this Chair has already dealt with. Mr. Asquith's address on Biography only became known to me on its very recent publication in his volume of *Occasional Addresses*. That volume appeared after I had fixed on my own theme.[3]

I have perhaps the less compunction in adhering to my original choice not merely because the field is a wide one admitting variety of treatment, but because Mr. Asquith largely devotes his address on biography to a branch of

[1] The Presidential Address to the English Association delivered on 10 May 1918. [The introductory section, containing chiefly personal references, has been omitted.]

[2] Although this address follows for the most part fresh lines, I have occasionally borrowed a few passages from three earlier essays of mine on the subject of biography, viz. 'National Biography', a lecture delivered at the Royal Institution on 31 January 1896, in *Cornhill Magazine*, March 1896 (reprinted separately); 'Principles of Biography', the Leslie Stephen Lecture (Cambridge University Press, 1911): 'At a Journey's End' in *Nineteenth Century And After*, December 1912.

[3] [The address by Mr. Asquith (as he then was) was delivered at the Edinburgh Philosophical Institution, 15 November 1901, and was included in *Occasional Addresses*, published in 1918.]

biographical writing which I judge to lie outside the strict biographical area. Mr. Asquith largely deals with autobiography, which, although obviously of the same family, is a collateral, and the family likeness is not in my view very close. Autobiography breathes a spirit and pursues an aim which, in my opinion, widely differs from that of biography. The man or woman who designs to describe himself and his own activities, writes in a vein which has little in common with the writer who sets out to describe another person and another person's activities. The autobiographer works from within outwards, while the biographer at least proposes to himself to work from without inwards. He is bound to start work from without, and he has been known to stay without all the time, never getting inwards at all. The autobiographer fixes his gaze mainly on himself. He is before all things an egoist. His success is proportioned to his self-absorption. His biographical kinsman is an altruist. His success is proportioned to his self-suppression. The general distinction is of the kind which separates the lyric poet from the dramatist.

'It would not be altogether absurd if a man were to thank God for his vanity among the other comforts of life.' Benjamin Franklin sets these words in the forefront of his autobiography, and they deserve to be set as a motto at the head of every successful autobiography. They are equally appropriate to autobiographical performances differing so widely in external circumstance as those of Samuel Pepys and John Wesley, of Jean Jacques Rousseau and Herbert Spencer.

Dr. Johnson may be right in his assertion that 'those relations are commonly of most value in which the writer tells his own story', but it is clear that a wide gulf separates a biographer's mental operations which are predominantly objective from an autobiographer's mental operations which are predominantly subjective. The one speaks the language of the plaintiff or defendant in the court of life, the other that of advocate or judge.

It is desirable to insist on this distinction because occasionally the failure of biographic effort is attributable to a confusion of the ultimately disparate aims of biography and autobiography. The biographer of the great Victorian novelist George Eliot, modestly anxious to suppress himself, and to let, as he says, his subject speak for herself, created out of quotations from George Eliot's letters and journals what he called, as I think erroneously, an autobiography. He wished his performance to be judged by an autobiographical standard. But a scrapbook of arbitrarily selected discontinuous extracts from letters and diaries, if they are worked into no connecting narrative, is neither fish nor flesh nor good red herring. The bricks stand piled in the builder's yard but the pile fails to serve the purpose of a building. An autobiographer alone can pen an autobiography, and no substituted service is allowable.

II

I do not propose to spend time in defining biography, or in tracing its historical evolution. It suffices to say that biography came into being at an early stage in the processes of civilization to satisfy a natural instinct in man, which may be called the commemorative instinct. Biography exists to satisfy the natural desire of civilized man to keep alive the memories of those who by character and exploit have distinguished themselves from the mass of humanity.

At a first glance biography may appear to be neither so imposing nor so generally effectual a mode of preserving the distinctive memories of buried humanity as portraiture or sculpture, or monumental architecture, or memorial foundations. Yet history shows that biography is, as Thomas Fuller, one of the early English practitioners, wrote, 'the safest way' to protect a memory from oblivion. Biographies wear better than pieces of pictorial or plastic art, or architectural monuments, or even memorial foundations, charitable or other. Memorial foundations have a habit of outgrowing the original tradition, of ceasing obviously to fulfil the commemorative intention. Biography is in any case a necessary complement, a protective corollary, of other forms of commemoration. In its absence the commemorative purpose, the personal significance, of a surviving portrait, or statue, or monument, or foundation lacks any certain guarantee of a long life.

> Vain was the chief's, the sage's pride,
> They had no memoir and they died.

Thus biography which exists to satisfy the commemorative instinct has for its aim the transmission to posterity of a full and fair history of a human being who by virtue of a combination of character and exploit has arrested contemporary attention and is likely to excite the curiosity or interest of a future generation. Biography is the endeavour to transmit as enduringly as is possible distinctive personality and achievement. In its most exalted aspect biography may be said in Milton's high sounding phrase to embalm and treasure up 'the precious life blood of a master spirit on purpose to a life beyond life'.

In the workaday world, however, biography does not confine its attention to the master spirits. As our chairman, Sir Henry Newbolt, once wrote of biographers when he was poring over the pages of the *Dictionary of National Biography*:

> Not of the great only [they] deign to tell
> The stars by which we steer,
> But lights out of the night that flashed and fell
> To night again are here.[1]

No person deserves a biography unless he be, in the literal sense, distinguished. The subject of a biography must be associated with a personality and with works which are distinguished, in the sense that they are not met with in the every-day range of human experience. But human action which can be credited with the biographic quality

[1] [From the poem, *Minora Sidera*, addressed by Sir Henry Newbolt to Leslie Stephen, when he was editor of the *Dictionary of National Biography*, with Sidney Lee as his assistant. The original has 'you' instead of 'they'.]

of distinction, varies infinitely in scale. It is not indeed only the master-spirits—the Shakespeares and the Miltons, the Drakes and the Nelsons—who in the interests of the present or the future justly invite biographic commemoration. Biography touches earth far below the stars. Although it leave out of account the vast majority of men and women, it can only justly satisfy the commemorative instinct by bringing a goodly sized minority within the biographic fold.

The Italian poet Ariosto imagined, with some allegorical vagueness, that at the end of every man's thread of life there hung a medal stamped with his name, and that, as Death severed Life's thread with its fatal shears, Time seized the medal and dropped it into the river of Lethe. Nevertheless a few, a very few, of the stamped medals were caught as they fell towards the waters of oblivion by swans, who carried off the medals and deposited them in a temple or museum of immortality. Ariosto's swans are biographers, whose function it is to rescue a few medals of distinguishable personality from the flood of forgetfulness into which the indistinguishable mass is inevitably destined to sink.

III

In the categories of creative art, biography can claim no foremost place. A touch of the portrait-painters' creative insight is essential to biographic eminence, yet the density of the raw material in which the biographer works hampers the exercise of the creative faculty in a degree unknown to other branches of art, literary, pictorial, or plastic. Efficient biography predicates a vast preliminary labour of a mechanical kind. 'Biography', wrote Boswell, the best of all biographers, 'occasions a degree of trouble far beyond that of any other species of composition.' The biographer begins his task by sorting heaps of written or printed papers, by exploring official records; by ransacking many a dark and dismal cavern of research. Boswell modestly refrained from detailing all his herculean labours

of investigation lest he might be judged, as he said, to be
'ridiculously ostentatious'. Carlyle, another biographic
giant, unashamedly showered floods of imprecations on the
obtuse tyranny of Dr. Dryasdust to whose car his biographic vocation bound him. These masters, Boswell and
Carlyle, set authoritative examples which humble disciples
ignore at their peril.

It is the biographer's first duty to sift and to interpret
his sweepings. Only when that process is accomplished
can he hope to give his findings essential form. Unity of
spirit, cohesion of tone, perspective, these are the things
which a due measure of the creative faculty will alone
guarantee. Otherwise, the delineation will lack the semblance of life and reality. Unlike the dramatist or the
novelist, the biographer cannot invent incident to bring
into relief his conceptions of the truth about the piece of
humanity which he is studying. His purpose is discovery,
not invention. Fundamentally his work is a compilation,
an industriously elaborated composition, a mosaic. But a
touch of the creative faculty is needed to give animation
to the dead bones; to evoke the illusion that the veins
'verily bear blood'.

The uninitiated tend to confuse a life or a biography
with a 'character' or character sketch. The character
sketch may form a useful segment of a biography, but as a
substitute for a life it has small or no value. Dr. Johnson
opens his great collection of the *Lives of the Poets* with the
warnings that 'a character is not a life'; that 'a character
furnishes so little detail, that scarcely anything is distinctly
known, but all is shown confused and enlarged through a
mist'. A 'character' is a nebulous impressionist study.
The method of the 'character' study is, at its best, that of
the impressionist artist who paints Venice in a hazy blur,
so that no palace or canal can be identified. The method,
however triumphantly the hand of genius may apply it to
canvas, is inapplicable to efficient biography. The method
of the efficient biographer is the more modest and mundane method of Canaletto, whose careful observation

shows with distinctness and in a true perspective every Venetian brick or pile.

The practice of the art of biography abounds in pitfalls. Although pictorial art and biography have only superficial affinities, the biographer may well digest the counsel which Ruskin authoritatively offered the pictorial artist. Ruskin's words run thus: 'There is only one way of *seeing* things rightly, and that is, seeing the whole of them, without any choice or more intense perception of one point than another, owing to our special idiosyncrasies.' It is the biographer's indulgence in the partial view, the giving an unchecked rein to his idiosyncrasies, which accounts for most of the wreckage in the biographic ocean. The biographer too often fails to see his facts steadily or to see them whole. His angle of observation excludes from his view much that is relevant, because it does not square with his personal predilection: his drawing is often out of perspective, not merely because he lacks the architectonic capacity of unifying or fusing detail, but because he suffers his private sympathies or antipathies to exclude much that is essential to completeness. Again, the writer's partialities will render his lights too brilliant and his shadows either too dark, or, as is a common experience, not dark enough. Right perspective both in a mechanical and moral sense is a primary condition of satisfactory performance.

The true principle of perspective in biography may be readily deduced from the triumphs of the art which belong to our literature. It is doubtful if any literature can claim such successful examples of the art as Boswell's *Life of Johnson*, and Lockhart's *Life of Scott*. For reasons which perhaps will not convince everybody, I would place beside these noble biographic monuments two others—Carlyle's *Life of Sterling*, and Froude's *Life of Carlyle*. True perspective comes of the twofold power of coherent arrangement and of unconstrained and undistorted vision. Boswell, Lockhart, Carlyle, and Froude may all be credited with the twin virtues or capacities. In the result each of their biographic performances is 'a satisfying whole', 'a perfect round'.

Whatever may be the effect on biographic perspective of moral or spiritual obliquity, it is of primary importance to note that there can be no glimmer of perspective when the architectonic faculty is absent or is idle. To my thinking, Carlyle not merely excelled even Dr. Johnson in the practice of biography, but he also expounded its theory more correctly and more comprehensively than the literary dictator. Carlyle thus described a biographic work to which perspective was lacking, owing to the absence of power or endeavour to bring consistency to the constituent elements. Carlyle depicted the result thus:

'A mass of materials is collected, and the building proceeds apace. Stone is laid on the top of stone, just as it comes to hand; a trowel or two of biographic mortar, if perfectly convenient, being spread in here and there, by way of cement; and so the strangest pile suddenly arises, amorphous, pointing every way but to the zenith; here a block of granite, there a mass of pipe-clay; till the whole finishes, when the materials are finished; and you leave it standing to posterity, like some miniature Stonehenge, a perfect architectural enigma.'

Carlyle was writing of Moore's long and full *Life of Byron*, where an unusually rich biographic opportunity was missed, not owing to any definable defect in the writer's vision, but because he lacked capacity to co-ordinate his raw material. Moore had access to ample evidence, both documentary and oral. He was a personal friend of the poet, and was on intimate terms with other personal friends. Reports of eyewitnesses were at hand to corroborate or correct written testimony. He enjoyed literary experience although it was gained in other than biographic fields. But in his *Life of Byron* he paid scant attention to the mechanical conditions of true biographical perspective. The outcome was a maze without a plan.

Yet disastrous as is the biographic effect of the neglect of the mechanical perspective, a worse fate befalls biography when the biographic perspective is distorted by an error in the biographer's angle of moral or spiritual or intellectual observation. The masters of biography and of biographic perspective, Boswell, Johnson, Lockhart, Carlyle, and Froude, were very conscious of the dangers incidental to the defectively narrow angle of biographic observation, and their example teaches the all-important lesson of broad and accurate vision.

IV

For purposes of detailed exposition here it may be convenient to substitute the short term 'bias' for the longer phrase 'distorting angle of observation'. My meaning will not be prejudiced by the exchange. The injurious forms of 'bias' seem to me to fall under five main heads which, although they may at times appear to encroach on one another, have each clearly distinguishable features. There is firstly the 'family' bias which connotes short-sighted domestic partiality. Next comes the 'official' bias, which connotes undue respect for conventional formulae of public or social life. There is thirdly the 'ethical' bias, which condemns biography to serve exclusively the irrelevant purpose of moral edification. Nearly akin is the bias of unconditional hero-worship which connotes undiluted panegyric and obsequious adulation. Finally there is the bias of the historian, which confuses the biographic aim with another only distantly akin to it. The 'historical' bias is calculated to repress unduly the element of personality which biographers exist to transmit.

The family bias, is best or worst discernible in biographies from a near kinsman's pen. The kinsman will rarely have made any previous experiment in the biographic art, and there is small likelihood that he has acquired any substantive architectonic faculty. The domestic biographer claims that his subject has been in life under his direct observation, and that his intercourse has been of the most intimate kind; but these conditions create in themselves no absolute or adequate qualification for biographic enterprise. Those who live in domestic relation with eminent men rarely see in the true perspective what is most worthy of remark about them. They tend to set in the forefront of their picture his domesticities, his domestic virtues. They take a domestic pride in his public service, with the detail and significance of which they are usually very imperfectly acquainted. They have knowledge peculiar to themselves—a partial knowledge which is only of biographic value when it is thoroughly fused with the whole available stock of biographic material. It may sound harsh to say that biography has no place for the widow's tears or the orphans' cry. On the other hand, the family bias often cherishes esoteric prejudices which may lead to the omission of essential facts. I have known biographies conceived in the distorting atmosphere of family prepossessions, which ignore the calling or status of the subject's parents, because, though these were quite creditable, they were humbler or more plebeian than the family bias found palatable. The uncorrected perspective of the family biographer often impels him to fashion a wooden idol, which may be adapted temporarily for domestic worship but can serve no larger and no lasting purpose.

V

The second form of bias, which I term *the ethical or edificatory bias*, will sometimes ally itself with the domestic bias, but it also manifests itself apart and equally distorts right biographic perspective. Sound biography of virtuous and valiant men will inevitably stimulate virtue and valour in its readers, but the aim of biography is misconstrued if edification be its deliberate goal. Many worthy persons harbour the delusion that biography should avowedly and exclusively inculcate moral principles. On this showing, there should be habitually chosen for biographic treatment only those men and women who could with any semblance of veracity be pictured as saints. Even so, the commemorative instinct, which biography exists to satisfy, will occasionally demand the admission of sinners to the biographic fold. The edificatory biographer will in that case be driven into one or other of two very dubious courses. The sins of his personage must be either so extenuated as to give the impression that he was a saint after all, or, if that device prove impracticable, the biographic theme must be contorted at all hazards into an awful example which by its repulsiveness shall keep the reader rooted in the path of virtue and orthodoxy. But the edificatory bias will also work with far greater subtlety. In the bulk of biographic subjects there will be lack of such strongly marked characteristics as will allow the boldest of biographers to present his model in the single and simple guise of either saint or devil. The edificatory bias works less obtrusively but no less deleteriously in the biographic treatment, for example, of one, who, although he be assuredly possessed of all the normal virtues, pains the friendly and orthodox biographer by heterodox deviation from established creeds and conventional practices. I shall describe a case of this kind where prompt steps were taken to arrest the error of biographic vision due to the edificatory bias, by the production of a second biography which presented the true perspective. A useful opportunity is thus offered of studying both poison and antidote together, of examining the same subject in both true and false biographic lights.

John Sterling, an attractive man of some literary power and much philosophic curiosity, at the age of 28, after a distinguished career at Cambridge University and various adventures in search of a regular occupation, took Holy Orders in the Church of England and served a curacy for eight months. His ordination was an ill-judged and precipitate step, from which he quickly retreated. It left no material or substantive impression on the moral or intellectual development of his personality. His temperament was always vivacious, enterprising, and eminently sociable. His brief career had no lack of happiness, although he fell early a prey to consumptive disease, and died at the age of 38. Sterling stands on the border line which separates those who do and those who do not merit biographic commemoration. His literary experiments and his varied associations give him the benefit of the doubt, but only a very exceptional set of posthumous circumstances could have justly made him the hero of two biographies instead of one.

Within four years of his death Archdeacon Hare, Sterling's lifelong friend and at one time his College Tutor and religious mentor, published a memoir, impregnated past cure with the writer's idiosyncrasies which were wholly religious or theological. Hare's biographic vision was blurred by the edificatory bias. He represented Sterling's career as a tragedy of spiritual torment, as a pathetic illustration of the misery incident to religious doubt. Hare's biography of Sterling is for the most part an edifying exposition of the alleged wretchedness which comes to those who question orthodox tenets. Carlyle happened to be another close and very affectionate friend of Sterling. To his mind Hare's edificatory bias wholly belied Sterling's personality, and gave an erroneous impression of the trend of his life's pilgrimage. Carlyle retorted in a portrait from his own easel. It was a case of Johnson writing Boswell's life; but Carlyle almost emulated Boswell's pertinacious industry in collecting the needful material. The result was a comprehensive and complete record of Sterling's short life in a perspective, unembarrassed by Hare's prepossessions. All taint of morbidity or mawkishness is absent from Carlyle's canvas, while there is no exaggeration of the modest interests attaching to Sterling's character and exploits. The organization of fact is admirable. Sterling was at one time, like Carlyle himself, a disciple of Coleridge, and the master is incidentally portrayed from personal observation with an unrivalled sureness of touch. Such shadows as truth demanded in Sterling's portrait are there, and they illustrate the all-compelling justness of Carlyle's angle of observation. A little vignette, in which Carlyle depicts Sterling reading to him and to Mrs. Carlyle some modest poetic exercise, is worth quoting as proof

that the biographer saw firmly and steadily all that there
was to be seen of Sterling, and saw it whole. Carlyle's
comment on Sterling's elocution runs thus:

'A dreary pulpit or even conventicle manner; that flattest moan-
ing hoo-hoo of predetermined pathos, with a kind of rocking canter
introduced by way of intonation, each stanza the exact fellow of the
other, and the dull swing of the rocking-horse duly in each; no
reading could be more unfavourable to Sterling's poetry than his
own. Such a mode of reading, and indeed generally in a man of
such vivacity the total absence of all gifts for play-acting or artistic
mimicry in any kind was a noticeable point.'

Carlyle's aim is not to edify, but to speak the biographer's
truth as he knew it.

VI

The official bias is usually innocent of conscious edificatory intention. It chiefly shows itself in an excess of
formal deference to the orthodoxies of social and official
convention. The official bias implies a blind faith in official or social decorum. It forbids any challenge of what
Carlyle called 'the respectabilities'. When Froude was
preparing in Carlyle's lifetime Mrs. Carlyle's correspondence for publication, he invited Carlyle's opinion as to
whether he ought not to omit some unflattering judgement on a public personage still living. Carlyle merely
said 'it would do the public personage no harm to know
what a sensible woman thought of him'. Here you have
a brutal defiance of the conventional reticence in biography to which the official bias clings.

It is largely in the supposed interest of men who have
played a prominent part in public and social life and of the
orthodoxies identified with public and social decorum that
the official bias is cherished. But the official bias is not
only seen to be operative in biographies of men who have
held public office—biographies of dignitaries of the official
hierarchies. It will often infect the biographies of writers
and artists when they have risen, as sometimes happens, on
the stepping-stones of artistic genius to social eminence.

It also tends to infect the biographic pens of those who themselves enjoy social eminence and are worshippers of the decorous orthodoxies, whatever may be their biographic themes. All who yield to the temptation of making a fetish of social convention are, when they turn biographers, the ready prey of the official bias.

The official bias is the foe of completeness; it sternly forbids the disclosures of the whole truth. It prides itself on a daring liberality when it suffers even scanty and partial glimpses of aught that lies behind the canonical scenes of officialdom. Unseemliness is often imputed by the official bias to any full notice of a public hero's private and personal predilections and experiences, as though biography can serve a genuine or satisfying purpose when a public man's idiosyncrasies or private activities are kept by the biographer behind a screen. Biography has small concern with the pomp and circumstance of public affairs or with social ceremony and pageantry. It is bound to attach a primary importance to the wires, often surprisingly slender, of motive and opportunity from which hang the great weights of public achievement. The perspective of biography is obviously all awry when private conduct and affairs are denied their share of the canvas or when they are imperfectly co-ordinated with public conduct and affairs. The demure voice of orthodoxy urges that it is above all things needful to preserve the dignity of a personage who has enjoyed public place and public renown. The fallacious cry works manifold disaster. A passion for sport, an indulgence in the lighter social pleasures, will often be judged by the victims of the official bias so to detract from the solid and serious fame of greatness that leading interests and characteristics of the hero will be ignored or vaguely and inconspicuously suggested in the biography. Either by suppression or by diplomatic evasion the sensitive susceptibilities of officialism will be saved, and appearances will be firmly installed in the place of realities.

It is almost sufficient condemnation of the official bias that it should be irreconcilable with a familiar biographic

law, which Plutarch framed and all his efficient disciples
have loyally obeyed. 'Nor is it', wrote Plutarch, 'in the
most distinguished achievements that man's personality
may be best discerned; an act of small note, a short saying,
a jest will distinguish the real character better than the
greatest sieges and most decisive battles.' To Plutarch's
'sieges' and 'battles', one might well add, the longest and
most belauded tenures of high office in church or state, or
the most exalted positions in the world of art, literature, or
science. Perspective depends on the presence of veracious
detail, of trifling circumstance. It is true that no more
space should be allowed to a man's littlenesses, to his
eccentricities, to his inconsistencies, to his lapses, than is
needed to convey a truthful impression of the whole
personality. But for the biographer under the fatal sway
of the official bias to dismiss altogether essential unheroic
evidence is to substitute a wooden effigy or plaster of Paris
model for a being of flesh and blood.

The official bias is widespread: its epidemic prevalence
is mainly responsible for the fallacy which imputes to the
biographer at large ghoulish propensities—a morbid desire
to tumble about helpless corpses and even to tear them
limb from limb. The poet Tennyson, who in early life
derided 'sleek respectability' in biographic and other fields
as a British idol, fell in later life under the obsession of the
official bias. He read into Shakespeare's imprecation on
his gravestone—'cursed be he that moves my bones'—a
warning against all biography save of the official kind.
Tennyson rather indiscriminately credited any free and
unofficial biography of a distinguished man with a design to

> Proclaim the faults he would not show;
> Break lock and seal; betray the trust;
> Keep nothing sacred.

The poet added by way of ironical plea for unofficial
frankness:

> 'Tis but just
> The many-headed beast should know.

Tennyson's taunt would be well merited by biography which is merely scurrilous and malicious, but that biographic species is so rare as to be negligible and censure is wasted upon it. The moral sense of all healthy communities is active enough to forbid its practice. In any case the moral energy of the community is better employed in a crusade against the official bias which fosters reticence at the expense of truth.

I forbear to give concrete illustrations of the working of the official bias and of the false errors in perspective which flow from it. I could mention a vast number of recent biographies of politicians, bishops, professors, heads of colleges, and other dignitaries which justifies Carlyle's ejaculation of eighty years ago 'How delicate, how decent is English biography, bless its mealy mouth'. As a rule it were better for the public interest to have no biography at all than a biography which is conceived in the official spirit of evasion or suppression, which distorts the perspective by economizing truth.

VII

I come now to the bias of hero-worship which commonly expresses itself in undiluted panegyric. The biographic aim of truthfulness disallows the claim to unvarying human perfection. Whenever that claim is accepted the biography becomes a beatific vision of a ghost instead of a living portrait of a human entity. Success in biography presumes sympathy with the biographic theme and admiration of heroic achievement. But mistrust is excited by the biographer who presents his hero in no mood other than the heroic, who never modulates the heroic key. The best practitioners in biography have readily checked the hero-worshipping distortion of biographic perspective, without injury, nay with benefit, to the just deserts of their subject. Boswell, when preparing his biography of Dr. Johnson, bluntly refused Miss Hannah More's request 'to mitigate some of the asperities of our most revered and departed friend' on the righteous ground that he would 'not cut off the doctor's claws nor make his tiger a cat to please anybody'. Boswell's retort suggests the proper frame of mind in which the biographer should approach his work.

Boswell's admirable precept is couched in the tone of his master whose own biographic labours illustrate to convincing effect the virtues of candour in a biographer and the futilities of hero-worship. In his *Lives of the Poets* strong personal prejudice occasionally provokes unwarranted censures, but, as a rule, Dr. Johnson is liberal in the praises of eminent achievement, and he is eminently fair in his estimates of mediocrity. He is prone to dwell on all the minute personal traits which he thinks to be essential to the presentation of a faithful likeness. The effect sometimes approaches the grotesque, but the biographic goal would not be reached otherwise. For example, the doctor harboured no doubt or disparagement of Swift's intellectual genius, but his appreciation would suffer had he omitted this living picture of Swift's person.

'The person of Swift had not many recommendations. He had a kind of muddy complexion, which, though he washed himself with Oriental scrupulosity, did not look clear. He had a countenance sour and severe, which he seldom softened by any appearance of gaiety. He stubbornly resisted any tendency to laughter.'

VIII

The historian's or historical bias stands on rather a different footing from the four other kinds of bias with which I have dealt. No less prejudicial than any of them to the right biographic perspective, it yet ministers to quite a different phase of distortion. A writer will never achieve the true biographic aim if he seek to serve at once two literary masters, History as well as Biography.

The distinction between history and biography lies so much on the surface that a confusion between them is barely justifiable. History may be compared to mechanics, the science which determines the power of bodies in the mass. Biography may be compared to chemistry, the

science which analyses substances and explains their operation by their composition. The historian has to describe
the aggregate movement of men, and the manner in which
that aggregate movement moulds political or social events
and institutions, and mainly political events and institutions, which, despite all recent argument to the contrary,
remain the historian's ultimate concern.

The biographer's concern with the crowd is secondary
and subsidiary. From the mass of mankind he draws apart
a unit who is in a decisive degree distinguishable from his
neighbours. He submits him to minute examination, and
the record of observation becomes a mirror of his exploits
and character from the cradle to the grave. The historian
looks at mankind through a field-glass: the biographer
puts an individual man under a magnifying glass.

It goes without saying that the biographer must frequently appeal for aid to the historian. An intelligent
knowledge of the historical environment—of the contemporary trend of the aggregate movement of men—is
indispensable to the biographer, if he would portray in
fitting perspective all the operations of his unit. One
cannot detach a sovereign or a statesman from the political
world in which he has his being. The circumstances of
politics is the scenery of the statesman's biography. But
it is the art of the biographer sternly to subordinate his
scenery to his actors. He must never crowd his stage with
upholstery and scenic apparatus that can only distract the
spectators' attention from the proper interest of the piece.
If you attempt the life of Mary Queen of Scots, you miss
your aim when you obscure the human interest and personal adventure, in which her career abounds, by grafting
upon it an exhaustive exposition of the intricate relations
of Scottish Presbyterians with Roman Catholics, or of
Queen Elizabeth's tortuous foreign policy. These things
are the bricks and mortar of history. Fragments of them
may be needed as props in outlying portions of the biographical edifice, but even then they must be kept largely
out of sight.

On these grounds I am afraid that that mass of laborious performances which bears the title of 'The Life and Times' of this or that celebrated person, calls, if not for censure, at any rate for faint praise. These weighty volumes can be classed neither with right history nor with right biography. The majority of them must be reckoned evidence of a misdirected zeal, of a misapprehension as to the true significance of biographic endeavour. Often such compilations are storehouses of raw material which are of great use to both biographer and historian in their own separate domains. But the perspective from the biographical point of view is seriously at fault.

IX

I come now to my last point, which touches a comprehensive condition of biographic perspective, and one which I have not so far handled. The efficient accuracy of the biographer's angle of observation will be substantially influenced by the distance of time which intervenes between the death of the biographic subject and the preparation of the biography. It is an essential quality of biography that the career of which it treats should be complete. Biography of the right kind excludes from its scope careers of living men, careers which are incomplete, because death withholds the finishing touch. No man is fit subject for biography till he be dead. Living men have been made themes of so-called biographies, but the choice inspires a limitation which forbids compliance with cardinal conditions of the art. The so-called biographers of living public men rarely make pretence of submission to the great primary principles. Consciously or unconsciously they aim at presenting some restricted view or interpretation of a prominent person's character and action. The design is either to increase or to diminish his reputation at the time of writing. There is no large intention of unfettered portrayal of personality. Apart from the essential defect of the material owing to the withholding of death's completing touch, the so-called biography of a living man is commonly steeped in raw partisan colouring which lacks endurance. Whether the outcome be lavish panegyric or, as is sometimes but more rarely the case, lavish vilification, the hues of the picture quickly fade. The ultimate hope of the writer is to create or stimulate sympathy or antipathy, an aspiration which is alien to conceptions of just biography. It is to the category of party pamphleteering that living biography may be logically relegated. It may stir a transient interest. It will in any case go to swell the heap of raw material which the true biographer will have to sift. But in itself the biography of a living man lacks biographic vitality.

The intervention of death alone brings the career within the lawful range of biography. It is not easy to state with precision the interval of time which should separate the operation of death from the production of the biographic record. There is a widely held belief that a biographer invites failure unless that interval be long, unless at least one generation has passed away before the biography be attempted. The inquiry reminds one of Pope's ironical discussion as to the number of years which is needed to convert an author who enjoys contemporary fame into a classic. Is there any better hope of fixing the exact point of time when a dead hero grows ripe for biography ?

> Shall we or shall we not, account him so,
> Who dy'd perhaps, an hundred years ago ?
>
> Suppose he wants a year will you compound ?
> And for a memoir deem him safe and sound.

While seeking some general definition, one may not demand too rigorous an enactment:

> We shall not quarrel for a year or two;
> By courtesy of England, he may do.

It would seem at first sight that two at least of the forms of bias to which I have called attention, the famliy and the official bias, will enjoy freer scope for their evil work when the interval is short than when it is long. The bias of hero-worship, too, may do the perspective greater harm when the hero has lately passed from life than when his death is a remote event. At any rate the family bias and the official bias can scarcely exert their full force save when persons are still alive to cherish first-hand memories of the hero. There seems plausibility, moreover, in the verdict that posterity takes a genuine interest in the description of a man's career only when its atmosphere is purged of the distorting influence of contemporary feeling or prejudice. The disturbing mists of partiality are more difficult to disperse or even penetrate while the partners or eye-witnesses of the man's activities survive.

On the other hand, there are wellnigh insuperable difficulties to be encountered if a life be delayed 'till interest and envy are at an end'. Among sources of biographic information the personal witness will always hold the first rank. In every case there will be details of importance to efficient biography which live in the memory of friends and colleagues, and with lapse of time will either perish or will survive in an inexact and hazy tradition. The personal knowledge which gives biography its opportunity of completeness is 'growing every day less, and in a short time is lost for ever'. On such grounds the motto of biography which seeks to satisfy the primary principles of the art would appear to be 'the sooner the better' rather than 'the later the better'.

This is substantially the creed of Dr. Johnson, who is a very high authority, if not the final oracle, on most points of biographic theory and practice. Dr. Johnson's earliest performance in the art concerned itself with Richard Savage, a poet of modest attainments, whose career was variously chequered. Johnson lived in close personal intercourse with Savage, and cherished a friendly feeling which, despite its sincerity, did not underrate his defects of character. Savage died on the 31st of July 1743. A bare week elapsed before Dr. Johnson, in an anonymous letter to *The Gentleman's Magazine*, stated that the poet's 'life will be speedily published by a person who was favoured by his

confidence'. Johnson's complete and satisfying biography
was published in the following February, within seven
months of the death of the subject. Johnson's *Life of
Savage* is a model of what the biographic commemoration
of a star of small magnitude should be. It is a faithful yet
candid narrative, extenuating nothing, and of course setting nothing down in malice. It owes wellnigh all its
excellence to the promptness with which it was taken in
hand.

Froude's *Life of Carlyle*, in spite of the storms of controversy which still beat about the book, supplies evidence
to much the same effect. Froude, who was the close personal friend of Carlyle for the last thirty-two years of
Carlyle's life and was his literary executor, published his
full biography within three years of Carlyle's death.
Froude's method is a combination of the methods of
Boswell and Lockhart. It gives very practical effect to the
biographic precepts of frank sincerity which Carlyle formulated and repeated with characteristic emphasis. It is
no discredit to the biography that some of Froude's readers
deemed Carlyle to be hoist by his biographer with his own
petard. The outcry which Carlyle's friends raised against
Froude's directness of speech was a tribute to his freedom
from the various biases of domestic partiality, moral edification, officialism, hero-worship, which were calculated
in Carlyle's tried judgement to ruin the perspective of
biography, and to reduce the art to futility.

In his biographic portrayal of Carlyle Froude suppresses
none of Carlyle's angularities of temper, of his sharpnesses
of tongue, of his defective sympathies, of his self-absorption. Froude painted the shadows darkly. But they do the
perspective no wrong, for the lights are also strong, and
glow with the reflections of direct personal scrutiny. The
portrait finally leaves a convincing impression of living
truth which a postponement of the work would have imperilled and in all likelihood would have frustrated.

There really seems little disagreement among the best
practitioners as to the serious risks of delay in the pre-

paration of biography. Boswell began his *Life of Johnson*
within a few months of the Doctor's death, and published
it, despite its bulk, within seven years—before any serious
inroad had been made on Johnson's circle as it was in his
day. Five years intervened between Sir Walter Scott's
death and the appearance of Lockhart's voluminous record. In recent times the interval has tended to grow even
briefer. Lord Morley, one of my most distinguished predecessors in the presidency of this Association, lately described as 'pernicious counsel' the familiar protest against
the publication of a biography until the subject's death
was forty or fifty years old. His own exhaustive *Life of
Gladstone*, in much of which the biographer is himself the
indispensable personal witness, was written within five
years of the statesman's demise. The current tendency
seems, indeed, to indicate a progressive abbreviation of the
interval between the death of a distinguished personage
and the composition of a biography. In the past three or
four years there have been published some six or seven full
memoirs of prominent persons who died less than two or
three years before the appearance of the biography. It is
to be admitted that some of these works show in active and
deleterious operation many of the forms of bias against
which I have declaimed. But there is no clear proof that
a delay of twice or thrice the duration would have exorcised the evil, while it is certain that a long postponement
would have entailed the loss of personal testimony. All the
biographic experience of our generation confirms the conclusions that the first-hand reminiscence of living contemporaries is the least dispensable ingredient, and that
the ever-threatening distortions of perspective are due to
causes by no means invariably traceable to the chronological conditions of production. Broadly speaking, despite the dangers to which the true perspective is always
liable, the balance of advantage seems to incline towards
early as contrasted with late biography. A lost opportunity of an early biography may never be recovered at a late
epoch. The wisdom of the world would have benefited to

the end of time had Thomas Heywood fulfilled his promise
of a biography of his friend and contemporary, William
Shakespeare, when the great dramatist was recently de-
ceased.

Again, if the commemorative instinct continue to be
active in the case of one who receives early biographic
commemoration, a later generation may ask for a fresh
biographic experiment on a more satisfying scale and in a
juster perspective. Fresh documentary material may well
become available in the long passage of years and may give
a new significance to the information already accessible.
At the same time, every late biographic effort will suffer
unless the personal witness has been enlisted in good time
in the biographic service.

X

I fear that much that I have said may be reckoned by
many to be 'counsels of perfection'. Yet the examples of
Johnson, Boswell, Carlyle, and Froude prove that such
'counsels of perfection' have been repeatedly turned to
practical account by those who enjoy a genuine biographic
faculty. Some of the familiar forms of bias which I have
censured—domestic partiality and hero-worship, for example—will often be blameless, if not praiseworthy, propensities, when they flourish outside the peculiar domain
of biographic effort. But the biographers who are unable
when at work to hold such impulses in check can hope for
no salvation; they will 'come like shadows, so depart'.

It is easier to preach than to practise. But the time is
appropriate to overhaul our conceptions of biography as
of wellnigh all other conceptions. The great events which
are stirring all our minds give the commemorative instinct
of all nations—not alone of our nation—a vital energy,
and a range for exercise, exceeding anything which has
been previously known. Biography will be called on—nay,
is being called upon, owing to the premature ending of so
many lives of high promise on the battle-fields of land, sea,
and air—to perform its peculiar commemorative function

on a vaster scale than ever before. In due time the statesmen and commanders who are controlling the nations'
and the world's destinies will themselves submit, at the
summons of the commemorative instinct, to biographic
scrutiny. All who have studied biographic principles in
the past owe it to the future to do what is possible to
ensure in the next era the observance of biographic truth.
None should be held to be qualified for biographic service
whose range of observation is unduly restricted, whose
vision is distorted by such forms of bias as are inimical to
the true biographic perspective. Biography can only justly
satisfy the commemorative instinct of humanity when it is
the fruit of conscientious industry combined with the
power of coherent and vivid delineation. Just and enduring biography means also sagacity and charity, dignity and
measure, but the breath of its life is candour.

'Tis not enough taste, judgment, learning join;
In all you speak, let truth and candour shine.

II. STUDIES IN SHAKESPEARE AND THE RENAISSANCE

SIR SIDNEY LEE

From a photograph included in a Shakespeare Tercentenary
Commemoration Volume, 1916, in the possession of the
Principal of East London College

THE IMPERSONAL ASPECT OF SHAKESPEARE'S ART[1]

I

IT has been said many times that it is mere futility to trouble one's head about the biographical or personal aspect of Shakespeare's entity. It should be sufficient for us to possess his works, and to enjoy them without seeking knowledge of the man behind them. Whether Shakespeare were born at Stratford-on-Avon or in Timbuctoo, whether he lived in the sixteenth century or the sixth, whether he were a collectivist or an individualist, a teetotaller or a wine-drinker, a monarchist or an anarchist, a monotheist or a pantheist, a puritan or a Roman Catholic, are, it is alleged, matters of no consequence, if not of irrelevance, for the student of *Hamlet* or *Macbeth*. When a dish of fine fruit is set before us at table, we should show ourselves almost unworthy of its sweet flavour and savour if we at once initiated investigation into the nature of the tree which produced it, and sought details touching the plant's growth and nurture.

There is much to be said for the attitude which seeks in literature pleasurable sensation, relief from sorrow, distraction from anxiety. It is not an attitude which is to be despised. But it cannot be the main position of the English Association. The scholar, critic, and teacher aim, in the study of literature, at something beyond experience of transient sensation. They aim at accuracy in the appreciation of an author's work; they try to measure its merits and defects, to estimate its originality or creative power. The critic and teacher examine the causes of literary achievement as well as its effects. It is pedantry to concentrate attention on the causes of literature to the neglect of its results; but there is scholarly virtue in a prudent

[1] A lecture delivered to the members of the English Association on the 11th of June 1909.

survey of the external circumstance which attends the
birth and life of literature.

In any case, to refuse to interest one's self in a great
author's history or personality is almost to defy a natural
instinct, which impels inquiry about those who prove
themselves our benefactors. We are not endeavouring to
gratify trivial curiosity. If we go the right way to work,
biographical research may be the best shape that a tribute
of admiration and affection can take.

When one seeks knowledge of the personality of an
author who died 300 years ago, one finds that the sources
may, as a rule, be roughly divided into two kinds. Firstly,
there are the records left by others concerning him.
Secondly, there are the records about himself of his own
making. We have to piece together external evidence and
internal evidence. To-night I chiefly inquire to what the
internal evidence amounts in Shakespeare's plays—What
is the revelation which Shakespeare made in his plays of his
private experiences and sentiments ?

The external evidence you know, and it need not detain
us long. I take for granted that the outward facts of
Shakespeare's life are familiar to you. The external circumstance of his career is, in my opinion, now accessible to
us in as full detail as is requisite. The traditional regrets
that the facts of Shakespeare's biography are scanty or
doubtful seem to me to lack substantial justification. At
the same time I fully admit that what is recorded of
Shakespeare's life at Stratford-on-Avon or in London
throws little or no light on his literary character, on his
spiritual nature. But to my mind it is unreasonable to
scorn revelations of him in the rough and tumble of the
workaday world, because they do not present him always
wearing the laurel crown.

A village youth, whose parents' material fortunes
steadily declined in his early manhood, he injudiciously
married as a mere boy, as boys sometimes will, a woman
eight years his senior. Then he left his family in the
country to make a career for himself in London. He was

stagestruck and longed to act and write plays. In London, after a short interval, his triumphs as a dramatist gained for him an assured position in theatrical circles. He never obtained much reputation as an actor. Evidence of his professional progress makes it clear that he was singularly industrious, singularly level-headed, and amply endowed with that practical common sense which enables a man to acquire and retain a moderate competence. His financial rewards were substantial. He husbanded his pecuniary profits; he purchased houses and lands in his native place, whither he returned while yet middle-aged to enjoy a placid retirement. A current popular fallacy would represent all men of poetic genius as despising the prosaic and conventional aim of making a livelihood. I have heard it argued that Shakespeare could not have written plays because he made good bargains with theatrical managers and saved money. There are, of course, notorious examples of poets proving bad economists, of poets living and dying in heart-rending poverty. Rarely are the profits of literature great, and the artistic temperament has been known to be incapable not only of comprehending the value of money when earned, but, worse still, even of earning any money at all. On the other hand, the examples of men of immense power in the highest field of literary effort proving efficient and rigorous men of business are so numerous, that there is nothing in the fully attested information regarding Shakespeare's business aptitude to rouse the smallest surprise. Chaucer and Sir Walter Scott, and, to take a foreign instance, Goethe, had all Shakespeare's sobriety in dealing with life's practical affairs. Almost all the great English novelists— and dramatic poets have some affinity with novelists— Richardson, Dickens, George Eliot, have illustrated the conjunction of imaginative power with some financial capacity. Great writers of recent times in other branches of literature—Carlyle, Macaulay, Tennyson, Robert Browning, and Herbert Spencer—did not defy the normal predilection for a balance on the right side at the bank.

There is nothing to disturb one's equanimity in a frank recognition that Shakespeare's colossal genius was linked with perfect sanity in his attitude to the fiscal problems which confront us all.

Shakespeare seems, in fact, to have had most of the bourgeois notions of comfort and respectability. Like many fellow actors, theatrical managers, and other parvenus, who by their own efforts became affluent, he acquired a rather dubious coat of arms. In his family relations he does not seem to have lived on very cordial terms with his elderly wife, but his will suggests that he maintained unbroken an affectionate intimacy with his elder daughter, and that he was a model grandfather.

Knowledge of this kind fails to define or illustrate Shakespeare's poetic individuality or his spiritual affinities. But it is not to be neglected. By bringing into prominent relief features in his character which set him on a level with other men, it makes our conception of his superiority in other directions the more real and actual. It does not explain or demonstrate the infinitude of his genius, which is another story, and loses nothing if it prove incapable of matter-of-fact, concrete explanation.

The study of Shakespeare's biography in the light of contemporary literary history shows that his practical experiences and fortunes did not materially differ from those who followed his profession of dramatist. His conscious aims and practices seem indistinguishable from those of contemporary men of letters. The mighty difference between his endeavours and those of his fellows must be assigned to the magical and involuntary working of genius, which, since the birth of poetry, has owned as large a charter as the wind to blow on whom it pleases. A very small acquaintance with the literary history of the world proves the hopelessness of seeking in details of birth or education, or in the common facts of life's everyday business, the secret springs of poetic inspiration.

The external biographic evidence also includes some early oral traditions and a few descriptions given of Shake-

speare by contemporaries. Such evidence mainly attests
the dramatist's modesty and amiability in ordinary social
relations. He won the affection of professional friends.
'I loved the man,' wrote his friend Ben Johnson, 'and do
honour his memory, on this side idolatry, as much as any.
He was, indeed, honest, and of open and free nature; had
an excellent fancy, brave notions, and gentle expressions.'
Another witness notes that he was 'very good company
and of a very ready and smooth wit'. There is ample corroboration of a genial and convivial temperament linked to a
quiet turn for good-humoured satire. According to some
early gossip, his father was 'a merry-cheeked old man', and
from him William inherited a gift for quick repartee, of
which his literary work offers abundant example. There
are one or two familiar anecdotes illustrating his love of a
jovial quip, even a turn for a harmless practical joke.
'Sweet', 'friendly', 'gentle', 'witty', are the epithets most
commonly associated with his name by his personal friends.
There survive, too, a few contemporary references to
Shakespeare's modes of work. These tell of 'his right
happy and copious industry', of the fertility and facility of
his pen. Some complain of his failure to correct his
manuscripts. He is said never to have erased a line. That
statement seems an exaggeration, for the text of his plays
indicates that he did not always refuse the labours of
revision. But in view of the mere amount of work he
completed in some twenty years of his working life, no
doubt is permissible of either his fluency or his powers of
application. Other evidence proves him to have been an
extraordinarily rapid reader, to have absorbed what he
read with a magical alertness, to have assimilated books
almost as easily as ordinary men inhale air.

Thus the external evidence reveals a genial, business-like
man, working rapidly and methodically; a modest man,
not overrating his own achievement at his friends' expense; one who outwardly betrayed sympathy with normal middle-class interests or ideals. Robert Browning,
among literary men of the Victorian era, was in these

regards not unlike Shakespeare. Browning in social intercourse proved, as a consequence, something of a disappointment to ecstatic worshippers.

II

It is to the internal evidence that I am directing your
attention to-night. Let me state my object precisely. I
propose to discuss with you—I am afraid somewhat summarily and perfunctorily—what are the reader's substantial chances of discerning in Shakespeare's plays clear,
definite, distinct testimony to the manner of man that the
dramatist was. I deal to-night with the plays alone, not
with the *Sonnets*. I omit the *Sonnets* of malice prepense,
and I hope you will agree with me, as I proceed to develop
the argument, that that omission is justifiable. Personally,
I believe that the luxuriance of Shakespeare's dramatic
instinct largely dominated that outburst of lyric melody
which gives the *Sonnets* their life. That is my personal
view. At the same time, I set in quite different categories
the relation in which a poet's personality stands to lyric
expression and the relation in which it stands to dramatic
expression. No general argument regarding the poet's
personality in the plays need therefore be materially
affected by a study of the *Sonnets*.

I have been the target of a good many critical arrows
in the matter of the *Sonnets*. If I admit, for the sake
of a quiet evening, that Shakespeare's *Sonnets* give voice
throughout to personal emotion (and to nothing besides),
the admission has no immediate pertinence save as tending
to create a presumption that there is no self-revelation in
the plays. The dominant topic of the *Sonnets*—an absorbing affection for a beautiful youth, an affection altogether transcending friendship—finds no place in the
plays. That fact of omission suggests that Shakespeare's
personality, if it lie on the surface of the *Sonnets*, is con-
cealed in the plays. For myself I believe that dramatic
forces are at work in the *Sonnets*, forces which produce the
potent illusion of a personal confession, without offering

sure evidence that Shakespeare is literally transcribing a personal experience. The poet's irresistible dramatic instinct was quite capable of presenting an affair of his art in a guise which would hardly make it distinguishable from an affair of his heart. But it would take me too far from my immediate purpose to pursue this thorny path.

I confine my present inquiry to the plays alone, and I ask, Does Shakespeare reveal himself to us there? I do not mean as Rousseau reveals himself in his *Confessions*, or as Johnson stands revealed in the pages of Boswell, but, say, as Cicero or Horace, as Burke or Shelley, lift the curtain on dominant predilections and prejudices in published words. Do Shakespeare's plays, like Cicero's or Burke's oratory, declare from time to time his precise likes or dislikes, his definite convictions and prejudices? Do we learn his private opinions on religion, on politics, and the other matters which more or less occupy every thinking man's attention? From 'personality' I here exclude physical characteristics and biographical details. I am not concerned with the everyday virtues and repugnances which most men of repute share alike. My inquiry is directed to distinguishing idiosyncrasies, to individual characteristics, to peculiar experiences of mind or heart.

At a first glance the theme may look simple enough. An author gives in the written page an expression of what is in him. He can have nothing else to give. Consequently all, it may be thought, one who seeks knowledge of an author's particular personality has to do, is to extract it from the verbal receptacle to which he committed it. But this is a superficial aspect of a highly complex question. There is a quibbling conundrum which asks, 'How can a thing be lost, when you know where it is?' and has for answer that the thing is at the bottom of the sea, or in the bottomless crevasse of a mountain. It may or may not be that the question I ask to-night may fairly provoke some such repartee. At any rate the speculation is difficult, and before we part with it, it imposes on us the obligation of glancing at the manner in which poetic genius works, and at the intellectual processes which are more especially involved in the creation of great drama.

III

On the main question, Does Shakespeare reveal a tangible personality in his plays ? diametrically opposite answers have been given by eminent critics. The doctors disagree. It may perhaps help us to appreciate the difficulties of the road along which we are travelling, if I report a few of the verdicts which have been already pronounced by judges whose decisions deserve attention. The theory of a personal note in the plays is of recent origin, and I can only quote in its support writers of comparatively youthful standing. I think that the earliest champion of a recognizable personality in Shakespearian drama is Emerson, the American essayist and moralist. These are sentences penned by Emerson near sixty years ago:

'Shakespeare is the only biographer of Shakespeare; . . . with Shakespeare for biographer, instead of Aubrey and Rowe, we have really the information which is material. . . . We have his recorded convictions on those questions which knock for answer at every heart. . . . What trait of his private mind has he hidden in his dramas ? . . . So far from Shakespeare's being the least known, he is the one person in all modern history fully known to us.'

Professor Dowden, Dr. George Brandes, and many German writers who are entitled to a respectful hearing, have written much to the same effect. Professor Raleigh has very lately ranged himself at Emerson's side and has asked, with more than Emerson's warmth, 'How dare we complain that Shakespeare has hidden himself from our knowledge in the plays ?' Professor Raleigh appears to detect neither ambiguity nor obscurity in Shakespeare's presentment of his personality in his plays. The impersonal view 'would', the professor alleges, 'never be entertained by an artist, and would have had short shrift from any of the company that assembled at the Mermaid Tavern'. At the Mermaid Tavern, you will remember,

Shakespeare and the great authors of his age were wont to assemble for convivial recreation. It would be unfair to discredit the Emersonian view because excess of enthusiasm has led a supporter into error. A good cause will not be killed by a bad argument. But Professor Raleigh's remark, that 'an artist' would never entertain anything but the personal theory, places his cause at some disadvantage. For it is 'artists' in literature who have asserted most confidently and persistently that Shakespeare was predominantly, supremely impersonal in his capacity of dramatist. Coleridge and Sir Walter Scott are among those who deny by anticipation the Emersonian verdict. Neither can be refused the title of 'artist'. Of later judges, let me summon Emerson's friend, Carlyle, who wrote, 'I will say of Shakespeare's work generally that we have no full impress of him there'. To much the same effect spoke Pater, one of the most penetrating of modern critics—'As happens with every true dramatist, Shakespeare is for the most part hidden behind the persons of his creations'. Carlyle and Pater's conclusions are irreconcilable with Emerson's words: 'We have his recorded convictions on those questions which knock for answer at every heart. . . . What trait of his private mind has he hidden in his dramas ?' Carlyle and Pater strike the note which, in spite of Professor Raleigh, is, with rare exceptions, habitual among 'artists' who have engaged in the discussion.

The most emphatic testimony to the 'impersonality' of Shakespearian drama comes from the most psychological of English poets and a dramatic artist of no mean order, Robert Browning. He bluntly declared that Shakespeare 'ne'er so little' at any point of his work 'left his bosom's gate ajar', and in his elaborate poem called *At the Mermaid*, he suggests prophetically the sort of 'shrift' which Professor Raleigh and his friends would have received at the tavern from the dramatist himself. In this familiar poem Browning presents Shakespeare in the informal and sociable confines of 'The Mermaid', addressing himself confidentially to his literary comrades on the very topic we are discussing to-night. The dramatist, after indulging in the pleasures of the convivial board just so far as to make him bring nothing but 'the truth out', is supposed to describe his creative mode of work as he hands the finished product to the circle of his intimate friends. Shakespeare's words, as Browning imagined them, run thus:

> Here's my work; does work discover
> What was rest from work—my life? . . .
> Blank of such a record truly
> Here's the work I hand—this scroll,
> Yours to take or leave; as duly
> Mine remains the unproffered soul . . .

The poet silences Emersonian criticism with the taunting interrogation:

> Which of you did I enable
> Once to slip inside my breast,
> There to catalogue and label
> What I like least, what love best?

Browning warns us that all sorts and conditions of life pass before us in procession in Shakespeare's plays, that Shakespeare's characters disclose to us all the secrets of their mind and heart. But as for the man who creates this mighty expanse of human comedy and human tragedy, he never wears his heart on his sleeve for daws to peck at, his own personality is his own secret, to which his pen is not the key. It is clear if Browning be in the right, Emerson and his followers are in the wrong.

To my thinking, the difficulties, even dangers, in Emerson's view of the omnipresence of Shakespeare's personality in his drama are insuperable. The dramatist's art obviously imposed on him the obligation of investing the great crowd of characters with all manner of emotions and sentiments which of necessity are irreconcilable one with another. His private opinions may be there; doubtless in a subtle sense they are there. But what is the critical test whereby we can distinguish Shakespeare's private utterances and opinions from the private utterances and opinions of his dramatic creations ? Where is the critical chemistry which will disentangle, precipitate, isolate, his personal views and sentiments ?

IV

I admit there are a few—a very few—plain and positive references to incidents which must belong to Shakespeare's experience. There is occasional mention in the two parts of *Henry IV*, in *The Taming of the Shrew*, and in *The Merry Wives of Windsor*, of places and persons with which only a native of Stratford-on-Avon could have been familiar. There are words and expressions which are peculiar to Warwickshire. There are references to country games and field sports of the graphic energy which testifies to sympathy with outdoor exercise. But I have larger topics in mind at the moment. I am seeking a clue to peculiar, spiritual or intellectual affinities, to individual experiences of emotion or passion.[1]

We shall all allow that Shakespeare's work shows sign of steady progress in art, and was clearly progressive in quality. His hand grew firmer, his thought richer, as his years increased. Throughout, there is steady development of dramatic power and dramatic temper. With his advance in age comes, in comedy and tragedy alike, a larger grasp of life. Humour and passion both grow larger in conception and scope. But this manifest feature of artistic development is not peculiar to Shakespeare; it indicates no definite idiosyncrasy. Such development is part of the universal law of growth. The mind of a man of thirty looks on life more seriously and with greater knowledge than a man of twenty; a man of forty improves in

[1] For a rather more 'personal' interpretation of Shakespeare's dramatic writings than I see my way to accept, I refer my readers to a lecture of admirable sanity by Mr. A. C. Bradley, in his *Oxford Lectures on Poetry*, pp. 311 sqq. I do not think on the essential issues the difference between Mr. Bradley and myself is, despite appearances, very great.

these regards on a man of thirty, and so on. We need not go to Shakespeare's plays to learn facts so generic as that he began life by being a boy, that he then reached adolescence and middle age, or that he exemplified in his work characteristics of various periods of human life. Such generalities do not help us to the knowledge of his peculiar personal views, to a realization of his individual experiences of mind and heart.

Nor are we likely to reach our goal through those philosophic commonplaces which are bountifully scattered over Shakespeare's work. It may be possible to deduce from the plays a broad practical philosophy which is alive with an active moral sense. Shakespeare often tells us in no faltering tones that men ought so to rise as to master their fate; that mercy in rulers is the brightest jewel in their crown; that vice leads ultimately to destruction. Such deliverances amount to little beyond the axiomatic comments of an intelligent spectator on the life outside himself. The case would be very different if we met in Shakespeare's writings with frequent pronouncements on religion, ethics, political economy, and the like, which qualified or questioned accepted beliefs, which had little or no relevance to the dramatic action or context, and which owed no suggestion to the story-books whence Shakespeare immediately derived his plots. If there were many inconsistencies between the character of the persons on whose lips was set a specific moral or political argument, and the argument itself, one could hardly avoid the deduction that there the dramatist spoke in his own person. But the enunciation of distinctive dogma is rare, and there is no unanimity among critics as to passages in the plays which are impertinent to the context. The few moral or ethical disquisitions which seem at a first glance nondramatic or strike an unaccustomed note frequently owe some suggestion to popular literature of the day. But Shakespeare's dramatic instinct is commonly so alert as to fuse the speech with the character completely enough to deprive of substance the charge of irrelevant self-revelation. A reiterated sentiment may strike a personal note. But the sentiments which Shakespeare is in the habit of reiterating are not distinctive. They have for the most part a proverbial veracity, and merely attest a healthy-minded sagacity which throws no light on individual personality.[1] There emerge no distinct clues to the idiosyncrasy which sets Shakespeare apart from the general run of humanity.

V

As soon as we search for the traits peculiar to individual character, for specific opinion on points of great and unending controversy, we are involved in a maze from which there is no sure exit. Let us be adventurous enough to assume that Shakespeare privately believed with Brutus that arbitrary despotic rule imposed on the subject the duty of assassinating the despot. We thereby condemn ourselves to hopeless perplexity as soon as we examine the doctrine of binding respect for authority which Shakespeare makes the bishops expound in his play of *Henry V*. Clearly, our minds will be torn asunder if we arbitrarily seek autobiography in mere dramatic poetry and mere dramatic utterance.

On Emerson's showing we ought to be able to discover from Shakespeare's flood of speech his private opinions on such a far-reaching topic as the nature and conditions of

---

[1] For example, Shakespeare is fond of ringing the changes, in plays of various dates, on the common proverb 'Self-praise is no recommendation'. Cf. *All's Well*, I. iii. 5–7: 'we make foul the clearness of our deservings, when of ourselves we publish them'; *Troil. and Cress.*, I. iii. 241–2: 'The worthiness of praise distains his worth, If that the praised himself bring the praise forth'; and *Coriolanus*, IV. vii. 51: 'And power, unto itself most commendable, Hath not a tomb so evident as a chair To extol what it hath done.' A more persistent reiteration of a proverbial sentiment is illustrated by the following quotations:

Two Gentlemen of Verona, II. iv. 188: 'one heat another heat expels';
Romeo and Juliet, I. ii. 45: 'one fire burns out another's burning';
Julius Caesar, III. i. 172: 'As fire drives out fire.'
Coriolanus, IV. vii. 54: 'one fire drives out one fire.'

property, a topic closely interwoven with the bases of human happiness. In one place Shakespeare bids wealth or comfort 'expose itself to feel what others feel', and then shake off all superfluities and show heaven's justice by sharing riches with the poor; 'so distribution should undo excess, And each man have enough.' Again, he makes poor people point out that 'what authority surfeits on would relieve us'. 'The meanness that afflicts us is as an inventory to particularize their abundance.' Poverty is due to the superfluity of wealth in high places.

Yet elsewhere we are told no less clearly that the division of society into ranks, with wealth and dignity nicely proportioned to each grade, is the keystone of society: that the current distinctions between high and low, rich and poor, are nature's laws: that the reverence involuntarily shown by the commoner for the peer, by the labourer for his employer, is 'the angel of the world', the salt of civilization. As soon as you reduce mankind to one uniform level of authority or property, you 'make a sop of all this solid globe' and condemn it to chaotic dissolution.

From the first series of quotations the collectivist might be tempted to infer that Shakespeare is of his party. If one isolate the second series, the individualists would be equally justified in claiming Shakespeare as one of themselves. I think it safer to conclude that he succeeded here in keeping in his own bosom the secret of his private partisanship.

Wellnigh every social topic is mentioned in his plays, but the oracle is for practical purposes always ambiguous. On that delicate question of the right of woman to share the work and privileges which are commonly allotted to men alone, Shakespeare speaks in many voices. Portia, in *The Merchant of Venice*, dons the barrister's wig and gown, and pleads in court of law with an eloquence and an astuteness which might well be held to prove that women are perfectly able to compete with men in at least one of the masculine professions. Yet Shakespeare elsewhere condemns without qualification women who ape the aspirations of men, and asserts that

> A woman mannish grown
> Is not more loathed than an effeminate man.

Who can say whether Shakespeare's heart beat in steadier unison with lawyer Portia than with Desdemona, whose intellectual horizon was limited by wifely duty?

Take a minor matter of social economy about which, on the Emersonian assumption, we ought to be in no doubt as to Shakespeare's personal predilection. Did he approve or disapprove of abstinence from strong drink? A man's attitude to that question is wont to shed light on his mental, moral, and physical constitution. In one place Shakespeare says, 'O God, that men should put an enemy in their mouths to steal away their brains; that we should with joy, pleasance, revel, and applause transform ourselves into beasts by drinking wine.' A military officer is credited by the dramatist with the remark: 'I could well wish courtesy would invent some other custom of entertainment.' Shakespeare makes a hale and hearty old man account for his good health thus:

> Though I look old, yet I am strong and lusty;
> For in my youth I never did apply
> Hot and rebellious liquors in my blood; . . .
> Therefore my age is as a lusty winter,
> Frosty but kindly.

Elsewhere we find commendation of 'honest water that never left man in the mire'. Well may it be argued that Shakespeare detected small virtue in grape juice or fermented liquors.

But what shall be said of him when we find that almost at the same time as he hymns the praise of 'honest water', he salutes the vine as 'the merry cheerer of the heart'? On sherris sack, a very strong potation, he bestows an unqualified benediction:

'A good sherris sack hath a two-fold operation in it. It ascends me into the brain; dries me there all the foolish and dull and crudy vapours which environ it; makes it apprehensive, quick, forgetive, full of nimble, fiery and delectable shapes; which, deliver'd o'er to the voice, the tongue, which is the birth, becomes excellent wit. The second property of your excellent sherris is, the warming of the blood; which, before cold and settled, left the liver white and pale, which is the badge of pusillanimity and cowardice; but the sherris warms it and makes it course from the inwards to the parts extreme; it illumineth the face, which as a beacon gives warning to all the rest of this little kingdom, man, to arm; and then the vital commoners and inland petty spirits muster me all to their captain, the heart, who, great and puffed up with his retinue, doth any deed of courage; and this valour comes of sherris. . . . If I had a thousand sons, the first humane principle I would teach them should be, to forswear thin potations and to addict themselves to sack.'

Surely the Emersonian theory puts us here in a new and inextricable dilemma. Very few years separate these self-contradictory utterances on the vice and virtue of drink one from another. There is no ground for arguing that they testify to a change of view, that Shakespeare, having first ranged himself with the water-drinkers, subsequently passed to the ranks of the alcoholists, and preached as 'the first humane principle' the duty of deep and strong potations,—or vice versa. Old Adam, Shakespeare's temperance advocate, belongs to the same epoch of Shakespeare's career as Falstaff, his colossal champion of powerful drink. We may form any conjecture that we please as to Shakespeare's personal likes and dislikes here. But it would be a conjecture mainly coloured by our own idiosyncrasy. Are we not once again driven, on the strict evidence of his own words, to the conclusion that whatever Shakespeare's convictions, preferences, or habits in the matter of drink, he did not choose to label and catalogue them consistently in drama ?

VI

Perhaps Emerson might admit that in the matter of these controverted questions of social polity there is need of qualifying the assertion that Shakespeare was his own biographer, his own confessor. In any case speculations about the personal significance of detached passages merely touch the fringe of the Emersonian argument. In a somewhat different plane stands the imposing central feature of Emerson's position from which no retreat is possible without yielding the citadel altogether. The main plank in the Emersonian platform, to which Emerson's disciples are deeply committed, may not be the identity between Shakespeare's personal views and isolated expressions of opinion in the plays on great controversies. From that assumption of identity the personal theory has arbitrarily borrowed much collateral support. But the fundamental basis of the personal theory lies elsewhere. It mainly rests on an alleged correspondence between the dominant mood or tone of a play taken as a whole, and the dominant mood or tone of Shakespeare's private sentiment or experience at the time of writing. Put broadly, we are asked to believe that some great sorrow, some overwhelmingly tragic incident in his own career, impelled Shakespeare to tragedy, while joyousness of mind and happy episodes impelled him to comedy and romance. It is common knowledge that Shakespeare, early in the seventeenth century, produced in quick succession that stupendous series of tragedies which, opening with *Hamlet*, was continued in plays like *Macbeth*, *Othello*, *King Lear*, and closed with such impressive embodiments of his genius as *Antony and Cleopatra* and *Coriolanus*. If we examine any recent exposition of the personal theory we learn that this prolonged absorption in tragedy was the outcome of a spiritual calamity, an episode of intensely tragic gloom in the dramatist's private life.

Some critics christen this alleged tragic passage the 'third period' of Shakespeare's working career. Only a crisis of personal tragedy can account, say the theorists, for the abandonment of the rich vein of romantic comedy which distinguishes the work (e. g. *Much Ado about Nothing*, *Twelfth Night*, and *As You Like It*) immediately preceding the great tragic series. The theorists draw the

further inference that the weight of gloom ultimately
lifted from Shakespeare's soul. The darkness dissolved.
The 'Sturm und Drang' disappeared. The 'third period'
ended, and with a serene brow he moved into his 'fourth
period', of which the main fruits were the three placid
romances *Cymbeline*, *The Winter's Tale*, and *The Tempest*.

It is, I think, generally admitted that there is no external evidence of any tempestuous catastrophes in Shakespeare's private career which have any kinship, figurative
or actual, with the crucial temper of *Hamlet*, *Othello*, *King
Lear*, and the rest. All the external knowledge that we
have of this epoch in Shakespeare's biography suggests uninterrupted progress in prosperity, the final farewell to
pecuniary difficulties, the final recognition of his eminence
by contemporary opinion, the steady growth of reputation,
the steady increase of worldly wealth and comfort. But it is
circularly argued that these tragedies of crime and grief are
there to indicate that, amid all outward signs of material
welfare, Shakespeare's spiritual being was a constant prey to
tragic torment owing to some unrecorded crisis in his private
affairs. Circular arguments never carry us far. The theorists,
to prove their point and to convert it into something other
than nebulous conjecture, must discover some solid biographic corroboration. Or, at least, by way of alternative,
they must look around literary history, and show that every
one who has written a series of great tragedies was himself at
the time in the grip of calamity, and that every one who
penned a romantic comedy was enjoying perfect peace of
mind. I believe the theorists will find no more support in
literary history than they have hitherto found in Shakespeare's biography. If research in literary history offered
them the requisite corroboration, most conceptions of
dramatic art would need drastic revision.

VII

Let us examine the problem free of Emersonian pre-
conceptions. Is there genuine necessity for a recondite,
for a personal or a biographical, explanation of the fact

that Shakespeare at the maturity of his powers devoted his genius for some years almost exclusively to tragedy? I say 'almost exclusively', because in almost every play where the tragic motive predominates there are strokes of comedy, even comic interludes, which seem inconsistent with the notion that Shakespeare in this 'third period' was sunk hopelessly and entirely in the slough of despond. There are bursts of pure humour, of playful merriment, in *Hamlet*. There is the Porter in *Macbeth*. The old criticism which would eliminate that broad comedian from Shakespeare's dramatis personae, on the ground that the sombre atmosphere of *Macbeth* required more uniform seriousness, is now reckoned obsolete and false. But the personal theorists find it hard to justify the burly humorist's interruption of the tragic crisis, save on some strained argument of sentimentality which urges that discordant laughter will at times, when the heart is breaking, alternate irresponsibly with tears.

A larger consideration, which has to be encountered, seems to weaken irrecoverably the personal theorists' foothold. It can never be forgotten that tragedy is the acme of dramatic art, that every supreme master (save Molière, the exception which proves the rule) has concentrated his mature powers on tragedy. No doubt is permissible that this was the accepted practice of the Elizabethan realm of letters. It was invariably on those who excelled in tragic drama that the greatest reward and the greatest applause were bestowed. Public taste was very different then from what it is now. Public taste then encouraged tragedy in the theatre. Theatrical performances at Elizabeth's and James I's courts reflected literary feeling of the day. They were very frequent, and tragedy was, as a rule, chosen for presentation there on great occasions. How high stood tragedy in the favour of the court may be judged from such a fact as this, that on Boxing Day (the day after Christmas) 1606, when festivities were furnished on an imposing scale, Shakespeare's company of players was engaged to produce in the royal presence no light comedy or farce, but the most appalling of all tragedies ever penned—Shakespeare's tragedy of *King Lear*. Such a fact graphically illustrates the interval that separates in the field of drama public sentiment of our own time from the public sentiment of Shakespeare's day. Such a fact suggests, too, the direction in which professional considerations were certain to lead an ambitious writer for the Elizabethan stage, as soon as he was fully conscious of his powers.

On this showing, Shakespeare devoted himself to tragedy because he was a great dramatic artist who was in close touch and sympathy with contemporary public feeling. It was not as though tragedy were a new venture for Shakespeare when he initiated that great series which ran from *Hamlet* to *Coriolanus* in James I's reign. He had experimented with tragedy from his earliest years. He had proved his tragic genius in *Romeo and Juliet*, in *King John*, in *Richard II*, in *Richard III*. All his history plays, save *Henry V* and *Henry VIII*, are tragedies in a great vein, an intense vein. Master as he was of comedy, he was so ardent in the pursuit of the nobler branch of dramatic art, that into his ripest comedies, such as *The Merchant of Venice*, *Much Ado about Nothing*, and *Twelfth Night*, he imports a tragic touch, and in his latest so-called romantic comedies, *Cymbeline* and *The Winter's Tale*, the tragic touch often conquers the spirit of comedy. It was in full accord with the artistic development of dramatic genius that tragedy should have claimed his main allegiance for many of his later years, consecutively and almost exclusively. It is difficult for those who have escaped the Emersonian yoke to perceive the need of another explanation of the predominant hold which tragedy exerted on the poet's thought.

VIII

But let us examine more closely the vitalizing processes of great dramatic art. To define those processes is to my thinking to come into open conflict with the personal theory of Shakespearian tragedy. When one considers the operative methods of great drama, the notion that Shakespeare's mind was absorbed during a long period of his career by an overwhelming personal grief, seems to lead straight to a conclusion which subverts all at which the personal theorists aim. In other words, I would contend that had Shakespeare been in this 'third period' the victim of a private calamity or the prey of searing anxiety, he could never have approached the highest pitch of artistic perfection, and could never have written the work assigned to him. No such unfaltering equilibrium, in treatment of plot and character, as distinguished, for example, *Othello* and *Coriolanus*, would have been within his power, had he sought expression in tragedy for agonies of his own heart, for moral and mental catastrophe within the scope of his own conscience.

In these two plays, at any rate, pursuit of artistic perfection is the manifest aim. Does emotional disturbance in the writer's own mind here cloud at any point his artistic path? That, in brief, is the ultimate question at issue.

In ordinary life, passion—more especially passion of tragic intensity—is never quite articulate. The turbulence of strong emotion invariably dims the intellect. The utterance loses proportion. Tragic art is consequently no outcome of a storm of passion, nor the recollection of a storm of passion, within the tragic poet's personal experience. The creative agent is imagination, the capacity to imagine passion rather than to feel it. In tragic drama the poet relies for his success on the potent pliancy of the imaginative faculty.

Shakespeare lay under no misconception on this cardinal point. He credited imagination with creative omnipotence, with the capacity of summoning out of nothingness all manner of emotion, with the power of inventing all manner of appearances of persons and things. Dramatic conceptions, dramatic passion, are, he implies, the coinage of the dramatist's brain and eye.

The poet's eye, in a fine frenzy rolling,
Doth glance from heaven to earth, from earth to heaven;

And as imagination bodies forth
The forms of things unknown, the poet's pen
Turns them to shapes, and gives to airy nothing
A local habitation and a name.
Such tricks hath strong imagination,
That, if it would but apprehend some joy,
It comprehends some bringer of that joy.

The tragic poet is in transient sympathy with the passions which he delineates. He is sensitive to emotion. He will assuredly have his own normal burden of human sorrow, his normal experience of passion. But it is not from that source that there comes the power of presenting emotion in terms of art. No triumph in dramatic art is accessible to one who is enslaved by colossal agitation, by overwhelming passion. The power of alert observation of life and literature, the power of analysing with calmness what is seen or read, is the main instrument with which the imaginative faculty does its work in dramatic poetry. When Shakespeare wrote that 'the truest poetry was the most feigning' he had these obvious truths in mind.

Indeed there seems no difference of opinion on these matters among those who are chiefly entitled to speak of them with authority. The great critics of antiquity, Plato and Aristotle, are at one in detecting in poetry imitations or appearances of things or sentiments, imitations or appearances which are quite distinguishable from the things or sentiments themselves. Aristotle's classical distinction between history (that which has been) and poetry (that which has not but might have been) excludes from the dramatic poet's province the poet's actual experience. Bacon's shrewd intelligence saw no less clearly that fiction is the essence of poetry, and he quoted approvingly an ancient apophthegm which represented poetry to be 'the shadow of a lie'. Lyric poetry seemed to fall outside Bacon's purview of literature. He applied his judgement exclusively to drama and epic, and those branches of the poetic art he defined collectively as 'feigned history'. The use of poetry, as he conceives it, is to give 'some shadow of satisfaction to the mind of man in those points wherein the nature of things doth deny it' (*Advancement of Learning*, Bk. II, ed. Kitchin, p. 125). Normal fact or experience is not, according to Bacon, in the plane of epic or dramatic poetry.

Coleridge made the vital point clear when he invented the word 'aloofness' to express the relations between a poet's, and especially a dramatist's, own feelings in private life, and those of which he is the painter or analyst. The dramatic poet is a spectator of the passionate tumult, and not an actor in it. He is a student of emotion. He tempers his presentation of tragic passion with rhythm and measure. His art sternly limits the active range of passion; its wildness or violence is curbed by figures of speech. He reproduces tragic passion not as it is, but so as to create an illusion of truth. Flashes of imaginative realism illumine his pen, and seem to give the words the vivid vigour of Nature. But these intuitions owe their effect to something which lies wholly apart from the poet's conscious external experience; they bear witness to the master's power of modulating language and of fitting it to thought. Artistic intellect or genius is never in great drama at the mercy of the emotional excitement in the artist's immediate environment. His triumphs are produced by a supreme command of his art. 'L'artiste,' wrote a few weeks ago M. René Doumic, the distinguished French critic 'l'artiste n'est pas celui qui a ressenti davantage, mais celui qui est le mieux doué, pour imaginer des états de sensibilité et pour en réaliser l'expression.' ('The artist is not the man who has felt the most, but he who is the best endowed to imagine states of feeling, and to give reality to the expression of them.') That seems to me to sum up fairly the whole situation.

Tragic intensity reaches the highest dramatic pitch in Shakespeare's work in the scene in *Macbeth* which deals with the murder of Duncan, and in the scene in *Othello* which portrays the death of Desdemona. The sentiments of the murderers in both plays are depicted with surest and firmest pencil and betray the loftiest inspiration of dramatic genius. Yet who would venture to suggest for one moment that Shakespeare knew and learned from private experience of murder, or from any personal murderous propensity, the smallest hint for his intimate portrayal of the sentiment governing men or women in the actual perpetration of a murderous crime. His power of vitalizing murderous moods might well throw light on his treatment of other episodes of tragedy, might well suggest that the tragic sentiment lay outside the scope of his personal activities or experiences.

There is in the realm of dramatic art something of the well-known paradox of acting. Artistic expression is not possible in an actor whose intellectual equilibrium is suffering continual disturbance from the vehemence of his own feelings or from his recollections of violent passion. The French have produced the greatest actors in the world—and the greatest of all French actors, Talma, has explained in detail how an actor who allows his personal feeling or emotion to sway his utterance on the stage loses all power of modulating his voice, loses his memory, strains his gestures, and destroys the effect of great acting. Shakespeare himself acknowledged this paradox of acting when he wrote his warning to actors: 'In the very tempest and, as I might say, whirlwind of passion you must acquire and beget a temperance that may give it smoothness.' 'Temperance' and 'smoothness' are the fundamental conditions of art. The supremely efficient dramatist is no more exempt from them than the supremely efficient actor, and no dramatist who wrote under the conscious impulse of private sensations of passion past or present is capable of due respect to these primary principles.

Another great French actor explained a temporary failure on the stage by remarking that he 'lived for an unlucky moment in the situation which the dramatist had created. I became the personage himself. I ceased to be the actor of him. I behaved as I should in my own room.

Loyalty to the conditions of the theatre means that one is different there from what one is at home.' Such reflections are, in a sense, true of the dramatic artist in the act of writing. He is not as he is in everyday life. Consequently he gives us in his dramatic work sparse or no clues to his personality.

Sir Walter Scott was once asked how he managed to present in his novels all manner of emotions and actions and scenes which were as remote as they well could be from his current experience. He was asked how, amid the preoccupations of his business and his profession, amid all his private anxieties and professional and financial cares, he could write *Waverley* and *Guy Mannering*. He replied that his 'fancy', by which he meant his imaginative faculty, did not concern itself with his private or personal affairs, but 'ran its ain rigs in some other world'. 'As soon as I get the paper before me', he went on, 'it commonly runs off pretty easily.' I suspect if Shakespeare had been asked the same question about his tragedies as Sir Walter Scott was asked about his novels, he would have answered in much the same terms. Very recently a novelist of eminence, whose power to portray the tragic and pathetic intensities of life is everywhere acknowledged, mentioned to me a tragic episode in one of his books—a moving description of the despair of a wronged wife. That sentiment (he assured me—making due allowance for difference of sex) he had never experienced. He had not met the situation or sentiment in any shape in his intimate experience, yet his portrayal of it gave his readers so perfect an illusion of the truth that some correspondents who had endured the misfortunes of my friend's imaginary heroine greeted him as a fellow sufferer, and invited more of his consoling confidence. The novelist told me that the passage, which had moved his readers thus, was penned almost unconsciously. When he went to his desk after breakfast to do his ordinary morning's work and wrote these words which were hailed as genuine sensation, he was at first quite uncertain how to continue the tale. As he put pen to paper the development came involuntarily. What my friend modestly called his 'professional faculty' was at work. He meant by 'professional faculty' what critics call the imaginative faculty. His powers of inspiration were active, and all the rest followed.

IX

Of course, the intensity of Shakespeare's dramatic presentments of life transcends those of my friend. But Shakespeare enjoyed, in a certain direction, an advantage which is denied the modern novelist, an advantage which rendered the dramatist even less dependent than my friend, or less apt than he to rely, on private experience. My friend's relatively smaller imaginative faculty enabled him to dispense with any suggestion of episode which his own affairs offered, although he lay under the obligation of improvising his fable and was bound by literary law to evolve all his plot out of his own ingenuity and intuition. Shakespeare was absolved from such necessity. He did not, like the modern novelist, invent the plots of his tragedies. He worked over old stories. He modified them, and frequently altered the final issue. He omitted some of the old characters and introduced some new ones. But the main theme—jealousy, ingratitude, ambition, sexual infatuation—was there ready to his hand, and its process of evolution was already on record. Had it lain within the conditions of his art, when he was delineating one or other of these great passions, for him to draw either suggestion or illustration from his private experience, the call must have lost its energy when history or legend or pre-existing fiction dictated the choice and development of topic. It was not as if Shakespeare went to Holinshed, or to Plutarch, or to the Italian novelists, merely for the bare outline of the plot which he filled out with wholly original incident and emotion. He borrowed almost all the incident and followed many an emotional cue. Nay more, at times, as in the case of *Antony and Cleopatra* and *Coriolanus*, when he depended on so excellent a piece of litera-

ture as North's translation of Plutarch, he took whole
speeches from his authority, merely converting with
wonderful ingenuity the prose into blank verse. When
Volumnia, Coriolanus's mother, pleads with her son in
accents of most moving pathos to take pity on his family
and fellow countrymen and to leave the Volscian camp,
both sentiment and language are Plutarch's, with the
smallest possible change. The indebtedness casts no
reflection on Shakespeare. It merely proves that artistic
purpose dominated his work in tragedy to the exclusion of
any predisposition to autobiographic confession or revelation. Wherever his critical sense taught him that Plutarch's sentiment and language satisfied his artistic need,
he wisely adopted them as his own. He knew the meaning
and significance of artistic restraint, the folly of painting
the lily or gilding refined gold. For the most part the
treatment of the tragic theme by the writers who supplied him with his plots fell below the requirements of
great tragedy. He allowed his imaginative faculty to
range over the details freely, and thereby transmuted
rough ore into pure gold, or something more precious than
gold. But in the process small room was left, small induce-
ment was present, for expositions of his personal experiences.

Little attention has been paid to a peculiarity which
colours Shakespeare's employment of his authorities in the
great series of his tragedies, and still further reduces the
probability of an alleged correspondence between these
masterpieces and the emotion of his contemporary private
life. *Othello* and *Measure for Measure*, *Macbeth* and *King
Lear*, *Antony and Cleopatra* and *Coriolanus*, main links in
this great tragic chain, came rapidly from his pen one after
the other. Each pair is based on one and the same authority. The stories of *Othello* and *Measure for Measure* were
both derived from a comparatively recent collection of
Italian novels by one Cinthio, a disciple of Boccaccio and
Bandello. The stories of *Lear* and *Macbeth* both come
from Holinshed's *Chronicles*. The stories of *Antony and*

Cleopatra and *Coriolanus* both come from North's translation of Plutarch. This constant duality of origin suggests the clearest of all refutations of the personal theory.

It is hardly possible to mistake the manner of Shakespeare's preparation for each pair of these six tragic labours. He found in Cinthio's recent collection of Italian novels a story of jealousy (*Othello*), which appeared to him to lend itself to dramatic treatment. He turned the page and discovered a story revolving about the virtue of chastity and the vice of incontinence (*Measure for Measure*), which impressed him with presenting similar pertinence to his dramatic purpose. It was the sequence in Cinthio which accounted for the order in which the dramatist dealt with the great topics of *Othello* and *Measure for Measure*. There was nothing else in Cinthio which equally deserved a dramatic artist's attention. Consequently Shakespeare looked elsewhere for the suggestion of his next tragedy. He turned to that encyclopaedic history by Holinshed, on which he had mainly relied in earlier days for his plays on English history. In a section preceding any that he had before consulted, he detected the narratives of *Macbeth* and *King Lear*, which invited him to the tragic themes of selfish ambition and filial ingratitude. An inferior dramatic hand had already dealt with Holinshed's legend of Lear. But there is no ground for doubting that *King Lear* and *Macbeth* marched together in the procession of Shakespeare's plays, because they both were already linked together in Holinshed's ample volume. So, too, of *Coriolanus* and *Antony and Cleopatra*, which were both tragedies from Plutarch's treasury, the one treating of pride of caste, the.other of illicit love in high place. Shakespeare's systematic dependence on his reading (and not on his personal circumstance) for his choice of tragic topic is nowhere so plainly indicated as by the evidence that the six masterpieces, which were produced at the zenith of his dramatic power, were, in point of origin, yoked together in pairs.

It is very tempting, though I fear most misleading, to regard this master of imagination as being specifically controlled step by step, in his dramatic career, by variations and alternations of private sensation and personal experience. The theory is not only in conflict with the fact of his reliance on plots which came accidentally under his notice in the course of his reading. It ignores his well-ascertained disposition to reconcile his dramatic work with the accidental calls of public taste, and with the requirements of the theatrical managers. His practical life shows that he never deliberately disregarded the bidding of his professional chiefs. The seductive theory that he selected his themes, not for their artistic capability or for their adaptability to popular taste or feeling, but for their correspondence with his transient mood, breaks down under every test.

One personal theorist has it that Shakespeare created Miranda in *The Tempest* because he was watching with parental affection at home at Stratford the blossoming girlhood and womanhood of his younger daughter Judith. It is hopeless to take seriously such alleged correlation of cause and effect. It defies chronology. *The Tempest* cannot have been written before 1610, when Miranda was portrayed as an ingenuous maiden of fifteen. Judith Shakespeare was baptized at Stratford-on-Avon on February 2, 1585, and when Shakespeare brought Miranda to birth she was a buxom woman of at least five-and-twenty. Records of her life negative, too, all suggestion of girlish innocence at that period of her career. The personal theory not only rests here on error in point of fact, but is supererogatory. The conception of Miranda was suggested by no episode in Shakespeare's private experience, but by popular romantic stories, for the time in great vogue, of girl princesses torn in infancy from home and civilized society and flung desolate by misfortune on the mercies of nature. Within a short period of the composition of *The Tempest* Shakespeare had experimented with this maiden type in two plays, first in the person of Marina in *Pericles*, and then in the person of Perdita in *The Winter's Tale*. In both those pieces he loyally followed the lead of old romances, and though we cannot point with equal assurance to the source of the plot of *The Tempest*, we need have no compunction in declaring Miranda to be the final and the ripened fruit of the dramatist's imaginative study of unsophisticated girlhood which he had found lightly sketched in fiction by feebler pens.

Again, it is suggested that only a mood of misanthropy in the author could explain such an intense portrait of the misanthropic temperament as is presented in *Timon of Athens*. The tragedy of *Timon of Athens* is not wholly of Shakespeare's authorship. The greater part is from the pedestrian pen of a play-writing hack coadjutor. The character of Timon and the scenes which he dominates are assuredly, however, from Shakespeare's pen. Timon is a tragic conception cast in the mould of Lear. It is an imaginative presentment of misanthropy in most lurid colours. But there is no justification for seeking its genesis in a phase of Shakespeare's personal temperament. Timon Misanthropos the Athenian, whom Plutarch's pen had graphically limned in his *Life of Mark Antony*, was already recognized in the literature of all Northern Europe to be the ultimate embodiment of the misanthropic tendency. Timon's history had already formed the plot of an Elizabethan play, and was acclaimed a fit topic for ambitious tragedy throughout the civilized world. His characteristic sentiment had been vividly described of old, not only by Plutarch but by Lucian, the Greek satirist, whose disposition was the reverse of sour. Shakespeare's Timon came into the day's work, and the tragic intensity of the portrait bears new witness to the omnipotence of his imaginative faculty. We should remember, too, that at the same time as the dramatist was painting the misanthropic Timon he was sketching, in *Pericles*, the charm and innocence of the girl Marina. That fact summarily confutes the fancy that Timon's cynical hatred of mankind had entered even temporarily the dramatist's own soul.

X

Thus I reach the conclusion that Browning's conception of Shakespeare is juster than Emerson's. In his work it is vain to look for his biography, for his specific personal sensation. His work did not 'discover what was rest from work—his life'. His work discovered the omnipotence of his imaginative faculty, his all-absorbing devotion to art. In his work he did not air his own woes. If he suffered from 'Weltschmerz' or 'world-smart', he made no precise or quite recognizable report of his sensation in the printed page. Like Sir Walter Scott, as soon as he took pen in hand, his 'fancy ran its ain rigs in some other world'. Like the great French actor, he was in his study a different being from the theatrical shareholder in London, or from the owner of house property at Stratford-on-Avon, or from the father of a family. Imaginative genius enables its possessor to live in fancy more lives than one. The number of Shakespeare's lives was greater than that of any other human being because of the supreme pliancy of his imaginative genius. To seek in his mighty drama close-fitting links with the life which he led by his own hearthstone, is in my view to misapprehend the most distinctive note of his miraculous gift of genius.

OVID AND SHAKESPEARE'S SONNETS[1]

FOR full eighteen centuries the *Metamorphoses* led in the race among Ovid's works for popular favour. Probably the vogue waxed greatest from the thirteenth to the seventeenth century. For those four hundred years generation vied with generation in proofs of admiring interest. The highest honours were steadily accorded to this spacious storehouse of myth and poetry, alike by laity and clergy through medieval western and southern Europe. The book was translated not only into French and Italian, but also into German and medieval Greek—languages then on the confines of culture. Separate fables, like those of Narcissus or Orpheus, Pyramus or Philomela, grew popular everywhere in vernacular renderings into verse. Dante in his treatise on rhetoric (*De vulgari eloquentia*) applauded both the poetic diction of the *Metamorphoses* and its allegorical value. Of the many medieval moralizations of classical poetry over which Rabelais made merry, the most popular were two allegorical interpretations of Ovid's poem—one by Dante's disciple, Giovanni del Virgilio, the fourteenth-century champion of scholarship, and the other by the French Dominican, Pierre Berçuire, who lived in friendly intercourse with Petrarch at Vaucluse. The Italian humanists of the late fifteenth and early sixteenth centuries, Politian and Bembo for example, accepted the *Metamorphoses* as a poetic model of indisputable primacy, and the prolific vernacular poets, Lodovico Dolce, the Venetian, and Clément Marot, the Norman, began new literal translations before the sixteenth was far advanced. The French scholar printer, Stephanus, saluted the author of the *Metamorphoses* as 'the poet of painters'. Tintoretto and Titian sought in Ovid's pages inspiration for their brush. At the bidding of

[1] Reprinted from the *Quarterly Review*, Centenary Number, April 1909.

Francis I, Primaticcio and Rosso adorned the walls of the palace at Fontainebleau with scenes of Ovid's fables. Meanwhile the most artistic of the early printers and engravers of Paris, Venice, and Bologna applied their skill to fine editions of the book. At Paris the first impressions of text or paraphrase bore the significant title 'La Bible des Poètes', for which was substituted in later issues the more sonorous designation 'Le Grand Olympe des histoires poétiques, du prince de poésie, Ovide Naso'. Both formulas bore witness to the vastness of the book's influence on contemporary literary effort. Tudor England shared the continental enthusiasm. Caxton turned the work into his own tongue so early as 1480. Near the opening of Queen Elizabeth's reign, two Englishmen, Thomas Peend and Arthur Golding, simultaneously and independently set to work on new translations into English verse. Peend withdrew from the competition in Golding's favour after publishing a single fable. Golding carried his enterprise through, and in 1567 he completed his publication of the fifteen books of the poem in English ballad metre. Golding's version held the field for half a century. During Shakespeare's lifetime seven editions enjoyed wide circulation; and, when the book's vogue was decaying, its place was filled by the rendering of George Sandys, whom Dryden described as 'the best versifyer of the former age'. Dryden himself was, at a later period, one of the 'most eminent hands' who laboured lovingly at the same oar. The *Metamorphoses* were acknowledged to be the poet's bible in seventeenth-century London no less than in sixteenth-century Paris.

Ovid's *Metamorphoses* appealed to readers of all ages. Boys delighted in its story-telling charm, while their seniors recognized its perfection of style and diction. Its usefulness as an educational manual was acknowledged universally from the medieval era downwards; and no school or college of western Europe in the sixteenth century excluded the work from its curriculum. Montaigne, who graphically presented the dominant literary sentiment of European youth in his epoch, describes in the following words an experience which every contemporary of culture might have echoed:

'The first taste or feeling I had of books was of the pleasure I took in reading the fables of Ovid's *Metamorphoses*; for, being but seven or eight years old, I would steal and sequester myself from all other delights, only to read them; forsomuch as the tongue wherein they were written was to me natural; and it was the easiest book I knew; and, by reason of the matter therein contained, [it was] most agreeing with my young age.'[1]

The differences of nationality caused no variation in the affection which Ovid's *Metamorphoses* excited in the budding intellect of Renaissance Europe.

Shakespeare's familiarity with Ovid's *Metamorphoses* was in inevitable conformity with the spirit of his age. The Latin text was part of the curriculum of his grammar school education. Golding's English translation was universally accessible during his boyhood and manhood. There is no straining of the evidence in the assumption that, had Shakespeare left a record of the literary influences of his youth, he would have described a personal infatuation with the *Metamorphoses* no smaller than that to which Montaigne confesses in his autobiographical reminiscences. There is in the Bodleian Library an Aldine edition of the Latin poem which came out at Venice in 1502, and Shakespeare's initials are scribbled on the title-page. Whether these letters be genuine or no, a manuscript note of unquestioned authenticity states that the volume was believed, as early as 1682, to have been owned by Shakespeare. At any rate, no Renaissance poet's work offers fuller or clearer testimony than Shakespeare's of the abiding impression which the study of Ovid's *Metamorphoses* made on poetic genius.

Shakespeare's earliest play, *Love's Labour's Lost*, introduces Ovid as the schoolboy's model for Latin verse (IV. ii. 127): 'Ovidius Naso was the man: and why, indeed, Naso,

1 *Essays*, Bk. I, cap. 25.

but for smelling out the odoriferous flowers of fancy, the jerks of invention ?' Elsewhere Shakespeare jests familiarly with the unhappy fate of 'the most capricious poet, honest Ovid', who died in exile among the barbarians (*As You Like It*, III. iii. 8). In another early play, *Titus Andronicus*, the book of Ovid's *Metamorphoses* is brought on the stage; and from it the tale of Philomel is quoted. But the proof of Shakespeare's minute knowledge of the *Metamorphoses* does not rest on specific mention of the poem or of its author. With exceptional vividness and completeness Shakespeare's writing assimilates numberless stirring passages of Ovid's mythological treasury. Nor does this bond mark the full limit of Shakespeare's indebtedness. Evidence which has been hitherto overlooked can be adduced to prove that the *Metamorphoses'* sporadic excursions into cosmic and metaphysical philosophy riveted the dramatist's thought with no slighter potency than the poetic figures and fables.

The phraseology of Golding's translation so frequently reappears in Shakespeare's page, especially by way of subsidiary illustration, as almost to compel the conviction that Shakespeare knew much of Golding's book by heart. At the same time it is clear that the Latin text of his schooldays recurred at times to his memory. In *King John* (v. vii. 26, 27) there is a curious verbal echo of Ovid's Latin at the opening of the *Metamorphoses* (i. 7), where 'chaos' is described as 'rudis indigestaque moles'. Shakespeare, in schoolboy fashion, when he speaks of England reduced by King John to chaos, reproduces Ovid's 'rudis indigestaque' as 'that *indigest* . . . so shapeless and so *rude*'. Golding merely renders Ovid's phrase by 'a huge rude heap'. None can mistake the source of Shakespeare's ἅπαξ λεγόμενον, the substantive 'indigest' (i.e. chaotic mass) with its epithet of 'rude' (i.e. the Latin *rudis*). Again, Ovid twice confers on Diana, in her character of goddess of groves, the name Titania (*Metamorphoses*, iii. 173, and vi. 346). In both places Golding omits this distinctive appellation, and calls Diana by her accustomed title.

Ovid's Latin text alone accounts for Shakespeare's designation of his fairy queen as Titania, a word which he first introduced into English poetry. A Latin quotation in *Titus Andronicus* (IV. iii. 4), from the *Metamorphoses* (i. 150), 'terras Astraea reliquit', may have a like bearing on the same issue.

But it is on the translation of the *Metamorphoses* that Shakespeare levies his heaviest loan. No commentator has yet done justice to the full extent of Shakespeare's dependence on Golding's version. Most of them have contented themselves with instancing, as an isolated feature of his plays, the close similarity of language between Prospero's recantation of his magical powers in the *Tempest* (v. i. 33 *seq.*):

> Ye elves of hills, brooks, standing lakes, and groves, &c.,

and Medea's incantation when making her rejuvenating potion in Golding's Ovid (*Metamorphoses*, vii. 197 *seq.*):

> Ye Elues of Hilles, of Brookes, of woods alone, of standing lakes, &c.

This kinship of phrase, far from being unique, admits of almost endless illustration. The strange and revolting ingredients which Medea, in the same passage of Ovid, flings into her miraculous cauldron, gave the witches of *Macbeth* many cues for their unholy compound.

It is perhaps in his easy allusiveness to Ovid's mythological personages and to the traits with which the Latin poet invests them, that Shakespeare attests the completeness with which the *Metamorphoses*, in Golding's version, swayed his mind. When in the Induction to the *Taming of the Shrew* (Sc. ii. 59–61), the Lord's servant promises the tinker Sly sight of a picture of

> Daphne roaming through a thorny wood,
> Scratching her legs that one shall swear she bleeds;
> And at that sight shall sad Apollo weep,

Shakespeare merely paraphrases Apollo's remorseful apostrophe of the irresponsive nymph in the *Metamorphoses* (i. 508–9) as he chases her through the woods:

> Alas, alas, how would it grieve my heart
> To see thee fall among the briers, and that the blood should start
> Out of thy tender legs, I wretch the causer of thy smart.

There is no more delightful tale in Ovid's work than that of Baucis and Philemon, rustic patterns of conjugal fidelity and simple hospitality, who, in their thatched cottage, 'their shed of straw', entertain unawares Jove himself when travelling on the earth in human shape. The story, doubtless, had a Greek origin, but none has been found; and Ovid is the virtual parent of the delightful fable. The episode fastened itself on Shakespeare's imagination. Twice does he airily employ its detail in metaphor. 'My visor is *Philemon's roof; within the house is Jove*,' remarks Don Pedro, in *Much Ado* (II. i. 100), at the masked ball when he introduces himself to the lady Hero; the latter playfully caps the allusion with the words: 'Why, then, your visor should be *thatched*.' To like purport is Jaques's comment on Touchstone's affectation of learning in *As You Like It* (III. iii. 10, 11): 'O knowledge ill-inhabited, worse than *Jove in a thatched house*.'

It is needless to accumulate evidence that Shakespeare's mind was steeped in the mythology of the *Metamorphoses* as Golding rendered it. A final reference deserves citation because it conclusively shows how literal could be Shakespeare's dependence on the English version. Frequently does the dramatist figuratively employ Ovid's touching story of the ardent hunter Actaeon, who, for spying on Diana in the bathing pool, was transformed by her into a stag, and was slain by his own hounds. In *The Merry Wives of Windsor* (II. i. 122) Pistol likens Master Ford to 'Sir Actaeon', and his patron Falstaff to '*Ringwood*', a mysterious hound in pursuit. Ovid gives names to Actaeon's hounds, calling the last 'Hylactor'. That word Golding arbitrarily and perplexingly renders 'Ringwood'.

R

It is difficult to question the inference to which Shakespeare's use of the same appellation points.

There is good reason to believe that Shakespeare's narrative poems, *Venus and Adonis* and *Lucrece*, were designed in very youthful days, before the poet's ambition centred in drama. In the former he not merely reflects Ovid's phrase and thought, with a completeness unparalleled elsewhere, but he casts the whole piece in an Ovidian mould. The plays freely assimilate Ovid in metaphor and allusion; but the poems reproduce the moving form and spirit of Ovid's work. *Venus and Adonis* bears on the title-page a couplet (from Ovid's *Amores*, I. xv. 35, 36) in which the poet prays Apollo for a draught of the pure Castalian stream. The work is as loyal a tribute to the Ovidian conception and fashion of poetry as any in the range of Renaissance literature. The theme of *Venus and Adonis* comes direct from the *Metamorphoses*, though Shakespeare has woven together more than one thread of story. Ovid's fable of Venus' pursuit of Adonis is fused with the Latin poet's vivid picture of the nymph Salmacis' wanton appeal to the coy and passionless youth Hermaphroditus; while the boar who slays Adonis in the hunt is described by Shakespeare in the language which Ovid uses of the Calydonian boar killed by Meleager. The triple skein is vivified by a voluptuous fervour, a graphic imagery, and a luxuriant diction, which echo the Latin poem with signal fidelity.

French and Italian sixteenth-century writers were prolific in more or less literal adaptions of Ovidian fables in their own tongues. The mythical adventures of Narcissus, Phaethon, and Pyramus had been poetized many times by Shakespeare's predecessors and contemporaries in France, Italy, and Spain. Ovid's tale of Venus and Adonis thrice underwent the ordeal in Italy between 1545 and 1561. English poets, at a little later date, turned to like purpose Ovid's characteristic tales of Glaucus and Scylla, of Cephalus and Procris, of Salmacis and Hermaphroditus. But Shakespeare's earliest publication, *Venus and Adonis*, catches more fully than any foreign or domestic effort the glow of the Ovidian fire. In that poem Shakespeare made his entry on the Elizabethan stage of literature as the best endowed and most ardent of Ovid's disciples.

Shakespeare's second poem *Lucrece* is in scarcely less degree an offspring of Ovidian study, although he does not therein lay the *Metamorphoses* under contribution. The story comes from Ovid's *Fasti*; and the philosophic embroidery, which mainly presents the varied activity of Time, is an echo of the *Tristia*. Neither in subject nor in style does the English poem stray far beyond Ovidian boundaries.

The only other separate volume of poetry of Shakespeare's authorship, apart from *Venus and Adonis* and *Lucrece*, is his familiar collection of sonnets. No critic has yet detected there any extensive trace of definite Ovidian influence. The source of two or three lines has been traced to the *Metamorphoses*. Even the significance of that small reconnaissance has been underrated. Many times in the Sonnets does Shakespeare develop with poetic fervour the classical conceit that the poet's verse resists Time's ravages and preserves eternally the name of him whom the poet commemorates. Ovid, at the close of the *Metamorphoses*, boldly adopts the proud vaunt, after the manner of Horace's ode, 'Exegi monumentum aere perennius', which itself owes much to Pindar. The classical conceit, as Ovid and Horace handled it, fired the imagination of all the Renaissance poets of western Europe. Ronsard was probably its most enthusiastic exponent. Shakespeare, in his fifty-fifth sonnet, presents the classical boast in gorgeous phrase, which draws directly on Ovid's peroration to the *Metamorphoses*. Shakespeare claims that his verse has so eternized his hero's fame, that

> Nor Mars his *sword* nor war's quick *fire* shall burn
> The living record of your memory.
> '*Gainst death* and all-oblivious enmity
> Shall you pace forth; your praise shall still find room
> Even in the eyes of *all posterity*
> That wear *this world out to the ending doom.*

These words reflect the closing flourish of the *Meta-morphoses* (xv. 871 *seq.*), which the Elizabethan translator Golding rendered thus:

> Now have I brought a work to end which neither Jove's fierce wrath
> *Nor sword nor fire nor fretting age*, with all the force it hath,
> Are able to abolish quite. . . . And *all the world* shall never
> Be able for to quench my name. . . . And *time without all end* . . .
> My life shall *everlastingly* be lengthened still by fame.

Under the same inspiration Shakespeare styled his Sonnets 'eternal lines' (xviii. 12), and told his friend (lxxxi. 9–12):

> Your monument shall be my gentle verse,
> Which eyes not yet created shall o'er-read,
> And tongues to be your being shall rehearse,
> When all the breathers of this world are dead.

The Sonnets' classical and conventional claim to eternity has been misread as an original tenet of Shakespeare's poetic creed; and even those who have recognized the likeness between Shakespeare's and Ovid's presentment of the fancy have treated the parallelism in isolation. Yet the many signs elsewhere of affinity between Shakespeare's and Ovid's poetic temperaments offer *a priori* evidence that the Sonnets absorb more Ovidian sentiment than this single turn of thought. There is, too, a piece of contemporary external testimony which points to a more extensive debt. When Shakespeare had reached the midmost stage of his working career, Francis Meres, keen-witted schoolmaster and acute observer of literary activity, wrote of the great dramatist in his *Palladis Tamia* (1598) thus: 'As the soul of Euphorbus was thought to live in Pythagoras, so the sweet witty soul of Ovid lives in mellifluous and honey-tongued Shakespeare; witness his *Venus and Adonis*, his *Lucrece*, his sugared sonnets among his private friends,' &c.

The critical preceptor gives many proofs of close acquaintance with Ovid's *Metamorphoses*, whence he borrows with precision his allusion to Euphorbus and

Pythagoras (xv. 161). Meres plainly detected in Shakespeare's Sonnets, no less than in the two narrative poems, a liberal touch of the Ovidian spirit. A closer comparison of the Sonnets with the *Metamorphoses* than seems to have been yet essayed proves the truth of Meres' verdict. The last lines of the last book of Ovid's long poem gave Shakespeare a cue for his vaunt of eternal fame. A mass of earlier lines in the same book presents a series of subtle conceptions about Time and Nature which Shakespeare's Sonnets absorb no less distinctly.

Tales of enchantment, wherein men and women undergo magical transformation into animals, flowers, trees, rocks, and fountains, fill a great part of the fifteen books of the *Metamorphoses*; and to the graphic energy with which these narratives are invested, Dante paid a lasting tribute in the *Inferno* (xxv. 97). The fables belong for the most part to Greek mythology, and were largely derived by Ovid from cognate Greek miscellanies compiled near his own time at Alexandria. Ovid was a borrower on a liberal scale, and on his Alexandrian canvas he embroidered reminiscences of Homer, of the Greek tragedians, and even of Latin contemporaries like Catullus and Virgil. Yet he can claim originality for his skill in weaving his scattered material into a homogeneous poetic panorama. At the same time mere story-telling did not exhaust Ovid's aim. Along with his tales of magic he seeks to satisfy, parenthetically, two extraneous purposes, one of which concerns politics and the other philosophy. In the penultimate and the last books he vaguely traces the political fortunes of the eternal city from Romulus' miraculous foundation to the death of Julius Caesar, whose metamorphosis into a star brings to a conclusion his records of transformation. His philosophic digressions are more widely distributed. At the opening as well as at the close of the poem, many hundred lines are devoted to speculation on 'the causes of things'. Ovid's work may be almost said to be framed in a philosophic setting. The proem deals with cosmology; it declares the world to be originally an emanation of chaos, and to have been first inhabited by a heroic race of humanity, who passed from the age of Gold to that of Iron, and left behind a colony of giants. These mysterious beings are reported to have made war upon the gods in heaven, who, to avert ruin, decreed a universal flood. A single pair of human beings is credited with having survived the Deluge, and they finally repeopled the earth by flinging stones, to be miraculously changed into men and beasts.

This strange thread of cosmological theory is abruptly suspended by the first series of metamorphic tales, and is kept out of sight until the poet has wellnigh exhausted his metamorphic themes. In the last book Ovid balances his cosmological exordium by a far more complex philosophical pronouncement. There he introduces the Greek philosopher, Pythagoras, as instructing the reputed progenitor of Roman law, Numa Pompilius, in the meaning of life and death. Through more than four hundred lines Pythagoras occupies Ovid's pulpit. The speaker is not content with explaining the orthodox Pythagorean doctrines of metempsychosis and vegetarian asceticism. He soon digresses into an energetic discourse, impregnated with metaphysical subtlety, on the essential imperishability of matter, of which only the outward forms undergo change. These principles of being are shown to serve a perpetual process of rotation among all the phenomena of Nature. The universe of matter is, on Ovid's hypothesis, an ever-turning wheel, which suffers nothing to be either new or old; the appearances of constant change or innovation are due to the effect of a regularly gyrating recurrence. So abstruse a solution of the mysteries of Nature is no part of the creed which is traditionally assigned to the Pythagoras of ancient Greek philosophy. Ovid ignores the mystical mathematical axiom that the essence of all things is number, which is the centre of the original Pythagorean philosophy. The so-called Pythagorean creed which Ovid presents is in fact a recent philosophic development of Alexandria, which, though called

Neo-Pythagoreanism, had small right to that title. It was fundamentally based on the Stoic platform, and was nearly akin to Neo-Platonism.

The last of the Stoic philosophers, Marcus Aurelius, summed up Ovid's doctrine in such sentences as 'all the occurrences in this world are the same from age to age and come round in a circle'; 'changes and vicissitudes roll on like one wave upon another'; 'all things were intended by Nature to change, to be converted into other forms, and to perish, so that other things may be produced in perpetual succession'. The ancient beliefs in metempsychosis and the virtue of vegetarianism, which Ovid also takes under his wing, were barely recognized by the new Pythagorean dispensation, of which the mainspring was the Stoic theory of universal 'revolution'. Elsewhere, too, Ovid travels beyond his metaphysical text. On his description of the wheel-like operation of nature, which he borrowed from contemporary metaphysicians of Alexandria, he loosely grafts geographical and geological observations, which he derives from more popular scientific manuals or reports of travel.

Ovid was in no sense a systematic philosopher. A worldling of acute intelligence, he accepted with readiness the first plausible solution at hand of metaphysical or physical puzzles. Nevertheless his fluent command of poetic diction lent charm to all he wrote; and careful readers of his *Metamorphoses* were hardly more impressed by his magical faculty of story-telling than by his unmethodized endeavour to unravel the mysterious process of being. Seneca quotes his philosophic dicta as well as his fables. The philosophic and allegorical interpreters of the poem during the Middle Ages had a specious warrant for their labyrinthine modes of exegesis. Many critics of the Renaissance detected in the *Metamorphoses* serious philosophic purpose no less than poetic charm. William Webbe, author of *A Discourse of English Poetry* in 1586, echoed a prevailing sentiment when he attributed to the *Metamorphoses* 'exceeding wisdom and sound

judgement'. Golding, the English translator, in some preliminary original comments on the *Metamorphoses*, twice
calls his readers' attention to Ovid's invention of Pythagoras' oration, wherein 'discourse' is made of 'dark philosophy' in its 'moral', 'natural', and 'divine' aspects.

No careful reader can overlook the thread of philosophical speculation which is woven dispersedly into the
texture of Shakespeare's Sonnets. In varied periphrasis
the sonneteer expresses a fear that 'nothing' is 'new';
that 'that which is hath been before'; that Time, being
in a perpetual state of 'revolution', is for ever repro-
ducing natural phenomena in a regular rotation; that
the most impressive efforts of Time, which the untutored
mind regards as 'novel' or 'strange', 'are but dressings
of a former sight', merely the rehabilitations of a past
experience, which fades only to repeat itself. The metaphysical argument has only a misty relevance to the
poet's plea of everlasting love for his friend. The writer
vaguely professes a fear that Nature's rotatory processes
deprive his passion for the beautiful youth of all flavour
of originality. With no very coherent logic he takes refuge
from this distasteful reflection in a bold claim on behalf of
his friend and himself to personal exemption from the
universal law of Nature's and Time's endlessly recurring
'growth' and 'waning'. The reality and individuality of
passionate experience are repeatedly admitted to be irreconcilable with the doctrine of universal 'revolution'.

Shakespeare's reasons for grafting these barely relevant
philosophic subtleties on a poetic scheme of emotional
confession of passion do not lie on the surface. Shakespeare, though a 'natural philosopher' in the general
sense of 'a philosopher by light of nature', was no professed metaphysician. The philosophic digression in the
last book of Ovid's *Metamorphoses* supplies the key to
the riddle. A poetic master's interpretation of Life and
Eternity involuntarily claimed the respectful attention
of a loyal disciple. Shakespeare in the Sonnets ignores
Ovid's association of his metaphysical doctrine with

Pythagoras, though in the dramas of early and middle
life he plays irresponsibly, in Ovid's manner, with the
proverbial 'opinion' of Pythagoras

> That souls of animals infuse themselves
> Into the trunks of men.[1]

Pythagoras' primordial warning (in the *Metamorphoses*)
—'forbear your *kinsfolk's ghosts to chase by slaughter*'—
seems echoed too in the 'fear' of the Clown in *Twelfth
Night* (IV. ii. 64) 'to *kill* a woodcock lest thou dispossess
the soul of thy grandam'. The worn-out creed of metempsychosis, however, finds no place in the Sonnets. It is
solely with Ovid's Stoic or Neo-Pythagorean musings
that Shakespeare there embroiders his emotional utterances. The result is something of a patchwork. The
warm tones of the diction obscure the philosophic inconsistencies, but do not dissipate them. At any rate
Shakespeare levies loans on Ovid's Neo-Pythagorean deliverances with a freedom which fully justifies Meres's
citation of the Sonnets as corroborative testimony that
'the sweet witty soul of Ovid lives in mellifluous and
honey-tongued Shakespeare'.

The English poet's discipleship to the Latin poet may,
with advantage to perspicuity, be first illustrated by the
use Shakespeare makes of two of Ovid's vivid physio-
graphic proofs of his central cosmic theory. The ceaseless
recurrence of natural phenomena is illustrated by Ovid
from the example of the sea-waves' motion. Golding
translates the passage thus:

> *As every wave* drives others forth, and *that that comes behind*
> *Both thrusteth and is thrust himself*; even so the times by kind
> Do fly and *follow* both at once and evermore renew.

Shakespeare (Sonnet LX, 1–4) presents the argument less
methodically, but he adopts the illustrative figure without
much disguise. Sonnet LX opens thus:

> *Like as the waves* make towards the pebbled shore,
> So do our minutes hasten to their end;

[1] *Merch. of Ven.*, v. i. 131–3.

> *Each changing place with that which goes before,*
> In *sequent* toil all forwards do contend.

Even more striking is Shakespeare's reproduction of Ovid's graphic description of the constant encroachments of land on sea and sea on land, which the Latin poet adduces as fresh evidence of matter's endless variations, and fortifies by a long series of professed personal observations. In Golding's rendering the passage opens thus:

> Even so have places oftentimes *exchanged their estate,*
> For *I have seen* it sea which was *substantial ground* alate.
> Again, where sea was, *I have seen* the same become dry land.

In Sonnet LXIV Shakespeare assimilates these words with a literalness which makes him claim to 'have seen' with his own eyes the phenomena of Ovid's narration:

> When *I have seen* the hungry ocean gain
> Advantage on the kingdom of the shore,
> And *the firm soil* win of the watery main
> Increasing store with loss, and loss with store;
> When *I have seen* such *interchange of state.*

The driving vigour with which Ovid pursues this corroborative theme of 'interchange' or 'exchange' between earth and ocean is well reflected in the swing of Golding's ballad metre:

> And in the tops of mountains high old anchors have been found,
> Deep valleys have by watershot been made of level ground,
> And hills by force of gulling oft have into sea been worne,
> Hard gravel ground is sometime seen where marish was beforne.

With especial force does Ovid point to the subsidence of land beneath the voracious sea:

> Men say that Sicil also hath been joined to Italy
> Until the sea consumed the bounds between, and did supply
> The room with water. If ye go to seek for Helice
> And Bury, which were cities of Achaea, you shall see
> Them hidden under water; and the shipmen yet do show
> The walls and steeples of the towns drowned under as they row.

The stirring picture so firmly gripped Shakespeare's imagination that he reproduced it in his drama as well as in his Sonnets. Under the Ovidian spell, the desponding King Henry IV passionately exclaims (*2 Henry IV*, III. i. 45 *seq.*):

> O God! that one might read the book of fate
> And see *the revolution of the times*
> Make mountains level, and the continent,
> Weary of solid firmness, melt itself
> Into the sea! and, other times, to see
> The beachy girdle of the ocean
> Too wide for Neptune's hips.

Shakespeare's treatment of the central tenet of Ovid's cyclical creed may be best deduced from Sonnets LIX and CXXIII. In both these poems the doctrine of Nature's rotatory process is the main topic, although the theme is developed to different purposes. In the first sonnet the poet seriously examines the theory without committing himself to it; in the second he pronounces in its favour, albeit with a smack of irony. The text of Ovid about which Shakespeare's thought revolves in these two poems is rendered by Golding thus:

> Things ebb and flow . . . Even so the times by kind
> Do fly and follow both at once, and evermore renew . . .
> Things pass perchance from place to place, yet all, from whence
>   they came
> Returning, do unperished continue still the same.

Shakespeare here concentrates all his attention on the hypothesis of 'revolution' in Nature. Sonnet LIX opens with the lines:

> If there be nothing new, but that which is
> Hath been before, how are our brains beguiled,
> Which, labouring for invention, bear amiss
> The second burden of a former child!

'If there be nothing new', if what we call birth or novelty is mere rotating return of an old state of being, then, the poet proceeds to argue, his friend's beauty would have had a former existence, and would have found 'backward' record five hundred years ago. A far older world would have passed its verdict on the present theme. The poet admits that 'five hundred courses of the sun' are conceivably capable of three sequels. Firstly, things and their appearances may progress; secondly, there is possibility of retrogression; thirdly, there may result the identity which is fruit of recurrence or repetition. The poet cannot determine

> Whether we [i.e. the present age] are mended, or whether better
> they [i.e. former ages],
> Or whether revolution be the same.

Then, somewhat lamely descending to lower levels of thought, he contents himself with the confident assurance that in any case 'wits of former days' spent their eulogy on less worthy objects than his friend. Ovid's creed is that 'revolution' *is* 'the same', and that things and their appearances are constantly returning to the same point whence they have come. Shakespeare, although tempted to assent, stays hesitatingly at the threshold.

In Sonnet cxxiii Shakespeare takes a bolder position, though again his intellectual courage evaporates when in face of the inevitable conclusion, and he weakly makes escape through an emotional commonplace. In the opening lines he apostrophizes Time and its massive structures thus:

> Thy pyramids built up with newer might
> To me are nothing novel, nothing strange;
> They are but dressings of a former sight.

In other words, Time's imposing manifestations merely rehabilitate what has been seen before. Time's apparent innovations, the poet continues, foist 'upon us' what 'is old'; we vainly imagine things to be 'born' afresh 'to our desire', although 'we before have heard them told'. The poet, wiser than his fellows, declares with some aggressiveness that he will henceforth refuse to distinguish between 'the present and the past'. Both the records of history and our own observations are lying deceptions;

the variations in natural phenomena, of which they offer delusive shows, are effects of the unending haste of Time's revolving wheel.

> For thy records and what we see doth lie,
> Made more or less by thy continual haste.

Here Shakespeare translates into his own vocabulary Ovid's dicta that 'times by kind do fly and follow both at once and evermore renew'; and that 'things . . . do unperished continue still the same'. Golding had·inquired if 'that *any noueltie worth wondring* be in' the miraculous birth and death of the recurring phoenix. Shakespeare, by way of response, describes himself in the present sonnet as 'not *wondering* at the present or the past'. When, in the final couplet, Shakespeare vows constancy of love, 'despite' Time's 'scythe', he ignores his previous argument, and breezily excuses himself by a conventional tag for indulgence in metaphysical subtlety. But the preceding quatrains show penetrating insight into the significance of Ovid's Neo-Pythagorean creed.

Some fifteen sonnets in all reflect Ovid's metaphysical or physical interpretation of the universe. In Sonnets XLIV and XLV Shakespeare develops the belief that life is constituted of the four elements, earth, water, air, and fire; all of which, he tells us, are necessary to 'life's composition'. Earth and water are described as oppressively 'slow' in action, while 'slight air and purging fire' are 'quicker' and more 'swift'. Here Shakespeare has adapted to his own purpose a leading principle of Ovid's natural philosophy:

> This endless world contains therein, I say,
> Four substances of which all things are gendered. Of these four
> The earth and water for their mass and weight are sunken lower.
> The other couple, air and fire, the purer of the twain,
> Mount up, and nought can keep them down.

Such a theory of the elements was common knowledge among the medieval and Renaissance poets; but Shakespeare's mode of contrasting the density of earth and water with that of fire and air sounds a peculiarly Ovidian note. A philosophic significance of more recondite nature attaches to Shakespeare's apostrophe, in Sonnet cxxvi, of *'Nature*, sovereign *mistress* over wrack' [i.e. decay], whose *'skill'* may Time disgrace'; whose 'skill' may, in other words, arrest Time's destroying power. Whatever be the poet's final use of the conceit, he here not only seems to have in mind the triumph over self-destructive Chaos, which Ovid's cosmological theory at the opening of the *Metamorphoses* assigns jointly to 'God and Nature', but would also appear to recall the *'cunning hand'* of *'Dame* Nature' in fostering human life, which figures in the Neo-Pythagorean manifesto of Ovid's last book.

Shakespeare's raids on the *Metamorphoses* are often too spasmodic or casual to respect the tenour of Pythagoras' complex discourse. He at times accepts at Ovid's hand a felicitous fancy without regard to its setting. Ovid elucidates his theory of 'revolution' by poetic pictures of the daily course of sun and moon, of the procession of the seasons, of the progress of man's life from youth to age, of Time's recurrent ruin and restoration of kingdoms and cities. From many of these vignettes Shakespeare snatches mnemonically a detached phrase or idea which carries little trace of the philosophic atmosphere. 'Tempus edax rerum' (*Metamorphoses*, xv. 234) becomes in Shakespeare's text 'devouring Time', which makes 'the earth devour her own sweet brood' (Sonnet xix). Golding renders the Latin here:

> *Thou Time, the eater up of things,* and age of spiteful teen,
> Destroy all things!

Shakespeare develops Ovid's defiant challenge of Time's voracity by a reference to the burning of 'the long-lived phoenix', on which Ovid also waxes eloquent. But here Shakespeare leaves Ovid's tale half told, and ignores his corollary of Time's counterbalancing forces of renewal.

In Sonnets LXIII and LXIV Shakespeare treats again of 'Time's injurious hand' and of 'Time's fell hand', which

defaces 'the rich-proud cost of outworn buried age' such,
᠎ ᠎ says, as '*I have seen*'. The 'lofty towers' which he
again asserts he has himself *seen* 'down-razed', are the
towers' of Athens and Thebes and other cities of Greece,
ruins of whose ancient works' were overgrown with grass
according to the Latin poet's glowing verse. Shakespeare's
observation was a vicarious experience for a second and
third time. Once more, too, Shakespeare misses Ovid's
philosophic assurance that this decay is merely the start-
ing-point of new growth:

> So see we all things changeable; one nation gathereth strength,
> Another weareth weak, and both do make exchange at length.

Yet in almost all his illustrations of Time's ravages he
follows Ovid's leadership with characteristic loyalty.

Shakespeare keeps closer to his guide's steps when he
adapts Ovid's sympathetic sketch of man's journey from
youth to age. In Sonnet LXIII he imagines the day when
his love's 'youthful morn' will have 'travell'd on to *age's
steepy night*'. Similarly Ovid notes how the boy, 'growing
strong and swift, . . . passeth forth the space of youth;
and . . . through drooping *age's steepy* path he runneth out
his race'. Not merely does Ovid's metaphor of travel
correspond with Shakespeare's reflection, but Golding's
phrase, '*age's steepy* path', is accepted with very slight
modification. The uncommon adjective 'steepy' tells
its own tale.

In Sonnet LX, Shakespeare, with an eye on the same
passages in Ovid, tells somewhat cryptically how

> Nativity, once in the main of light,
> *Crawls* to maturity.

This is a difficult mode of saying that the newborn babe,
when it has once emerged into the full expanse of the
day's light, passes on to manhood through a period of
crawling. 'The main of light' echoes Golding's 'light-
some sun' and 'daystar clear and bright'. The ambiguity
frequently attaching to Shakespeare's habit of using
abstract for concrete terms (i.e. 'nativity' for 'newborn

babe') is here increased by an insistent reminiscence of Ovid's graphic description, in the same connexion, of the baby's early endeavour to crawl. On the infant's crawling processes the Latin poet lays curious stress in his account of man's progress from infancy. Golding's version runs:

> The child newborn lies void of strength; within a season though
> He, waxing fourfooted, learns like savage beasts to go;
> Then, somewhat faltering, and as yet not firm of foot, he stands
> By getting somewhat for to help his sinews in his hands.

Another instructive verbal echo of Golding is heard in Sonnet xv. The four ages of man are likened by Ovid to the four seasons—to 'spring-tide', which decks 'the earth with flowers of sundry hue', to 'summer waxing strong . . . like a lusty youth', to 'harvest', and to 'ugly winter', which, 'like age, steals on with trembling steps, all bald or overcast with shrill thin air as white as snow'. In Sonnet xv Shakespeare writes, again claiming another's vision:

> I perceive that men as plants increase . . .
> Vaunt in their youthful sap, at height decrease.

Nothing very distinctive can be alleged of such comparisons between human life and nature. But Shakespeare here, with singular precision, goes on to define his presentation of this law of growth, in language of Golding's coinage; he calls it 'the conceit of this inconstant *stay*'. Golding repeatedly adapts a negative periphrasis, of which the word 'stay' is the central feature, when he writes of the Ovidian theory of Nature's unending rotation. Golding's usage, which is none too felicitous, was probably due to exigencies of rhyme. Thus he asserts that 'in all the world there is not that that standeth at a *stay*'. At different points he notes that 'our bodies' and 'the elements *never stand at stay*'. Shakespeare's 'inconstant *stay*' (Sonnet xv, 9) is Golding's clumsy vocabulary. He shows a keener artistic sense, and a better appreciation of Ovid's argument, when he replaces 'this inconstant stay' elsewhere by such variants as 'nature's changing course' (XVIII, 8), 'revolution' (LIX, 12), 'interchange of state' (LXIV, 9), and 'the course of altering things' (CXV, 8). This terminology, which also echoes Golding (e.g. 'the *interchanging course*' and '*exchange*' of 'estate'), does better justice to the lucidity of the Latin poet.

Some of the ideas common to Ovid and Shakespeare are the universal food of poetry. But the majority of the cited parallelisms have individuality; and their collective presence both in the Sonnets and in one short passage of the *Metamorphoses* establishes Shakespeare's debt. He by no means stood alone among Elizabethan poets in assimilating Ovid's Neo-Pythagorean doctrine. Nor is the cyclical solution of Nature's mysteries the exclusive property of Ovid, or of his Neo-Pythagorean tutors; it is shared by the Stoics and the Neo-Platonists. But the poets of Europe first learnt its outlines in Ovid's pages, even if curiosity impelled some of them subsequently to supplement Ovid's information by resort to metaphysical treatises of one or other of the Greek schools and to current Italian adaptations of Neo-Pythagoreanism or Neo-Platonism. Such was clearly the experience of Shakespeare's great poetic contemporary, Edmund Spenser, who twice in his *Faerie Queene* repeats Ovid's account of the processes of Time and Nature in the *Metamorphoses*, but subtilizes it by references to Plato or Plotinus, to Ficino or Bruno. In Spenser's third book, where Adonis personifies the productivity of Nature, and the garden of Adonis is pictured as a treasury of Nature's seeds, the poet champions the doctrine of the imperishability of matter, despite the variations of its forms, in lines like these:

> That substance is eterne and bideth so:
> Ne when the life decays and form does fade
> Doth it consume and into nothing go,
> But changed is and often altered to and fro.

Ovid's influence is more clearly visible in the extant fragments of the seventh book of Spenser's moral epic, the unfinished canto of Mutability. There Spenser depicts the regular rotation of Nature and Time,

> The ever-whirling wheel
> Of Change, the which all mortal things doth sway.

Spenser's and Shakespeare's phrasings of their accounts of the cyclic workings of 'Dame Nature's' activities differ. But there is sufficient resemblance in thought to prove the suggestive energy of Ovid and to confirm the right of the *Metamorphoses* to its French title of 'La Bible des Poètes'.

The cryptic problems commonly associated with Shakespeare's Sonnets lie beyond the scope of this demonstration of the Ovidian temper which colours the Sonnets' philosophy. The new proofs of Shakespeare's dependence on Ovid support the belief that the bulk of the Sonnets came from Shakespeare's pen in his early life, when his memory of the *Metamorphoses* was freshest. In that elegy of Ovid from which Shakespeare drew the motto for his *Venus and Adonis*, the Latin poet pays a noble tribute to Lucretius, the greatest of all poets who made philosophy their theme. Ovid's fine reference to Lucretius must have been familiar to Shakespeare in very early life, and may well have stimulated an effort to fuse lyric emotion with the philosophic speculation of Ovid's own pages.

In any case, an examination of the philosophic sentiment which courses through the Sonnets renders indefeasible the claim of those poems to rank with the richest fruits of the pagan Renaissance. The main themes of the Sonnets are beauty's obligation to propagate itself in offspring, the supremacy of masculine beauty, faith in the immortality of verse and in its capacity to eternize its subject. All these themes belong to the paganism of Greek lyric poetry, which flowed from Greece through Latin literature into the vernacular poetry of the Western Renaissance. But the philosophical reflections which pervade the poems offer the plainest evidence that has yet been adduced of the pagan tone of the poet's voice. The doctrine that, in spite of all appearances to the contrary,

Time is an endless rotatory process, and that what seems 'new' is mere recurrence of what has 'been before', is fatal to all Christian conception of the beginning and end of the world, with its special creations at the outset and its day of judgement at the close. No notion of the soul's immortality is quite consistent with the cyclical workings of Time and Nature. There is no possibility of reconciling these pagan cosmic views with Christianity. Such a conclusion is of importance because it brings Shakespeare's spirit into closer kinship with the intellectual development of the European Renaissance than is sometimes acknowledged. But critical lovers of the Sonnets, who recognize in them the flower of poetic fervour, will probably be content to draw, from the fact of Shakespeare's absorption of the Ovidian philosophy, fresh evidence of that miraculous sympathy and receptivity whereby

> all the learnings that his time
> Could make him the receiver of, . . . he took,
> As we do air, fast as 'twas minister'd,
> And in 's spring became a harvest.

SHAKESPEARE AND THE ITALIAN RENAISSANCE[1]

I

LITERATURE, philosophy, science, law, and art are the five main currents of the tide of civilization. All the five trace much of their healthful flow in modern times within and without Europe to the impetus of Italian example—to the comprehensive energy in the fourteenth, fifteenth, and sixteenth centuries of Italy's imaginative, intellectual, and artistic accomplishment. Modern Italy's political history was until the middle of last century a record of gloom, a tale of cruel dismemberment; but her intellectual and artistic fortunes never ran higher than in the days of Shakespeare's youth. Literature and art gave a genuine meaning to the conception of Italian unity, even when the country was politically torn asunder by the strife of faction and by domestic or foreign tyrannies. A degenerate era of Italian culture opened at the close of the sixteenth century, but before that date Italy—by virtue of her art, poetry, and philosophy—had won unfading laurels for herself, and had helped many foreign brows to chaplets no less lasting. To change the metaphor, Italy may be fairly likened, in the fourteenth, fifteenth, and especially in the sixteenth century, to a copious fountain whence the sparkling waters of civilization spread in broad streams over modern Europe, and thence at later epochs, over a great part of the world. So honourable a tribute can be paid to no other country.

Italy set out on her modern career with advantages which she shared with no other part of Europe. Civilization in liberal measure illumined the land while mists of barbarism enveloped the rest of Europe.

The intellect of ancient Italy was largely fertilized by forces older and more lucent than those of her own

[1] The British Academy Annual Shakespeare Lecture, 1915.

breeding: by the thought and style of Greece. But the native land of Virgil and Catullus, of Cicero and Tacitus, insured herself near 2,000 years ago against a denial at any era of her literary genius or power. The country which harboured the Republic and Empire of Rome, the country which was the nursery of Roman law and the birthplace of Latin Christianity, claimed in the fifth century of our era a civilized and a civilizing tradition, which Attila and his Huns, with other scourges of kindred race, vowed to perdition in vain. The successes and failures of the Gothic warlords of the fifth century in their assaults on Italy graphically illustrate the virtual futility of relying on brute violence to annihilate the fruit of man's intellect and spirit.

The barbarian invaders of Italy effected a very incomplete conquest of the country, very incomplete when it is compared with their conquests elsewhere in Western Europe. In spite of the invasion and settlement of Teutons in the North, in spite of the later immigrations of Normans and Saracens in the South, the Latin race can still claim in the peninsula an ethnical predominance. On the lips of the people at large the old Latin language suffered in course of time transformation, re-formation. Yet the Latin tongue in select circles survived without radical decay and came to serve the greatest purposes of human intercourse, the purposes of social organization and of education, not in Italy alone, but wherever government was built on sure foundations by the barbarian conquerors. The triumph of the Latin language over the perils of extinction which menaced it in Europe of the fifth and sixth centuries is a complementary testimony to the impotence of brute matter in conflict with unconquerable mind.

Some 1,500 years ago Italy proved herself the saviour of such civilization as the world then knew, and during some eleven succeeding centuries she discharged the proud function of protecting the old elements of civilization and reinforcing it with new elements. The missionary activities of civilizing Italy never suffered arrest before the close of the sixteenth century. Yet the Teutonic influence bred in the Middle Ages sentiments and ideas which clouded the mental and spiritual atmosphere of all Europe and cast their shadow on Italy. One should not exaggerate the darkness of the Dark Ages; one should not disparage or ignore medieval culture. Much Latin literature and all Greek literature save Aristotle's philosophical works were for the time lost. The Greek language fell out of knowledge, and the lapse tended to impoverish the intellect. On the other hand, a substantial amount of Latin poetry and prose was studied, and gave a cue to intellectual exertion. Virgil and Ovid never lacked medieval readers or commentators. Aristotle in a Latin garb was reckoned the prophet of scholastic philosophy. In Italy especially clear gleams of light broke the medieval sky. There was in the thirteenth century the poetry of Dante, a brilliant radiance. None the less the teaching of the old civilization endured in Italy a partial eclipse. The medieval Church enshrouded life and learning in a dim, mystical gloom of which the ancient world knew little. The mind of man abandoned itself to dreams and reveries.

The medieval sentiment may be comprehensively defined as an amalgam of dogma and asceticism. The mind and the body were alike condemned to unprecedented restraints and austerities. The monastic vows of obedience, poverty, and chastity well reflect the medieval aspiration. The piece of literature which best satisfied the general temper had for its title 'the contempt of the world and the miseries of the human condition'. Even Dante, who caught many Pisgah-like glimpses of later enlightenment, saddened man with his pictures of the Inferno, and he made his final goal peace or quietism in all spheres of human endeavour. Dante's only hope of realizing his ideal lay through universal recognition of a single supreme authority, soaring above all calls of nationality as well as individuality, a single supreme authority which should find embodiment in an omnipotent emperor.

In the fourteenth century there sprang from Italian soil a movement which had for its effect, if not for its first aim, the emancipation of human life and human aspiration from the fetters of medieval conceptions. The movement which we call the Renaissance sprang up and matured on Italian soil, and confirmed Italy's old title of saviour or champion of European civilization.

It was the gradual discovery by Italy of the true range of classical Greek literature and philosophy which was the spring of the intellectual and spiritual revival. That discovery was begun in the fourteenth century, when Greek subjects of the falling Byzantine Empire brought across the Adriatic manuscript memorials of Greek intellectual culture, of which the West had lost nearly all knowledge for some 1,000 years. Petrarch and Boccaccio, the fathers of modern Italian literature, although they were in no true sense Greek scholars, vaguely heralded the new Greek revelation. But close study of Greek texts was needed to bring home the significance of the new learning. It was not till the overthrow of the Byzantine Empire by the Turks in the fifteenth century that the literary art of Athens was driven westward in full flood, and the scope of Greek enlightenment was definitely acknowledged by Italy. It was then there first came into the modern world the feeling for form, the frank delight in life, the unrestricted employment of the reason. An ancient literature and an ancient philosophy had come to light to prove that the human intellect possessed capacities which were hitherto unimagined, and to convict of futility the dogmatic and ascetic ideals of the Middle Ages.

Perhaps the Greek author whose influence on the new movement was largest was Plato. Some dim knowledge of his theories is visible in medieval literature; but Aristotle in a Latin garb was the only Greek philosopher who enjoyed any genuine allegiance in Europe before the fifteenth century. On foundations, which the Latinized Aristotle had laid, the Roman Church indeed built up its intricate scheme of scholasticism. Direct study of the work of Plato and of the Neo-Platonists, his late Greek disciples, was an innovation of the Renaissance. At Florence, in the villa of the Medici, the old Athenian Academy was revived in the fifteenth century for the discussion of Plato's conception of life and love and art. Under the banner of Florence the sway of medievalism received its first challenge.

At the outset the true issues of the strife were obscured. The Platonists of fifteenth-century Florence were slow to recognize the revolution which they were putting in train. Plato's predilection for abstractions and for allegory was not out of harmony with the intellectual tendencies of the Middle Ages, and medieval processes of thought were very gradually abandoned by the Florentine academicians. The new literature and speculation abundantly illustrate the tenacity of the old spirit. The Florentine Platonists thought to reconcile the new enlightenment with the old scholasticism, and their jumbling of incompatible ideas drawn respectively from paganism and Christianity hindered for a generation a clear outlook. A wild incongruity infected Florentine art as well as Florentine speculation. Even Michael Angelo brought on canvas into the presence of the Madonna fauns disporting themselves in Dionysiac revels. Yet in time the Platonic light pierced the haze. At any rate the earth ceased to connote for the Italian Platonists gloom and misery; the human body was no longer a synonym for corruption; the reason grew impatient of servitude to any preconceived theory.

It was the idealization and worship of beauty that lit, in the groves of the Florentine academy, the flame which at length dispelled the medieval vapour. The identification by the thinkers—first of Florence, then of other Italian cities, and afterwards of all the Western continent —of the highest good with beauty, the assumption that a true appreciation of beauty was the least disputable of virtues, went near shattering the dominant medieval conceptions of the world and of humanity. The doctrine which found exponents through the length and breath of

Italy soon had its apostle in the papal curia itself. Cardinal Bembo summed up the new gospel by declaring that only when one said of the world that it is 'beautiful' did one serve the cause of truth. 'Beautiful' was, the cardinal argued, the only epithet which accurately described the heaven or the earth, the sea or the rivers, trees, gardens, or cities.

One of the practical fruits of the new Italian conception of beauty merits a special emphasis. Italian painting is one of the insistent facts in the history of the Renaissance. Italian painting is the first satisfying realization in the human economy of the significance of colour. The Italian painters of the Renaissance first interpreted life with any approach to perfection in terms of colour. The moving cause lay in Italy's new search in the creation for beauty. The Italian painters were fortunately placed. A relevant inspiration lay in the blue of the Italian sea and of the Italian sky, in the mingled hues of the native marble, in the gay plumage of the birds, in the immense variety of iridescent flowers, in the fruit of the vines, in the trees of the olive and the orange and the palm, and, last but not least, in the brilliant tints of Italian women's hair and complexion. Beauty of form was fully realized by the Greeks; but the Italian sense of colour was denied them. A full appreciation of colour in all the richness of its range is to be reckoned among the innovations of the Italian Renaissance. It is an original gift to the world of Titian and Tintoretto and other great painters of Italy to which poetry as well as art lay under obligation.

The new conception of beauty which challenged the old ideals of asceticism greatly stimulated the new conception of man's intellectual faculty which dealt a heavy although by no means a fatal blow at the medieval principle of dogma. The creed of the Renaissance frankly acknowledged the earthly elements, the animal senses, in man's being. The fleshly instincts were often allowed freer play than before. Yet without pause did the missionaries of the Renaissance urge that man differed from all terrestrial creatures by virtue of his endowment of reason, and that that endowment was capable of lifting him high above the animals, and of setting him ultimately on a level with the angels. The final purpose of reason harmonized in the creed of the Renaissance philosophy with the new faith in beauty. The mind of man was destined to discover and reveal the ultimate beauty and order which lay behind the outer shapes of matter.

Pico della Mirandola, a Renaissance philosopher, seems first to have invented for himself the proud title of 'interpreter of nature'. The title suggests the comprehensive potentiality which was attached to man's intellectual faculty. There were more avenues than one by which he might arrive at an interpretation of nature. A wide choice was offered him. Poetry, art, and philosophy might each prove a pathway, and there was a fourth road which gave equal promise of the desired goal. The fourth approach lay through scientific inquiry. The intellectual restlessness of the Renaissance was impatient of specialization, and many Italian sons of the movement trod all the ways which seemed to incline in the right direction. Leonardo da Vinci is the most familiar type of the intellectual versatility of the era; he sought with almost equal enthusiasm to conquer the domains of science as well as of poetry and art.

Scientific curiosity issued from the new sense of beauty and the new plea for intellectual enfranchisement, in as compelling a flow as the artistic or literary achievement of the Renaissance. Nowhere in sixteenth-century Europe was scientific exertion more active or more fruitful than in Italy. The year that witnessed the birth of Shakespeare at Stratford-on-Avon witnessed the birth in Pisa of Galileo, the greatest Italian man of science in a line of succession which was already long and distinguished.

No reference, however cursory, to the scientific activity of the Renaissance would be complete without passing mention of its chief practical outcome in the era, the discovery of the New World. The first voyages across the

Atlantic, which resulted in the momentous discovery of the Western hemisphere, were undertaken by way of testing a scientific theory or guess which was propounded in Italy in the early years of the Renaissance. The first two navigators who touched American shores—Columbus in the south and Cabot in the north—although they served foreign masters on their Atlantic explorations, were both natives of the great Italian seaport of Genoa. The intellectual stir, which came of the discovery of an old civilization (that of Greece) and put a new valuation on nature and man's intellectual capacity, was reinforced at no distant interval by the discovery of a new world which gave a new estimate of man's physical environment. The dark curtains which had hitherto restricted man's view of the physical world to a small corner of it were torn asunder, and the stimulating fact came to light that that which had hitherto been regarded by men as the whole sphere of physical life and nature was in reality a mere fragment of a mighty expanse, of the greater part of which there had been no previous knowledge. The intellectual revelation came first. The physical revelation followed. It was not a wholly accidental conjuncture of events. The new intellectual curiosity was first conspicuously justifying itself. Each revelation powerfully reacted on the other, and increased the fertility of Renaissance thought and action.

An English critic has written: 'Producers of great literature do not live in isolation, but catch light and heat from each other's thought. A people without intellectual commerce with other peoples has never done anything conspicuous in literature.'

The Greek influences of the Italian Renaissance adequately establish the pronouncement as far as Italy of that era is concerned. What Greece did for Renaissance Italy, Renaissance Italy did for contemporary Europe. The Italian influences of the Renaissance moved in the sixteenth century the imagination of her neighbours, France and Spain. Germany and England owed great part of their literary and artistic aspiration in the sixteenth century to intellectual commerce with Italy. In England, France, and Spain great heights of literary endeavour were in due time scaled. There was no complete reciprocity with Italy in the exchange of literary or artistic stimulus. The star of Italian influence was in the ascendant throughout the epoch, and while she shared her radiance with the other countries of Western Europe, she received for a long time little compared with what she gave. Yet Italy was not inattentive to contemporary advances of culture outside her own boundaries in the sixteenth century, especially in the way of scientific speculation. Ideas enjoyed a freedom of intercourse which surmounted all the practical obstacles. In none of the intellectual and artistic fields did nationality prove a bar to communication. In the result Western Europe of the sixteenth century formed something like a single federation of thought and art, a fact which Bacon recognized when he left by will his name and memory to foreign nations. Voltaire subsequently wrote to an English friend: 'Ceux qui aiment les arts sont tous concitoyens. Les honnêtes gens qui pensent ont à peu près les mêmes principes, et ne composent qu'une seule et même république.' Voltaire's vision was amply realized in the days when Shakespeare was setting out on his mighty career.

II

The term 'humanist', when it was first invented in Italy, merely denoted a student of human or secular literature as distinguished from sacred learning or theology. The first 'humanist' was above all things a classical scholar, and 'humanism' was little more than a synonym for classical scholarship. But classical study, as we have seen, sharpened and widened all human faculty, and the word 'humanist' may be justly extended to apply to all who in the sixteenth century were inspired by the new faith in beauty and reason, to all who sought to realize the new exalted hopes of human progress.

England was somewhat slow to enlist in this mighty march of mind. The culture of the Renaissance blossomed late in the British isle, far later than in Italy, or indeed in France. Nor did the English soil prove equal to fostering the humanist development in all the fields of endeavour which the new spirit fructified in Italy. No original painting, no original music, were cradled in Tudor England. There the Renaissance sought distinctive expression in literature and poetry alone. Nor was it till the last years of the sixteenth century that the literature or the poetry of Tudor England acquired true distinction. But although her pace was sluggish through the earlier decades, England was steadily garnering, as they passed, foreign stimulus, chiefly Italian stimulus. Not all the foreign impetus was the exclusive gift of Italy. On the one hand, Englishmen came to study the classics for themselves, and, on the other, they soon had at their disposal the Renaissance literature of France. Yet French literature of the sixteenth century was itself to a large degree fruit of the Italian tree. Much of the spirited teaching which France offered her neighbour had been learnt in Italian schools. The French liberality of suggestion helped to reinforce in literary England Italian influence. But the foreign influences, whencesoever they came, worked efficiently. They braced the native genius to triumphant exertion which left Elizabethan literature a match for the world.

Humanism in England may be dated from the visit of the three Oxford scholars, Linacre, Grocyn, and Colet, to Florence and other cities of Italy at the end of the fifteenth century. Colet's friend, Sir Thomas More, showed at the opening of the following century a sensitiveness to the new enlightenment which entitles him to be regarded as its earliest English apostle. His *Utopia* ranks with the 'richest fruits of the new Renaissance study of Plato; but it should be borne in mind that More's first publication was a translation into English of a pregnant biography of Pico della Mirandola, a Florentine pioneer of that interpretation of Platonic philosophy which was reforming the human intellect. Sir Thomas More justly called Pico 'a great lord of Italy and an excellent cunning man in all sciences'.

Englishmen acquired early that habit of Italian travel which they have not yet lost. English visitors to the great Italian cities always make careful report at home of the new revelations of Italian thought. In the middle years of the century one Sir Edward Hoby visited Venice, then in all her splendour, as well as Padua and Mantua, Ferrara, Siena, and Rome. It was Hoby who rendered into English the very textbook of the Renaissance culture of Italy, *Il Cortegiano* ('The Courtier') by Baldassare Castiglione. That volume pictured in minutest detail the scholar and the gentleman as he had been fashioned by the new ideals, and the theme was rounded off by a rapturous oration assigned to Cardinal Bembo on the new conceptions of beauty and of love.

English travellers in sixteenth-century Italy, despite political and religious controversy, were hospitably entertained. They were impressed not merely by the country's intellectual and artistic triumphs, but by the refined amenities of her social life. Academies on the Florentine model had made the literary club for conversation and discussion a prominent feature of civic organization. Art had touched the domestic furniture and equipment, and had brought into use devices and implements which were barely known in England. Many an English visitor to Italy was surprised to find forks habitually taking the place of fingers. Throughout Shakespeare's lifetime Englishmen explored Italy in numbers which increased year by year. There were protests from time to time on grounds of morality or religion. Rome, it was urged, was no fit place of pilgrimage for an English Protestant. The practical ethics of the Italian people were held to falsify conspicuously the lofty standards of their ideal philosophy. Some stern English moralists judged that the opportunity of vicious indulgence, the notorious enchantments of Italian Circes, were the main incentives to Italian travel. Englishmen in Italy were reckoned indeed by some to better the Italian instruction in sin, so that men occasionally spoke of an Italianate Englishman as a devil incarnate. The Italian Renaissance, despite its high ideals and brilliant accomplishments, had a dark side which insular prejudice or intolerance was not likely to underestimate. Yet it was a negligible minority of Englishmen in Italy who suffered serious moral or religious deterioration. The most efficient leaders of public opinion never ceased to preach the value of travel as a necessary part of a good education, and it was to foreign Italian cities, with their memorable antiquities, libraries, colleges, theatres, and academies, that the young Englishmen were chiefly advised to bend their steps. If they were confronted by temptation there was benefit in the discipline of resistance. 'Homekeeping youth have ever homely wits,' wrote Shakespeare. A perfect man, he added, was one who was tried and tutored in the world outside his native country. The dramatist laughingly detected in the travelled Englishman no worse failing than a predilection for outlandish manners and dress which offended insular taste. When it was said of an Elizabethan that he 'had swum in a gondola', the intention was to pay him a compliment on his polished deportment—on his urbanity, a trait which was first identified with Italian cities.

Sir Philip Sidney was perhaps more sensitive to the varied manifestations of the spirit of the age than any contemporary, and in his short life he illustrated by his own activities as graphically as any Englishman the versatility of the new forces of culture. His visit in youth to the home of the Renaissance, to Italy—while all the artistic, literary, and scientific impulses of the era were in full glow —attests the stimulating purpose which Italian travel commonly served. In Italy Sidney learned sonnetteering of the school of Petrarch. The pastoral romanticism which the Neapolitan Sanazzaro had brought to birth in his Italian *Arcadia* impelled Sidney to furnish his fellow countrymen with an English Arcadia—a region which it would rather puzzle serious geographers to find on the

map. Sanazzaro first applied the geographical Greek name
of Arcadia to an imaginary realm of pastoral simplicity,
where love-making was the sole concern of life. It was
largely, too, under the sway of Italian criticism that Sidney sought in his *Apology for Poetry* to shame the earth-
creeping mind 'into lifting itself up to look into the sky
of poetry'. But Sidney's craving for knowledge under
Italian skies passed beyond these bounds. He did not
limit his observation to literature in his Italian tour. At
Venice, where he remained longest, he devoted a great
part of his time to astronomy and music, a science and an
art which absorbed immense Italian energy despite other
distraction. Furthermore Sidney enjoys the rare distinction among Elizabethans of coming into personal contact
with the two great Italian painters, Tintoretto and Paolo
Veronese. With those men the pictorial art of Venice
came near perfection. Each offered to paint Sidney's
portrait, and he was embarrassed by the choice. Whether
he was wise in selecting Paolo Veronese I leave to the
judgement of those who know more of art than I do. The
portrait was completed by Veronese, and all lament that
it is not known to survive.

Yet it was not essential for an Englishman of Shakespeare's era to visit Italy in order to keep in touch with her
literary activities or philosophic progress. There were
from time to time Italian visitors to England, who were
capable of giving to Englishmen in their own country
instruction in the new Italian culture by word of mouth.
An Italian professor of law, Alberico Gentili, an Italian
jurist of the highest reputation in his own country, taught
Roman law for many years at Oxford, and gave a new
impulse to its study in England. But the most notable of
the Italian visitors to this country while Shakespeare was a
youth was the Platonic philosopher, Giordano Bruno,
whom Coleridge classes with Dante and Ariosto as one of
the three most characteristic Italians of all time. Bruno
was a philosopher and a scientific inquirer of the type dear
to the Renaissance. He sought out the beauty of the

world and discovered it in a light flowing from heaven. He defended the new Copernican system of astronomy which makes the earth a satellite of the sun. In a mystical allegory, *Spaccio de la Bestia Trionfante*, he foretold how the elements of man's lower nature were to vanish, and their places to be filled by truth, prudence, and wisdom— wisdom whose daughter is law. In his *Gli Eroici Furori* Bruno distinguished two kinds of enthusiasm, one which bred blind and unreasoning fanaticism, and the other which bred that love of truth and justice which turns some men into prophets and teachers and other men into creative artists. This noble prophet of enlightenment, who delivered his message to the chief universities of Europe in turn, arrived in England in 1583 and stayed here nearly two years. A warm welcome was accorded him by Sir Philip Sidney and his friends, and in many a debate on mighty themes did he engage them under their own roofs. Not all England was prepared to accept his ethereal teaching. He obtained permission of the Vice-Chancellor of Oxford to lecture in that University, and announced himself as 'the awakener of sleeping souls' ('dormitantium animarum excubitor'), but his audience disappointed him by their somnolence. He consoled himself by bitterly describing Oxford as 'una costellazione di pedantesca, ostinatissima ignoranza, e presunzione mista con una rustica inciviltà, che farebbe prevaricar la pazienza di Giobbe'. Nor could he refrain from complaints of the bad manners of the English people, their uncouth language, and their detestable climate. Yet whatever the discouragements of academic Oxford and the discomforts of his English sojourn, Bruno, while he lived in stimulating converse with men of letters in London, wrote or planned the philosophic and scientific books on which his fame mainly rests. The dedication of two of these works— *Spaccio de la Bestia Trionfante* and *Gli Eroici Furori*—to Sir Philip Sidney is a tribute to a fellow countryman in which we may all take pride. Elizabethan England at large may hardly have been ready for Bruno's gospel; but she at any rate placed no restriction on his freedom of thought. He enjoyed here, in his own phrase, an inestimable 'libertas philosophandi'. In his own country the forces of dogma had been checked but not crushed, and scientific originality was a chief abhorrence of the conservative temper. Bruno's boldness of utterance finally exposed him to the cruel reproof of the Inquisition, that blind protector of the ancient creeds. In the last year of the sixteenth century Bruno was burnt at the stake in Rome. He cheerfully sacrificed life in the cause of knowledge. It is some satisfaction to know that since 1889 there has stood a statue of this Italian guest and friend of Sir Philip Sidney in Rome itself, on the very spot—the Campo di Fiore—where the faggots once blazed about his helpless frame.

But beyond the visit of Englishmen to Italy or of Italians to England, there lay a far vaster opportunity of acquiring in England a knowledge of Italian poetry and philosophy. At the moment that Shakespeare was absorbed in the great work of his life, the domestic facilities may be gauged by the issue in English renderings of the two most imposing manifestations of the Italian poetic genius of the era. The most characteristic verse of sixteenth-century Italy was the epic poetry of Ariosto and Tasso. Each poet's temperament illustrates to perfection a salient phase of the Italian genius of the Renaissance, and together they present its whole range. Both tell a story with spirit; both are masters of verbal melody; both have the painter's eye for imagery. But the boundless energy and kindly irony of Ariosto are replaced in Tasso by romantic pathos and deep-toned lyric harmony. To both their idiosyncrasies Elizabethan translators were found capable of doing justice. The greatest English epic of the period, Spenser's *Faerie Queene*, owes much to the inspiration of these Italian poets. Spenser avowedly set himself to 'overgo' or excel Ariosto, and an admission of his success is quite consistent with a liberal appreciation of the many stirring episodes and fancies which he borrowed from

Ariosto's pages. The most exquisite canto which Spenser penned, the sixth of the second book, is touched in nearly every line by Tasso's sensuous enchantment.

Time will not permit of more than a hint of the Italian influences which worked immediately on Elizabethan lyric or sonnet. 'The sweet Tuscan', as Petrarch was called by Elizabethan poets, was the confessed master of the Elizabethan sonnet. Spenser was reckoned by Elizabethan critics so expert a pupil that he was often called 'the English Petrarch'. Spenser's lyric fancy was steeped moreover in the philosophy of the Florentine Platonists, while Tasso was one of a hundred other Italian poets who trained the lyric inspiration of Shakespeare's contemporaries. Samuel Daniel's lyric charm is not in question. Yet it is doubtful if without the tuition of Tasso and some other foreign masters (French as well as Italian) he would have won his high place in our literature. Here are some beautiful lines from his pen:

> Let 's love, the sun doth set and rise again;
> But when as our short light
> Comes once to set, it makes eternal night.

Although Daniel gave no hint that he owed the verse to any outside suggestion, he was translating, as literally as the two languages admitted, the pensive words of Tasso:

> Amiam, che 'l Sol si muove, e poi rinasce.
> A noi sua breve luce
> S' asconde, e 'l sonno eterna notte adduce.

If we pass to prose, especially to prose on speculative topics, we find the processes of assimilation, translation, or adaptation from the Italian at work with equal vigour. When Bacon declares his hostility to Aristotle, and insists on the superiority of experiment and induction over deduction or ratiocination untested by direct observation, he admits indebtedness to a philosopher who lately lived and wrote in the extreme south of Italy, to Telesio of Cosenza. Bacon curiously calls Telesio an Italian 'novelist', meaning an Italian innovator of scientific method.

When Bacon dubbed himself an 'interpreter of nature', he borrowed the title from the Florentine Platonist, Pico della Mirandola. As in poetry, so in science, Italian hints often blossomed in English minds into imagination or thought of unexpected power and scope. William Harvey, the discoverer of the circulation of the blood, graduated in 1602 in the medical school of Padua University, after attending the lectures of the Italian professor who was the greatest anatomist of his day. The help of his great Italian teacher is not to be gainsaid. Yet Harvey passed far beyond the range of his Italian study when he gave medical and physiological knowledge a new certitude.

III

I claim Shakespeare as the greatest of humanists in the broad sense which the term justly bears in the history of the Italian Renaissance. I believe that in Shakespeare the spirit of humanism worked to supreme effect. Were I casting a discourse on humanism in the mould of a sermon and prefacing it with texts, I doubt if I could do better than choose two passages from Shakespeare. There are two familiar passages in the play of *Hamlet* each of which expresses with admirable point one or other of the two most significant phases of the Renaissance—the cry for intellectual enfranchisement on the one hand and the enthusiasm for man's physical and mental endowments on the other. The first passage runs:

> Sure He that made us with such large discourse,
> Looking before and after, gave us not
> The capability and god-like reason,
> To fust in us unused.

The second runs:

'What a piece of work is a man! how noble in reason! how infinite in faculty! in form and moving how express and admirable! in action how like an angel! in apprehension how like a god! the beauty of the world! the paragon of animals!'

It would be easy to match the first passage in the

writings of Giordano Bruno. The second passage seems to echo the raptures of Pico dello Mirandola. Elsewhere Shakespeare makes himself responsible for yet another opinion which precisely reflected the intellectual tendency of the era. From his pen came the words: 'Modest doubt is called the beacon of the wise.' Many times too does the dramatist reinforce Hamlet's salutation of the potential beauty of human nature by enthusiatic greetings of the beauties of physical nature in which the new Italian sense of colour seems to be craving an original utterance. When Shakespeare wrote,

> Full many a glorious morning have I seen
> Flatter the mountain tops with sovereign eye,
> Kissing with golden face the meadows green,
> Gilding pale streams with heavenly alchemy,

or when he hailed

> daffodils,
> That come before the swallow dares, and take [i. e. bewitch]
> The winds of March with beauty,

he testified to the same impulse which moved Cardinal Bembo, a generation before, to say that beauty is the essential attribute of the heavens and the earth, of rivers and gardens. Shakespeare's definition of man as 'the *beauty* of the world', and the power which he detects in the daffodils of infatuating with their 'beauty' the March winds, powerfully accentuate the Renaissance apostle's teaching. Every reader of Shakespeare will be able to add to these quotations, which interpret with all Shakespeare's gift of language paramount principles of the Italian Renaissance.

Intellectual receptivity, assimilative capacity, is an invariable mark of poetic genius. The popular apophthegm that the poet is born and not made needs much qualification before it can be credited with truth. The originality of genius is no mere spontaneous emanation or exhalation of the poet's mind. It is rather the magical power of absorbing very rapidly, even instantaneously, pre-existing thought and fancy, and of delivering them to the world again in a new and arresting shape or expression. Shakespeare's pre-eminence resides in his catholic sensitiveness to external impressions, whether they came from reading or from observation, and in his power of transmuting them in the crucible of his mind into something richer and rarer than they were before. All modes of thought and style wrought thus upon him. Among the many foreign influences to which he proved susceptible, I believe the teaching of the Renaissance looms as large as any in a just estimate of the sources of his achievement.

The needful recognition of the foreign element in the constitution of Shakespeare's achievement is quite compatible with the fullest acknowledgement of his patriotic sentiment which is clearly unassailable. While he must be absolved of all taint of insularity he cannot be suspected of cosmopolitanism in its undesirable significance. The bracing air of toleration fed his spirit; but that virtuous sustenance never impaired his love of his own country or his confident faith in her destiny. It was he who apostrophized his country and countrymen in his own magnificent diction as:

> This happy breed of men, this little world;
> This precious stone set in the silver sea,
> Which serves it in the office of a wall,
> Or as a moat defensive to a house
> Against the envy of less happier lands:
> This blessed plot, this earth, this realm, this England.

At the same time Shakespeare, with almost equal fervour, deprecates the shortness of vision which ignores the patriotism of other countries, and refuses all fellow-feeling with them:

> Hath Britain all the sun that shines? Day, night,
> Are they not but in Britain? . . . Prithee think
> There's livers out of Britain.

Shakespeare is at once the noblest expositor of patriotism, and the most resolute contemner of insularity.

No one who has closely studied Shakespeare's writings

can harbour any doubt of the breadth of his reading, or can view with any other than impatience the persistent fallacy, which Milton rashly stamped with his authority, when he wrote of Shakespeare as

fancy's child
Warbling his native woodnotes wild.

The extent to which Shakespeare studied Italian literature in the original admits of discussion. He quotes in Italian a proverbial compliment on the beauties of Venice in his earliest play, *Love's Labour's Lost*:

Venetia, Venetia,
Chi non ti vede, non ti pretia.

Hamlet, when he talks to Ophelia of 'the players'' play, remarks that 'the story is extant, and written in very choice Italian'. There is clear evidence too in the history of the composition of *Othello* that the dramatist had access to at least one tale which had never worn any but an Italian garb. But the range of his linguistic power does not matter very much. He was in any case far better versed in English than in any other tongue. A large part of Italian poetry and prose of the Renaissance was accessible to him in English translation. As students of Spenser know, the fundamental ideas of the Renaissance and many literary processes of the Renaissance—the Platonic interpretation of life and the world, the decorative usage of classical mythology—were already woven into the web of Elizabethan writing when Shakespeare was serving his apprenticeship to his art. There were many keys to open the gates of knowledge to a man of his alert intuition.

To a large extent the Italian affinities of Shakespeare's work were in all probability a vicarious endowment, but they were none the less effective on that account. The Elizabethan atmosphere was so charged with Italian thought and fancy, that no sensitive poetic genius, even if Italian books were wholly sealed for him, could well escape an ample draught of inspiration. In the familiar scene in *The Merchant of Venice*, where Lorenzo talks through the moonlit night with Jessica in the gardens of Portia's villa, one hears throughout the dominant notes of the Italian Renaissance in all their sweetness. The setting of the scene catches completely the Italian spirit. The mythological reminiscences, the praise of music, the neo-Platonic and pseudo-scientific theory of the spheres, are all Italian or Greco-Italian echoes.

When Lorenzo points out to Jessica the floor of heaven, and tells her

> There 's not the smallest orb which thou behold'st
> But in his motion like an angel sings,
> Still quiring to the young-eyed cherubins:

the scholarly reader may be forgiven for recalling the mystical speculation of a famous South Italian contemporary, Tommaso Campanella, poet and man of science, who out of a Platonic fancy elaborated a beatific vision of spirit-inhabitants of the stars, communicating thought to one another in words of light. But I think we should be content to ascribe this and other surprising likenesses of thought and fancy between Shakespeare's poetry and Italian Renaissance speculation to agencies other than immediate recourse to Italian texts.

Shakespeare's specific references to Italian art are rare. They do scant justice to the scope of the Italian triumphs in the realms of painting or of sculpture. Yet Shakespeare on occasion makes vague reference to art at large which supplements the story of his intuitive relations with the doctrines of the Italian Renaissance. Once, and once only, Shakespeare paid an enthusiastic tribute to the life-like excellence of Italian sculpture. But his praises seem to lack the precision which betokens first-hand knowledge. In *The Winter's Tale* (v. ii, 93–9), the supposed statue of Hermione is described as 'a piece many years in doing, and now newly performed by that rare Italian master, Julio Romano; who, had he himself eternity and could put breath into his work, would beguile Nature of her custom, so perfectly he is her ape'. The speaker finally asserts that Romano 'so near to Hermione hath done Hermione, that they say one would speak to her and stand in hope of answer'. Shakespeare's 'rare Italian master' was an eminent pupil of Raphael. Vasari, the sixteenth-century biographer of Italian artists, cites an epitaph which imputes to him skill as a sculptor, no less than as a painter; but it is by his pictures alone that Romano is now known, and Shakespeare's panegyric cannot be literally corroborated. Nowhere else does the dramatist make a like categorical reference to an Italian artist of the Renaissance. More than once elsewhere, however, he grows almost ecstatic over the living illusion of great portraiture. He fails to associate the perfect art directly with Italy. Of the portrait of Timon of Athens by a painter who is nominally an Athenian, a critic who is also presented as an Athenian, exclaims (*Timon*, I. i. 38–9):

> It tutors Nature: artificial strife
> Lives in these touches, livelier than life.[1]

Whatever the limitations of Shakespeare's personal acquaintance with the artistic fruits of sixteenth-century Italy, he clearly assimilated a popular philosophic axiom of Italian criticism which represented the great sculptor or painter as a rival of creative Nature, and Nature herself as cherisher of a fear that the artist by improving on her handiwork might discredit her. Bembo, the Cardinal of the Renaissance, invested the theory with extravagance when he wrote on Raphael's tomb:

> Hic ille est Raphael, metuit quo sospite vinci
> Rerum magna parens, et moriente, mori.

(Here lies the famous Raphael, in whose life-time great mother Nature feared to be outdone, and at whose death feared to die.)

It is curious to note that the identical conceit was

---

[1] Cf. *Venus and Adonis* (289–92):
> Look, when a painter would surpass the life,
> In limning out a well-proportion'd steed,
> His art with nature's workmanship at strife,
> As if the dead the living should exceed.

chosen to decorate Shakespeare's own epitaph in Stratford-on-Avon Church. The elegist, when he wrote of—

Shakespeare, with whom
Quick nature died,

placed the dramatist in that category of creative artists, to which Bembo had assigned Raphael. Shakespeare's poetic art was thus identified by his own countrymen with the same conception of creative genius as that called into being by the pictorial art of the Italian Renaissance.

I have spoken of some ancillary glories of Shakespeare's dramatic poetry, and of the exalted conception of his artistic powers, which justly identified him with the sons of the Italian Renaissance. When we descend to the more material foundations of his work, the problem enters a somewhat different phase. It is familiar knowledge that Shakespeare hewed many of his plays out of Italian stories. The most superficial studies of his plots show him to be beyond doubt a close student of a very distinctive species of literature which is peculiarly characteristic of Renaissance Italy. Boccaccio, of Florence, the herald of the new Italian movement in many of its directions, may be reckoned to have rendered his most conspicuous service to the amenities of civilization by his creation of the art of the short story. In musical language, which eliminated once and for all the crudities of the old Tuscan dialect, Boccaccio pictured, with a softly glowing serenity, experiences of love and life of which he had read or heard or seen. He treats human nature with a frankness which often shocks the prudish. He is prone to dwell with a cheerful irony on the infidelities of husbands and wives. Yet he is a master of pathos as well as of gaiety, and blends varied ingredients harmoniously. Boccaccio the novelist founded in Italy a long-lived school, and though none of his scholars equalled his own powers, many who were especially active in the sixteenth century caught some touch of his vivacity. Bandello, a Lombard, who was a bishop in the south of France at the time of Shakespeare's birth, turned into lively fiction of Boccaccio's type episodes in the social life of his day. Although he lacked his master's gift of style Bandello excelled Boccaccio in lubricity. A third six-teenth-century Italian novelist, Giraldi Cinthio, of the cultured city of Ferrara, also enjoyed a wide reputation in his day. In his methods, merits, and demerits he may be linked with Bandello. The Italian novel, indeed, engaged almost as much energy in Renaissance Italy as the drama subsequently engaged in Elizabethan or Jacobean England. It found readers, not in Italy alone, but, either in the original or in translation, in all countries of Western Europe. Imitations as well as translations soon abounded in France, Spain, and ultimately in England.

The Italian novel rendered the English drama the practical service of supplying it with a treasury of plots, and Shakespeare, like all the fellow dramatists of his time, welcomed with enthusiasm such practical help. Most but not all the Italian stories which he emplóyed were ready to his hand in his own language or in French. His indebted-ness to Italy is not, however, greatly reduced thereby. The English and French renderings at his command, though differing among themselves in efficiency, were usually literal. Their temper was little changed. In what-ever shape Shakespeare gained access to them, the main stories of *All's Well that Ends Well* and *Cymbeline*, of which Helena and Imogen are the respective heroines, remain the ripe fruit of Boccaccio's invention. Bandello is the parent of the leading episodes of *Romeo and Juliet* and *Much Ado About Nothing*. Cinthio was the first to tell the tragic adventure of Isabella in *Measure for Measure* and the tragic trials of Othello and Desdemona. Even where Shakespeare seeks his plot in romances of English authorship, as in *As You Like It* and *The Winter's Tale*, the Italian influence is not wholly absent; for the English novelists commonly marched along the Italian road: they rarely travelled far from it.

The Italian fable, it goes without saying, formed as a rule the mere basis of Shakespeare's dramatic structure.

Having studied the Italian tale and examined its dramatic possibilities, Shakespeare altered and transmuted it with the utmost freedom as his dramatic spirit moved him. It is by his changes rather than by his literal transferences that the greatness of his faculty, the breadth of his intuitive grasp of human passion and sentiment, may best be gauged.

Yet the scenes of his chief comedies and of many tragedies rarely leave Italy. The episodes are assigned to Venice or Verona, to Milan or Mantua, to Florence or Padua. He rarely takes the names of his characters from the Italian novels of his immediate study. He rechristens his *dramatis personae*, but the new designations are no less Italian than the old. It is curious to observe that, when in *As You Like It* Shakespeare is dramatizing a piece of English fiction by his fellow countryman, Thomas Lodge, he rejects Lodge's amorphous name of Rosader for his hero and substitutes a name so rooted in the traditions of Italian literature as Orlando. I think it provable that Shakespeare's Orlando, the hero of *As You Like It*, was deliberately christened after the Orlando of Ariosto's great Italian epic. Shakespeare's Italian nomenclature may not always suggest quite so much as that; but it invariably proclaims him the pupil of an Italian school, paying homage to his masters.

At times Shakespeare's choice of Italian plot sets his work in the full tide of the Italian literary stream. The story of Romeo and Juliet, which Bandello first told to Europe, was made familiar to Italy by earlier pens. The tale, which has a right to be reckoned a national legend of Italy, was the theme of Shakespeare's earliest venture in tragedy of the great romantic kind. In his dramatic treatment of it, he gave indubitable promise of his glorious fertility and power. Manifold are the original touches of poetry, insight, and humour in Shakespeare's version of the Italian novel. Yet who can deny the Italian glow which lives in Shakespeare's radiant picture of youthful love ?

The play of *Twelfth Night* is cast in a very different mould from that of *Romeo and Juliet.* Everybody knows the main plot, how a girl is disguised as a page; and how, while her master moves her love, she is sent by him to plead his suit with a proud beauty, who on her part is fascinated by the supposed boy. The fable is a fantasy of which all the elements are dyed in Italian colours. Bandello, although he gave the story its European vogue, was, as in the case of *Romeo and Juliet,* but one of its Italian narrators. No English alchemy could free the sensitive and intricate amours of their Italian note. Shakespeare's play, in spite of his manipulation of the Italian plot and his fusion with it of much original comic episode, echoes the strains which Boccaccio's youths and maidens voiced in the garden overlooking Florence at the dawn of the Italian Renaissance. What atmosphere, save that of sensuous Florence, does Duke Orsino breathe when, in the first speech of the play, he makes languorous appeal to the musicians:

> That strain again! it had a dying fall:
> O, it came o'er my ear like the sweet sound
> That breathes upon a bank of violets,
> Stealing and giving odour.

Shakespeare's tragedy of *Othello,* the best constructed of all his tragic dramas, presents life in its sternest aspect and passion in its fiercest guise. Yet it is based as directly as *Romeo and Juliet* and *Twelfth Night* on Italian foundations, and, unlike the other Italian stories whence Shakespeare drew his plots, the fable of *Othello* is not known to have circulated out of Italy, or rather out of the Italian language, before Shakespeare handled it. The author of the story of Shakespeare's tragedy of *Othello* is the sixteenth-century novelist, Cinthio of Ferrara. Some of his tales had been rendered into French, and at least one into English. Before Shakespeare wrote *Othello* he had himself made a first draft on Cinthio's store of fiction. The plot of *Measure for Measure* was of Cinthio's devising; but that painful Italian story was ready to Shakespeare's hand in an English version. Not so the little novel of the Moor of

Venice. In the Italian alone was that tragic history to be studied. In adapting the incidents to his purpose, Shakespeare here if anywhere exerted all his powers. With magical subtlety he invests the character of Othello with passionate intensity, of which the Italian novelist knew little. Iago is transformed by the English dramatist from the conventional Italian criminal of Cinthio's page into the profoundest of all portraits of hypocrisy and intellectual villainy. At every point Shakespeare has lifted the theme high above the melodramatic level on which the Italian had left it. New subsidiary characters are added. The catastrophe is wholly reconstructed. The master spirit is everywhere at work with magnificent energy. Yet Cinthio's guidance is not to be disparaged. His story holds the sparks which Shakespeare's genius fanned into brilliant flame.

Finally, let me supplement what I have already said of the tinges of Platonic philosophy, which the Italian Renaissance conveyed to Shakespeare's pages, by a concluding reference to his Sonnets. It would be irrelevant to my present purpose to mention, let alone discuss, any of the difficult problems which attach to these poems. At the moment I merely cite them as consummating evidence of the genuine strength of Shakespeare's affinities with Italian Platonism. Responsive as he proves himself elsewhere to varied influences of the Renaissance, I believe that the Sonnets prove even more convincingly than any other of his writings how deeply he had drunk of the spring of Italian philosophy. All the sonneteers of Europe, from their father Petrarch downwards, enlisted under Plato's banner and preached the ideality of beauty, isolating it from its physical embodiment. As Platonic or Neo-Platonic study widened in Italy, much lyric poetry there and elsewhere assimilated in greater and greater degree the technicalities of Plato's or the Neo-Platonists' mystical conception. Michael Angelo, one of the noblest Italian champions of the Renaissance, wrote sonnets, in which the loveliness of earthly things is invariably held to reflect an ethereal light from heaven. Shakespeare immersed himself as a sonneteer in even deeper metaphysical subtleties Constantly he credits the beauty of the friend whom he celebrates with the qualities of a 'shadow'—the English rendering of the technical Latin word *umbra* which Giordano Bruno and other Italian Platonists applied to the mundane reflection of their idea or ideal of perfection—an idea or ideal which lay outside the material world. The beauty of Shakespeare's friend is (he tells us) a 'shadow' of the true 'substance' of perfect beauty; the substance is not visible to mortal eye, only the shadow is seen on earth. Shakespeare goes even a step further in his metaphysical theorizing in the Sonnets. Beauty in its unearthly perfection he identifies with truth, again an entity which is independent of matter and indeed of time. Constantly Shakespeare links truth and beauty together, as of the same ethereal significance and quality. The meaning of his phraseology is, as is common in such debate, often obscure. But there is no reason to doubt that one of the doctrines by which he stood when he penned his sonnets was an anticipation of Keats's mystical creed:

> Beauty is truth, truth beauty; that is all
> Ye know on earth, and all ye need to know.

It was by way of Italy that such doctrine reached Shakespeare in England.

Shakespeare's work is a vast continent, and I this afternoon am only endeavouring within the limits of my power and my hour to explore a single stretch of the territory. There are many, and my sympathies are with them, who detect in Shakespeare's humour his greatest gift. That endowment and his manner of exercising it owe nothing to Italy. Italian humour was pitched in another key. Nor can Italy claim any influence on his masterly reform of the methods of drama, and on his triumphant broadening of its bases. Italian drama of the sixteenth century was too closely wedded to the classical canons to touch at many points a dramatic ambition, which sought to realize in the theatre the highest ideals of romance, and to set adrift theatrical conventions in manifest conflict with the representation of sentient life. The brisk dialogue of Shakespearian comedy and the portrayal there of some veteran types of eccentricity may occasionally echo an Italian note. But the profundities of Shakespearian tragedy lay beyond the Italian range. The Italian Renaissance was but one of the forces which went to the making of Shakespeare's mighty achievement. But I hope I have said enough to show that Italian thought and invention lent a well-defined sustenance to his unmatchable genius.

Shakespeare's indebtedness to Italy has many parallels in the history of English poetry. Chaucer, Shakespeare's greatest poetic predecessor, was an admiring disciple of the work of both Dante and Boccaccio. Milton, Shakespeare's successor on the throne of English poetry, was an appreciative and a grateful student in many Italian poetic schools. When we leap a century and face the great revival, of which Byron and Shelley were two exponents, we meet in English poetry with a passionate devotion to Italy, which was accentuated by Italy's contemporary suffering and oppression. The Brownings bore on high the same torch until it reached the hand of Swinburne, who was stirred by Italy's past and present fortune to his noblest poetic utterances. Swinburne was profoundly sympathetic with Italy in her manful struggles for liberty and unity, and he greeted exultingly her restoration to a place among the great nations. He saw in the colours of her flag, green and white and red, symbols of hope and light and life. Had he lived to be with us to-day we may say with confidence that he would have applied to Italy at this moment his own words of earlier date:

> She feels her ancient breath and the old blood
> Move in her immortal veins.

Swinburne's poems on Italy worthily pursue a great tradition of English poetry. The Italian allegiance of Shakespeare, emperor of English poets, gives that tradition its most dazzling glory.

TASSO AND SHAKESPEARE'S ENGLAND[1]

I

THERE is some special appropriateness at the moment in recalling attention to Tasso's association with English poetry—with that manifestation of English genius whence Great Britain derives no inconspicuous part of her renown. For Tasso made his chief bid for immortality as the poetic chronicler of the First Crusade whereby the City of Jerusalem was first wrested from the Moslem sway and restored to Christian rule. The army which achieved the hardly-won victory was drawn from the chivalry of all Western Europe, but the chief command was in French hands, and Godfrey of Bouillon, a nobleman of France, is the hero of Tasso's epic. The Italian poet credits the French generalissimo with every moral and military virtue. His courage goes hand in hand with a dignified caution. He is pious, humane, far-seeing in counsel, resolute in action, modest in bearing. The stirring military adventures which Tasso narrates with abundance of romantic embellishment and magical episode end on a strikingly subdued note. The last stanza of the long poem shows Godfrey with his aides-de-camp, just after the last strenuous resistance of the enemy had been overcome, reverently walking in the light of the setting sun through the captured city. Without pausing to change their war-stained habiliments, Godfrey and his companions enter the Holy Sepulchre, and there, hanging up their arms, they offer on their knees humble prayer. Godfrey's conquest did not prove lasting. In less than a century the banner of the Crescent replaced the flag of the Cross, and held its own for the prolonged period of 630 years. The recent capture of the Holy City by an army under English leadership, which France and Italy fervently acclaimed, lends a new and prophetic significance

[1] Reprinted from *The Anglo-Italian Review*, September 1918.

to Tasso's epic panorama. Well justified would be a revival in England of that sympathetic interest in the *Gerusalemme Liberata* and its author, the beginnings of which go back to the day when the work first issued from the press, and first uplifted the spirit of Italy and Western Europe.

II

No insularity of sentiment restricted the literary sympathies of Elizabethan Englishmen. Their sturdy patriotism was proof against any narrowness of vision in the world of thought or fancy. Shakespeare and his fellow-countrymen were fully alive to the great fact that Britain had not (in the dramatist's phrase) 'all the sun that shines'. When the star of Torquato Tasso first illumined the literary skies of Italy, the gaze of the British poets turned eagerly towards it and sought to catch something of its light and heat.

Tasso, the youngest of the four supreme masters of Italian poetry, was for Shakespeare's England a living force in a sense which fails to apply to any other of the great Italian company. The Elizabethan knew little of Dante save as a mysterious medieval luminary which brightened the land of Italy before English literature came into coherent being. Petrarch was the contemporary of Chaucer, who did homage to his 'sweet rhetoric', and although the fame of Petrarch, notably as a sonneteer, ran high among Shakespeare and his friends, a touch of antiquity clung to the great Tuscan's achievement. Ariosto exerted a lively influence on Elizabethan poets, but his career was over and done in the days of their great-grandfathers, and his work enjoyed the seasoned respect of veteran standing. Tasso, as far as chronology goes, might have been the elder brother of Spenser, Shakespeare, and their fellow-workers, and they regarded him with something like fraternal sentiment.

When Spenser, who was destined to be Tasso's most faithful English disciple, was born in the City of London in 1552, Tasso was a precocious child of eight rapidly developing under Jesuit tuition at Naples a marvellous enthusiasm for things of the mind. When some twelve years later Shakespeare's birth shed a new radiance on Stratford-on-Avon and on England, Tasso had just won his first fame as the juvenile poet of *Rinaldo*, an ambitious epic of Carlovingian chivalry, and he had planned that work's illustrious successor, *Gerusalemme Liberata*, which was soon to challenge comparison with all pre-existing epic triumphs from Homer's *Iliad* onwards. Sir Philip Sidney, an Elizabethan who was notably sensitive to every aesthetic impulse, was studying literature on a tour through northern Italy in the year 1573, when Tasso's pastoral drama of *Aminta* saw at the art-loving Court of Ferrara the light of the stage, and surprised all Italy with its new evidence of the music of words.

Six years later Elizabethan thought and fancy blossomed in their first glory with the simultaneous production of Spenser's melodious *Shepherd's Calendar*, of North's rendering into virile English of Plutarch's *Lives*, of Lyly's fantastic romance of *Euphues*, and of Sir Philip Sidney's impassioned *Apology* for the true worth of poetry. It was in the very same year that Tasso put the finishing touch to the original version of his epic story of the rescue of the Holy Sepulchre by the most knightly of Christians, the French general—Godfrey of Bouillon. There in rich tones of melody he sought to satisfy the twofold claims of romance and classic orderliness, and at the same time to stimulate Christian ardour in its still pending struggle with Mohammedan aggression. Thenceforth Tasso's name was a household word wherever poetry and romance were honoured, or Christian piety held sway. English poets and critics hailed the young author as the living 'wonder of Italy', and his 'poem of Jerusalem' was declared to be comparable 'to the best of the ancients'. 'There is no man doth satisfy me more than that notable Torquato Tasso' wrote a contemporary Scottish student. One English admirer breathed the hope that 'an English Tasso' might arise to equal the renown of the Italian. During the next two decades the poet's verse was sedulously assimilated, adapted, and translated by the most highly cultured subjects of Queen Elizabeth and King James I.

But it was not Tasso's poetic achievements alone which excited the stirring interest either of his own fellow-countrymen or of the Elizabethans and their successors. The shadows which darkened the poet's life intensified the wonder which the merit of his work roused at home and abroad. Shelley tells us that poets learn in suffering what they teach in song. To no poet does the pathetic apophthegm apply more poignantly than to the author of *Aminta* and *Gerusalemme*. As soon as he completed his world-renowned epic, a development of that melancholy form of insanity by which he was always menaced caused, to the dismay of Europe, his removal to the madhouse of Ferrara. Seven years of agony and torture passed before his sorrowful petitions for release were granted.

A widespread but unsubstantial legend long assigned Tasso's defect of reason and consequent imprisonment to a hopeless passion for a lady of rank above his own—for the Princess Leonora, sister of his patron Alfonso D'Este, Duke of Ferrara—and to the poet's fears of the vengeance of the lady's brother, in whose eyes so presumptuous an aspiration might well be construed as an act of treason. Tasso is the poet of love, and gave rare poetic expression to varied phases of the great emotion. Very often does he create a potent illusion of passion. But Tasso's amorous verse, like most of the love-poetry of the era of the Renaissance, is far too lavishly imbued with idealization of feeling, with imaginative embellishment, with adulatory eulogy of his patrons' or patronesses' mental and physical endowments, to warrant acceptance as the literal confession of a personal experience. Tasso's sonnets and madrigals, in which the voluptuous note strangely alternates with ethereal fancy and extravagant flattery, give no more certain clue than Shakespeare's sonnets to the precise adventures of the poet's own heart. It is a strained inter-

pretation of these illusive poems which has bred the
familiar fable of Tasso's private tragedy of love. Elizabethans knew of Tasso's 'fury' or 'melancholy' as they
called it, but they wisely refrained from tracking it to so
romantic a source as a Princess's refusal to requite his
affections. As in the case of our own poet Cowper, Tasso's
physical inheritance included a nervous derangement
which betrayed itself in varied delusions and occasional
outbreaks of violence. His seclusion, however painful,
became at times desirable in his own interest. No more
occult explanation is required.

Happily the catastrophe, which roused the sympathy of
all Europe, wrought little injury to Tasso's literary power.
From the lunatic asylum at Ferrara he poured into the
world fresh verse and prose, which kept alive the enthusiasm of his admirers and drew many of them to his dismal
cell as to a sanctified shrine of the Muses. The French
essayist, Montaigne, was among the visitors, and the sad
sight stirred in him the thought that happiness was more
accessible to ignorance than to wisdom. Montaigne's
account of his visit and his grim comments were soon
circulating in the still-cherished Elizabethan translation of
the Frenchman's essays. Tasso's fame, too, was heightened
by the controversies in which he actively engaged with the
rigorous critics of Italy who scented heterodoxy in his
conceptions of both art and religion. His genius was
eagerly contrasted with that of the earlier national poet
Ariosto, and a comparison of the two men's merits and
defects became a theme of urgent and universal concern.

On Tasso's release from captivity he spent the remain-
ing nine years of his life in restless wanderings about his
native country. He was still subject to tormenting sus-
picions and to hallucinations which recall the mystic
visions of Blake, but he was suffered to go where he would,
voluntarily experiencing all the hardships of poverty,
although many hospitable doors were open to him. To the
satisfaction of hosts and friends his literary energies never
slackened. While Shakespeare was gaining his first hold

on the London playgoer, and while Spenser was proving his wealth of poetic genius in the published volumes of the *Faerie Queene*, Tasso, despite his misfortunes, was maintaining, as dramatist, critic, philosopher, sonneteer, and writer of pious verse, a supreme place in the continental world of letters. A welcome promise of a public laureation, for which he had long yearned, brought him to Rome in the spring of 1595, and he awaited the official ceremony in the peaceful haven of Sant' Onofrio Monastery on the slope of the Janiculum. There before the appointed date death put a sudden end to all his hopes and sufferings. He had just entered his fifty-second year. His life reached almost the same limit of time as Shakespeare's. Somewhat ironically, the body of the dead poet, clad in splendid robes, with the belated laurel wreath about his brow, was borne by his friends on an open bier through the crowded streets of Rome. A private burial followed in the church of the monastery of Sant' Onofrio, and the tearful lamentations have not yet ceased to echo. More than two centuries later Byron, while sojourning in Italy, paid the unhappy poet the elegiac tribute:

> ... Glory without end
> Scattered the clouds away; and on that name attend
> The tears and praises of all time. ...

III

Amid all his griefs Tasso cherished a confident belief in the immortality of his name and work. In the Europe of his own day he acknowledges only one serious rival to the throne of the contemporary world of letters—the Portuguese Camoens, whose *Lusiad*, the epic eulogy of Portugal's exploration of India, was very little older than Tasso's *Gerusalemme*. Of England Tasso knew little, and of her high literary promise nothing. In his great poem he bestows little notice on the English contingent in the army of the First Crusade. His Crusading heroes mainly belong to France and Italy. In early life he had visited France and was elated by the fervent reception of Ronsard, the prince of French poets of his century. Had fate allowed him a few years later to cross the English Channel, he would have been cheered by a welcome every whit as friendly. Through the decade preceding his death the foundations of his English fame were laid, and in spite of later alternations of literary taste, the Elizabethan estimate has since known in England no serious reverse. Only one English writer has ventured to stand pertinaciously by the critical verdict of Boileau, the pedantic dictator of the *Grand Siècle*, whose love of epigram led him to label Tasso as the poet of tinsel and Virgil as the poet of gold. Milton's regard for Tasso induced him on his Italian tour to seek out Manso, the grand seigneur of Naples, who in his youth, near half a century before, had befriended the great Italian in his crying need and had won the respect of the poet's admirers by penning an adoring biography. Milton in a fine Latin poem celebrated with touching sympathy Manso's devotion, and in many impressive passages of his own great religious epic gave evidence of his grateful indebtedness to Tasso's fertile inspiration.

A long succession of Milton's juniors who justly claim high honour in the realm of English poetry—Dryden, Gray, Collins, Wordsworth, Byron, Keats, Shelley, and Landor—have borne no less imposing tributes of honour and affection to Tasso's memory and achievements. Dryden characterized Tasso as 'the most excellent of modern poets'. Keats linked him with Homer, Virgil, Milton, Shakespeare, and Spenser as one of the six best-beloved sons of Apollo.

It was as the author of the pastoral play of *Aminta* that Tasso first fascinated the Elizabethan ear. That piece was the first completely successful endeavour to give a genuinely dramatic touch to the classical dialogue of pastoral simplicity, and the musical quality of Tasso's language made his little play the harbinger of Italian opera where drama and music were to be completely fused. Very delicate are the harmonies of word and fancy in which Tasso recounts the amorous pursuit by the shepherd

Aminta of the disdainful shepherdess Silvia. At the outset
an Elizabethan admirer paid the poem the misconceived
compliment of publishing a Latin paraphrase, but soon a
wiser endeavour was made to echo Tasso's lyric melodies
in our own tongue. One of the finest choric songs in
Aminta tells how in the golden age love ruled the world
without rival, before the social conventions of honour and
expedience had arisen to hamper the freedom of its flow.
The Elizabethan lyrist, 'well languaged' Samuel Daniel,
made by way of a youthful poetic experiment an ingeniously literal version of Tasso's tuneful invocation 'O bell'
età de l' oro'. Elsewhere Tasso's chorus of shepherds in-
quires in what school the art of love may best be learned.
Gaily they reach the conclusion that women's bright eyes
are the only efficient teachers, compared with which the
academies of the Greek philosophers, and even Phoebus
Apollo himself, are neophytes. Shakespeare in his second
youthful comedy, *Two Gentlemen of Verona*, seems to
christen his heroine Silvia after Aminta's ladylove. But
even better worthy of notice is the circumstance that the
great dramatist echoes Tasso's greetings of love's best
school when the amorous hero of Shakespeare's first
comedy, *Love's Labour's Lost*, makes his lyric confession of
a lover's faith:

> From women's eyes this doctrine I derive:
> They sparkle still the right Promethean fire.
> They are the books, the arts, the academes,
> That show, contain and nourish all the world:
> Else none at all in aught proves excellent.

Tasso, in his role of pastoral dramatist, soon found a
formidable Italian rival in his disciple Guarini, whose
Pastor Fido brought complexity of plot and conceited
intricacies of phrase and thought to burden the simple
structure and style of *Aminta*. Shakespeare's friends and
contemporaries, Beaumont, Fletcher, and Ben Jonson,
when they first sounded the pastoral note in English
drama, acknowledged allegiance to Guarini as well as to

Tasso. Perhaps the influence of the *Pastor Fido* seems more pronounced than that of *Aminta* in the *Faithful Shepherdess* and the *Faithful Shepherd*. Such pastoral experiments have a very questionable claim to the praise which Tasso's critics bestowed on his own pastoral endeavour that it never deserted the countryside. Yet the lyric delicacies of fancy and sentiment which figure in the earliest of England's pastoral plays recall the liquid tones of Guarini's master as surely as their artificial subtleties are reminiscent of Tasso's disciple.

IV

Interesting as is the early English history of *Aminta*, that piece was far from rendering the most impressive of the varied services which Elizabethan England owed to Tasso's activities. In the stirring year of the Spanish Armada, the Italian poet played two rather different parts on the English literary scene. In a treatise on the style of great poetry (fantastically called *The Arcadian Rhetorike*) the writer hailed Tasso as the 'light of Italy', and claimed for him, not as pastoralist alone, but as epic poet and as tragic dramatist in addition, a supreme authority which ranked him with Homer and Virgil, with the renowned Spaniards Boscan and Garcilasso, with Du Bartas, the popular idol of Huguenot France, and with Sidney and Spenser, then the brightest stars in the literary firmament of the writer's own country.

Again, in the same year, 'that excellent orator and poet, Signor Torquato Tasso', was introduced to the English reader no less admiringly in a humbler guise. An isolated chapter of the poet's autobiography in prose was rendered into English, and the translator's 'home-born mediocrity' could not obscure the charm of the personal reminiscence. Tasso narrated how, while riding on a solitary ramble from Novara to Vercelli, he chanced on a small farmer of rare courtesy and intelligence, who, with his family, entertained the poet for the night, and how after supper the sympathetic and enlightened host discussed with his guest themes of agriculture and fruit-growing and the management of a farm and family. The work—called in Italian *Il Padre di Famiglia* and in English *The Householder's Philosophie* —well illustrated Tasso's versatility and broadened the appeal which he made to English interests.

In Edmund Spenser's epic allegory of *The Faerie Queene* the luxuriant beauty of the poetic spirit found its ultimate expression in Elizabethan England, and Spenser is better entitled than any other Englishman to the description of Tasso's English disciple and apostle. In his sonnets Spenser occasionally adapts Tasso's amorous fancies and turns of phrase, but it is in some of the most characteristic splendours of *The Faerie Queene* that he echoes with admiring frankness many fascinating notes of his Italian master's devising. Like Tasso himself, Spenser drank deep of the great poetry which was accessible to him in various tongues before and while he wrote. When he describes the plan of his poem to his sympathizing friend, Sir Walter Raleigh, he admits that he follows in many foreign footsteps. He specifically acknowledges the help of his contemporary Tasso, as well as of Homer, Virgil, and Ariosto. Substantial are Spenser's debts to the two classical poets, and numerous are the exciting episodes of *The Faerie Queene*, which reflect the exploits of Ariosto's *Orlando Furioso*. It may not be easy to compare and balance Spenser's debts to Ariosto's *Orlando* and those to Tasso's *Gerusalemme*. But it is abundantly clear that the habitual seriousness of Spenser's temper has a kinship with Tasso's genius to which the lighter-hearted muse of Tasso's Italian predecessor can lay no claim. Spenser's richest conceptions of loveliness and the supreme melodies of his poetic speech draw from Tasso a sustenance which Ariosto was in no position to offer. Much may be inferred from the dominant fact that the surpassing fascinations of Spenser's enchantress, Acrasia, reflect the glowing lights and shades of Tasso's unmatchable Armida, the most alluring of all poetic presentments of beautiful witchery. Neither Homer's Circe nor Ariosto's Alcina, to both of whom she

is of near kin, is Armida's compeer in voluptuous charm.
Spenser's Acrasia, in spite of her manifold attractions, has
less human interest.

It is in Spenser's description of his Bower of Bliss,
Acrasia's home, that *The Faerie Queene* shows the full
measure of the English poet's dependence on Tasso's
inspiration. Spenser's Bower of Bliss is a replica of the
dazzling beauties of the garden and palace of Tasso's
Armida. At times he accepts the Italian poet's guidance
to the length of merely translating the Italian words.
Spenser repeats with an almost touching fidelity Tasso's
subtle claim that in his ideal realm of beauty art has
tutored nature and has breathed into the forces of nature
the quintessential spirit of art. The languorous music
which fills the air of the two poets' enchanted demesnes
sound precisely the same note. The song which binds in
fatal spells the wanderers in Armida's garden is heard again
with little verbal changes by the visitors to Acrasia's Bower
of Bliss. Tasso had framed the bewitching words thus:

> Così trapassa al trapassar d'un giorno
> Della vita mortale il fiore e'l verde:
> Nè perche faccia indietro april ritorno,
> Si rinfiora ella mai nè si rinverde.
> Cogliam la rosa in sul mattino adorno
> Di questo di che tosto il seren perde;
> Cogliam d'amor la rosa: amiamo or quando
> Esser si puote riamato amando.

Spenser did no injury to the music of the stanza when
he contented himself with this English rendering:

> So passeth, in the passing of a day
> Of mortal life the leafe, the bud, the flowre:
> No more doth flourish after first decay
> That earst was sought to deck both bed and bowre
> Of many a lady, and many a Paramowre.
> Gather therefore the rose whilst yet is prime
> For soone comes age that will her pride deflowre;
> Gather the Rose of love whilest yet is time,
> Whilest loving thou mayst loved be with equall crime.

V

All the light and heat which Spenser drew from Tasso's verse came from his study of the original Italian. While Spenser was composing his sonnets and the early books of *The Faerie Queene*, where Tasso's influence is most discernible, there was no English version of Tasso's main work for the help of those unversed in the Italian tongue. But it was not long before that want was supplied. In 1594, while Tasso was still alive, an English rendering of the first five cantos of the *Gerusalemme* in the original eight-lined stanza was issued in London with the Italian text alongside. The translator, Richard Carew, a cultured Cornishman 'of good sort and quality', followed too literal a method and had too limited a gift of poetic diction to allow him to do justice to Tasso's rich utterance. But at the end of a century a genuine success was scored in a rendering of the whole poem by the better endowed pen of Edward Fairfax. This work ranks high in the great series of Tudor translations. Fairfax dedicated his version to Queen Elizabeth in adulatory strains which remind one of Tasso's own courtier-like tones. Fairfax described his Sovereign as embodying in her own person the distinctive features of Tasso's own performance:

> Wit's rich triumph, wisdom's glory,
> Art's chronicle, learning's story.

Fairfax works on paraphrastic lines and even introduces similes for which his original gives him no cue. But he catches much of Tasso's poetic fervour, and, in spite of his manifest inequalities and awkwardnesses, so charmed many generations of English readers as to give Tasso an English vogue which he could hardly have otherwise enjoyed. King James I, we are told, valued Fairfax's rendering above all other English poetry, and it is known to have solaced the anxieties of King Charles I's imprisonment. On a later generation it made a profound impression. Edmund Waller, who was credited with reforming English versification in the mid-seventeenth century, confessed to Dryden, 'that he derived the harmony of his numbers from Godfrey of Bulloign, which was turned into English by Mr. Fairfax '.

Dr. Johnson, in his biography of Waller, cites an ample specimen of Fairfax's work by way of illustrating Waller's debt, but Dr. Johnson was no lover of Tudor archaisms, and he reckoned a new English version of the *Gerusalemme* of his own day by his friend, John Hoole, more 'elegant' than that of the Elizabethan. Some years later Charles Lamb bore new testimony to Fairfax's merits, and although Fairfax is now one of many English interpreters of Tasso's message his translation still ranks high among English classics. To 'British Fairfax', as the English poet William Collins called him, must be assigned a material part of the influence which Tasso exerted on British poetry from the days of Shakespeare to those of Wordsworth. Keats's library contained a copy of Fairfax's Tasso, but none of the Italian original.

Finally, it is worthy of note that the popular Elizabethan drama, whose highest developments gave English literature its chief glory, sought some of its raw material not merely in the work of Tasso but also in the tragic story of his life. It is disappointing that two of the three plays which were clearly wrought in his lifetime out of his poetry or his biography should be only known from extant records of their theatrical performance, and that the texts of the pieces should have perished. There is no question that Shakespeare's own company of actors produced early in the year 1592, just when Shakespeare was acquiring his first fame, a lost drama called *Jerusalem*, and that Tasso's chronicle of the city's recovery by Christian warriors furnished the anonymous dramatist with his theme. The topic appealed to the Elizabethan temperament. A year or two later a fresh attempt was made to dramatize some of the exploits in the Holy Land which Tasso put to the credit of his leading characters, Godfrey of Bouillon and his companions. The author was Shakespeare's admiring friend, Thomas Heywood, and the play, which is still extant in print, enjoyed a long and successful run.

Even more notable is the fact that Tasso's personal history while he was yet alive was also turned to dramatic purpose on the London stage, when Shakespeare's powers were nearing their maturity and his popularity was already assured.

On the 11th of August, 1594, there was produced at the Theatre of Newington Butts, on the south side of the Thames, yet another lost play by an unknown hand, called *Tasso's Melancholy*, and there were many revivals during the nine months succeeding its first production. The piece lived indeed on the stage for the rest of Queen Elizabeth's reign. Some of the properties employed, 'Tasso's Picture' and 'Tasso's Robe', figure in an inventory of the company's wardrobe dated four years later, in 1598. Another four years later, in 1602, when Shakespeare's tragic masterpiece of *Hamlet* was first produced at the Globe Theatre, Thomas Dekker, a professional playwright of repute, was employed to revise the old play of *Tasso's Melancholy* for yet a further run. The playgoer of Elizabethan London was thus offered during the same theatrical season an opportunity of contrasting in mimetic representation the pathetic melancholia of Tasso with the no less moving melancholy of Shakespeare's Prince of Denmark. Shakespeare at any rate supplied the only apt words for the rival show when he put into Ophelia's lips her familiar lament over Hamlet's 'antic disposition':

> O! what a noble mind is here o'erthrown . . .
> That unmatch'd form and feature of blown youth
> Blasted with ecstasy.

In 1798 Goethe sought to interpret in drama Tasso's aberrations, and the German poet is commonly credited with an effort which lacked all precedent. In point of fact he was treading, however unconsciously, a path which an Englishman of Shakespeare's period had first followed with sufficient skill to arrest the interest of Shakespeare's own friendly audience. England well deserves the credit of honouring Tasso's genius and of lamenting his misfortunes with a promptitude and a sincerity which have few parallels in the comparative history of literary appreciation.

SHAKESPEARE AND THE INQUISITION:
A SPANISH SECOND FOLIO [1]

I

SHORTLY before the war there was lent to me a copy of the Shakespeare Second Folio of 1632 to which there was attached a surprising and a unique interest. This copy underwent near the date of publication the strange experience of official expurgation under the authority of the Spanish Inquisition.

Eight years ago the volume was temporarily brought to England with a view to valuation. It had previously lain for the best part of three centuries in the library of the English College at Valladolid. The book has since returned to its ancient home, and is not likely to travel again. A wish was expressed on the part of the English College that I should describe the book at the time that I examined it in my London study. Many valuable extracts from the College registers and archives were also forwarded to me. But the war supervened and I put aside my notes, only to consult them again during the past few weeks. With the approval of the corporate owners of the book, I now draw public attention to the singular and hitherto unsuspected adventure which befell an early copy of Shakespeare's collected works within two decades of the author's death.

II

The English College at Valladolid, which was christened St. Alban's, was founded by the great Jesuit agitator, Father Parsons, in 1589. King Philip II. of Spain was an enthusiastic patron of the foundation, which had for its

---

[1] Reprinted from *The Times*, 10th and 11th of April 1922, with some rearrangement of the order of the contents of the two articles.

object the training of young Englishmen for the priest-
hood, with a view to their returning as missionaries to
England in the hope of reconverting their fellow-countrymen to the Catholic faith.

The Valladolid College was one of a number of similar
Continental foundations. Such establishments, which
were under Jesuit supervision, were so many counterblasts
to the persecuting policy of Queen Elizabeth's Government, which construed the acceptance by Englishmen of
orders in the Catholic Church into the capital offence of
treasonable sedition.

The first English seminary college was founded at Douai
in 1568, and when political disturbances drove the professors and students temporarily to Rheims, a detachment
migrated to Rome to inaugurate the well-known English
College there. The Douai College returned in 1593 to its
first home, where it remained till its dissolution by the
French Government of 1795. But the English Catholic
leaders on the Continent, who could always count on
King Philip II's zealous patronage, regarded Spain as their
chief place of refuge. Valladolid was their first and most
notable foundation.

It was opened on 1 September 1589, with six students,
all young men of good English family, of whom three had
already spent some time at Rheims and three at Rome.
A house was hired in the Calle de Don Sancho, and was
soon purchased by the munificence of a Spanish bene-
factress. The College still occupies the same site. Between
1589 and 1640, 476 English students were entered at the
College. Among them was Henry More, Sir Thomas
More's great-grandson, afterwards an active Jesuit and
historian of the Jesuit Mission to England (1580–1659).
He joined the Valladolid College on 20 June 1603, ran the
risks of the English mission for some 25 years from 1622
onwards, and died in 1661, at the age of 75, Rector of the
English College at St. Omer, another sixteenth-century
foundation of English Catholics.

Almost all the students on leaving Valladolid faced like

Henry More the perils of the English mission in the dark days of the penal laws. Between 1600 and 1643 seventeen suffered either capital punishment at Tyburn or elsewhere, or died in English prisons. In 1632, the year of the publication of the Shakespeare Second Folio, as many as eleven new students, undeterred by the menacing experience in store for them, came out from England to Valladolid; nine followed two years later, and ten in 1636. The College had clearly no lack of courageous and devoted *alumni* when Shakespeare's work was first put at their disposal in the College library.

The instruction at the College was mainly theological. It naturally included scholastic philosophy, by which the students appear to have set much store. In 1637 six entrants fresh from England left the College on the ground that they were refused permission to join at once the philosophy class.

The library was specially well equipped in dogmatic theology and scholasticism, but some secular literature was admitted in early days, chiefly books on English history. No catalogue appears to exist of the volumes in the library in the first decades of the 17th century, but there still remain on the shelves from that period many standard works on the medieval history of England, like Archbishop Parker's edition of Mathew Paris's *Chronica Majora* (1571); an edition of Froissart's *Chronicles*, issued at Lyons in 1588, and Sir Henry Savile's massive collection of medieval chronicles (*Rerum Anglicanarum, post Bedam scriptores praecipui*), which appeared at Frankfort in 1601.

Of more modern Latin literature from English pens the chief volume was the collected edition of the works of Sir Thomas More, Henry More's great-grandfather (Louvain, 1566). Literature in the English tongue, apart from Shakespeare, seems to have been represented some two centuries ago only by first editions of Sir Walter Raleigh's *History of the World* (1614) and of Francis Bacon's *History of Henry VII* (1622).

III

There were many obstacles to the circulation of books in Spain, especially those written in foreign languages. In conformity with its primary function of stamping out heresy, the Spanish Inquisition, early in its career, took literature under its harsh protection. Before any printed book could find admission to a Spanish public or private library it had to pass under an Inquisitor's eye. On the Inquisitor's report to the local tribunal, a book was either prohibited and destroyed or it was subjected to the mutilating process of expurgation.

Official Indexes, which were issued at irregular intervals, supplied the titles of both prohibited and expurgated volumes. At all ports, familiars of the Holy Office made search for books among incoming cargoes, and though the cunning of smugglers occasionally evaded the espionage, very few literary importations escaped the penal toils of the Inquisitors.

Ownership of a condemned book usually exposed its possessor to all the barbaric tortures of the Holy Office. Those tortures were proverbial in England, where at the very time that Shakespeare's Second Folio was published, James Howell, a man of letters, who had travelled in Spain, was writing to a friend (30 August 1632): 'The very name of the Inquisition is terrible all Christendom over.'

In the result the Inquisition, through its censorship of books, kept the intellect of Spain in abject servitude. Yet the obscurantist tyranny had its moments of relaxation. Works of the imagination excited less suspicion on the part of Inquisitors than works on theology, philosophy, or science. Although many Inquisitors deemed themselves protectors of morals as well as of faith, they were less stringent in their censorship of morality than of doctrine.

It is curious to note that the far-famed dramatic narrative called *Celestina*, which dates from the extreme end of the fifteenth century, and passed through numberless editions in the sixteenth, escaped, despite its gross improprieties, all censure from the Inquisition until 1640. Then some fifty lines were ordered to be excised, and it was not until the end of the eighteenth century that the book as a whole was prohibited.

When the power of the Inquisition was at its height early in the seventeenth century the outspoken satires of Quevedo suffered no injury at the hands of the Holy Office, while the dramatic work of Cervantes, Lope de Vega, and Calderón circulated without hindrance. One dramatist, Tirso de Molina, as popular at the time as any of these great masters, long and successfully doubled the roles of dramatist and ecclesiastic. His main title to fame rests on his creation of the witty freethinker and profligate, Don Juan, who later became a hero of literature in every country of Europe. Yet Tirso's frank interpretation of human nature failed to disqualify him for occasional service as censor of books for the Inquisition.

The English College at Valladolid enjoyed no exemption from the sway of the Inquisition. Valladolid, the ancient capital of the kingdom of Castile, was the birthplace of the far-famed Torquemada, the founder of the institution, and of King Philip II, one of its most fanatical supporters. The tribunal of the Holy Office there was highly organized early in the seventeenth century, and its activities were incessant. The publication of new editions in 1632 and in 1640 of the *Index Librorum Prohibitorum et Expurgandorum* whetted the literary activities of the tribunals throughout Spain.

Books, before they were admitted to the library of the English College, were submitted to all the rigours of examination by the local tribunal.

IV

The Shakespeare Second Folio at Valladolid, which has been rebound at a recent date, is in fair condition, and is undefaced by irresponsible scribbling, save for the appearance of the signature 'Joannes Lucas' on one of the preliminary pages, and of the words 'Finis Coronat Opus' at the end of *Coriolanus*.

At the foot of the title-page appears in very distinct handwriting the licence of the Holy Office. The book had safely weathered the perils of prohibition. It was subjected to the minor penalty only of expurgation, which was carried out by a Jesuit named Guillén Sanchez, with the full authority of the Holy Office. The words of the licence run thus:

Opus auctoritate Sancti Officii permissum, et expurgatum eadem auctoritate per Gulielmum Sanchaeum e Soc^te Jesu.

Little seems to be known of the Jesuit Inquisitor, beyond the fact that he expurgated near the same date some other English books, which still remain in the College library. A copy of the third edition of Speed's *History of England*, which appeared in London in the same year as the Shakespeare Second Folio, bears in the Inquisitor's handwriting these words:

Historia haec expurgata est et permissa auctoritate Sancti Officii huius Tribunalis Vallisoletani anno 1645 per Gulielmum Sanchaeum.

Inquisitor Sanchez fails to date the Shakespeare licence, but there is reason to believe that it belongs to a somewhat earlier year than that mentioned in the Speed licence.

The expurgator of the Holy Office treats Shakespeare's work with lenience. For the most part he does his spiriting gently. His forbearance lends small support to the claim of some modern Catholic writers to identify Shakespeare's religion with their own. It is highly improbable that the Spanish Inquisitor considered the question of Shakespeare's personal creed. His conciliatory mood was doubtless due to the tolerance commonly bestowed at the time by the Censors of the Holy Office on dramatic literature. The contemporary native drama was enjoying a special popularity throughout the orthodox cities of the Peninsula.

Strange to relate, there is good ground for believing, in

spite of the normal policy of the Holy Office, that a copy of Shakespeare's works had, at a somewhat earlier date, found admission to a private library in the same city of Valladolid. There the Casa del Sol was, and is, the family residence of the Counts de Gondomar, of whom the most famous was Spanish Ambassador in England from 1613 to 1622. The Count de Gondomar, who played, during those nine years, no small part in English political and social history, was a noted bibliophile, and according to trustworthy evidence, he added to his fine library in the Casa del Sol a copy of the Shakespeare First Folio soon after its publication. He was probably in a position to gain the special indulgence of the Holy Office. Some eighty years ago the Spanish historian, Señor Gayangos, examined the volume in its ancient Spanish home, and made a full and careful report of its condition, which showed much marginal manuscript comment. The present Count de Gondomar bears witness to the fact of the presence of the book at the Casa del Sol until 1873. He adds the information that, on his grandfather's death in that year, the heirs presented the whole library to the royal family of Spain.

V

Inquisitor Sanchez apparently set out on his task of expurgating the Shakespeare Second Folio with a twofold aim. He thought to delete words and passages which offend either against morality or against Catholic doctrine. Especially does he seek to protect Pope, priests, monks, and nuns from damaging insinuations. But he fails to apply his principles with any strict uniformity, and much that one would expect to fall under either his dogmatic or his ethical ban escapes his attack. Only a single play does he wholly condemn, and that on moral rather than on doctrinal grounds. The twelve leaves which supply the text of *Measure for Measure* are torn out bodily in accordance with a common usage of expurgators of the Holy Office.

But twenty[1] of the 36 plays which the volume contains are

---

[1] Lee, by mistake, wrote 'nineteen'.

left untouched—viz., seven of the 14 comedies, five of the 10 histories, and eight of the 12 tragedies. The unexpurgated pieces are: *Two Gentlemen of Verona, Merry Wives, Comedy of Errors, Midsummer Night's Dream, Taming of the Shrew, Twelfth Night, Winter's Tale, Richard II, 2 Henry IV, Henry V, 3 Henry VI, Richard III, Coriolanus, Titus Andronicus, Timon of Athens, Romeo and Juliet, Julius Caesar, Othello, Antony and Cleopatra,* and *Cymbeline.*

Four comedies, *The Merry Wives of Windsor, The Comedy of Errors, Much Ado,* and *The Merchant of Venice,* receive a special mark of commendation. At the head of the text of each of these plays the Inquisitor has inserted the word 'good'. *The Merry Wives* and *The Comedy of Errors* are wholly untouched, and *Much Ado* and the *Merchant* come off scot free, save for the deletion in the first comedy of some frank remarks by Margaret, Hero's waiting woman, while she is dressing her mistress for her wedding (III. iv), and the excision from the *Merchant* of a licentious reflection on the Jew when he is lamenting his daughter's elopement.

The rest of the comedies are mildly handled. In *The Tempest* only two expressions are inked out—viz., 'an unstanched wench' (I. i. 51) and the epithet 'holiday' in the phrase a 'holiday foole' (II. ii. 30). In *Love's Labour's Lost* Boyet's free jesting with Rosaline, the lady-in-waiting on the French Princess, is scored through (IV. i), and *Saint Cupid* is deprived of his canonization by the erasure of the word 'Saint' (IV. iii. 366 and v. ii. 87); nor is 'Saint Denis' allowed to retain his prefix when the Princess couples him with 'Saint Cupid' (v. ii. 87).

In *As You Like It* (III. iv. 14) Rosalind's remark about Orlando, that 'his kissing is as full of sanctity as the touch of holy bread', disappears, like the Clown's remark in *All's Well* (II. ii. 28), 'as the nun's lips to the friar's mouth', when the speaker is jesting about the harmonies of nature.

The History plays provide fuller scope for the Inquisitor's censure, but even there much that one would expect to offend his susceptibilities is untouched. Falstaff's ribaldry in *Henry IV* provokes no remark, but his oath, 'By the Mass!' suffers deletion. So in *1 Henry VI* (i. iii. 49–50) Gloucester is allowed to hurl at Cardinal Beaufort all his passionate virulence, with the exception of a single line. When the Duke exclaims:

> Under my feet I stamp thy Cardinal's hat,
> In spite of Pope or dignitaries of Church,

the second line is obliterated. In *2 Henry VI* the scene dealing with the Duchess of Gloucester's practice of the black art of raising spirits is slightly censored, and in the later passage where Gloucester exposes the pretended miracle of the restoration of sight to a blind man there is much mutilation, and many lines are effaced.

The only two history plays which excite the Inquisitor's sustained disapprobation are *King John* and *Henry VIII*. In the former play King John's speeches defying the Papal legate, Cardinal Pandulph, and the Bastard's sarcasms at the Legate's expense, are all freely expurgated. References to the 'usurped authority' of the Papacy, and the insinuations of corruption in the sale of pardons, all go out. The dramatist's allegation that the evil king died of poison remains, but the suggestion that the poison was administered 'by a monk' is erased.

In *Henry VIII*, apart from some excision of the Old Lady's frank obscenities (ii. iii), it is against the religious and political partisanship of the piece that the Inquisitor chiefly aims his well-inked darts. He will not allow Henry VIII to complain of 'tricks of Rome', and all praises of Archbishop Cranmer are expunged.

The epithets 'virtuous', 'good', and 'honest', which are applied to the Archbishop, are heavily scored. When the King bids the courtiers 'use him (i. e. Cranmer) well; he's worthy of it,' the last clause is removed. The Inquisitor treats with exceptional sternness the prophetic eulogies which the Archbishop pronounces on the Princess Elizabeth, Anne Boleyn's daughter, just after her baptism. He

And like a Mountaine Cedar, reach his branches,
To all the Plaines about him: Our Childrens Children
Shall see this, and blesse Heaven.

Kin. Thou speakest wonders.

Cran. She shall be ~~to the happinesse of England~~,
An aged Princesse; many dayes shall see her,
~~And yet no day without a deed to crowne it.~~
Would I had knowne no more: But she must dye,

~~She must, the Saints must haue her; yet a Virgin,~~
~~A most vnspotted Lilly shall she passe~~
~~To th' ground, and all the World shall mourne her.~~

Kin. ~~O Lord Archbishop~~
~~Thou hast made me now a man, neuer before~~
~~This happy Child, did I get any thing.~~
~~This Oracle of comfort ha's so pleas'd me,~~
~~That when I am in Heauen, I shall desire~~
~~To see what this Child does, and praise my Maker.~~

I thanke ye all. To you my good Lord Maior,
And you good Brethren, I am much beholding:
I haue receiv'd much Honour by your presence,
And ye shall find me thankfull. Lead the way Lords,
Ye must all see the Queene, and she must thanke ye,
She will be sicke els. This day, no man thinke
'Has businesse at his house; for all shall stay:
This Little-One shall make it Holy-day.   *Exeunt.*

In her dayes, Every Man shall eate in safety,
Vnder his owne Vine what he plants; and sing
The merry Songs of Peace to all his Neighbours.

~~God shall be truely knowne, and those about her,~~
~~From her shall read the perfect way of Honour,~~
And by those claime their greatnesse, not by Blood.
Nor shall this peace sleepe with her: But as when
The Bird of Wonder dyes, the Mayden Phœnix,

~~Her Ashes new create another Heyre,~~
~~As great in admiration as her selfe.~~
~~So shall she leaue her Blessednesse to One,~~
~~(When Heauen shall call her from this clowd of darknes)~~
~~Who, from the sacred Ashes of her Honour~~
~~Shall Star-like rise, as great in fame as she was,~~
~~And so stand fix'd. Peace, Plenty, Loue, Truth, Terror,~~
~~That were the Seruants to this chosen Infant,~~
Shall then be his, and like a Vine grow to him;
Where-ever the bright Sunne of Heaven shall shine,
His Honor, and the greatnesse of his name,
Shall be, and make new Nations. He shall flourish,

THE EPILOGVE.

'Tis ten to one, this Play can never please
All that are heere: Some come to take their ease,
And sleepe an Act or two; but those we feare
W'haue frighted with our Trumpets: so 'tis cleere,
They'l say 'tis naught. Others to heare the City
Abus'd extreamly, and to cry that's witty,
Which we haue not done neither; that I feare

All the expected good w'are like to heare,
For this Play at this time, is onely in
The mercifull construction of good women,
For such a one we shew'd 'em: If they smile,
And say 'twill doe; I know within a while,
All the best men are ours; for 'tis ill hap,
If they hold, when their Ladies bid 'em clap.

FINIS.

A CENSORED PAGE OF *KING HENRY VIII*

In a copy of the Shakespeare Second Folio, in the Library
of the English College, at Valladolid

strikes out such lines as these, which foreshadow Queen
Elizabeth's beneficent reign:

> God shall be truly known, and those about her
> From her shall read the perfect ways of Heaven.

Where the dramatist put into Cranmer's mouth the
words:

> She shall be, to the happiness of England,
> An aged Princess, many days shall see her,
> And yet no day without a deed to crown it.
> Would I had known no more! But she must die,
> She must, the saints must have her; yet a virgin,
> A most unspotted lily, shall she pass
> To the ground, and all the world shall mourn her.

The Inquisitor, with comically ironic effect, allows the
speaker to say no more than:

> She shall be
> An aged Princess, many days shall see her,
> Would I had known no more! But she must die.

He is no less drastic in his revision of Archbishop Cranmer's panegyric on Queen Elizabeth's successor, King
James I. Similarly, Henry VIII is deprived of the address
to his Court in which he fervently acknowledges Cranmer's flattering outlook. The speech in the Folio text
opens:

> O Lord Archbishop,
> Thou hast made me now a man (&c.).

All that the King is suffered to retain are the concluding
words, 'I thank ye all', which, deprived of their setting,
hang limply in air. The whole of this censored scene is in
all probability from the pen, not of Shakespeare, but from
that of his coadjutor, John Fletcher. Such knowledge,
which the Inquisitor doubtless lacked, was not calculated
to affect his judgement.

The Inquisitor's energy or interest was apparently
exhausted by his work on the history play of *Henry VIII*.
There is rebuke of the obscenity of Pandarus in *Troilus and
Cressida*, which in the Second Folio is wrongly placed

among the tragedies. But the genuine tragedies are practically undefaced by his pen. There the Inquisitor only
obliterates some indelicate jesting of Hamlet with Ophelia
(*Hamlet*, III. ii), and some coarse expressions from the lips
of Lear's Fool (*Lear*, III. ii. 27 and 40).

Another kind of interest attaches to one marking of old
date in the section of the tragedies. Special attention is
called by means of a thick line drawn in the margin to
a passage in *Macbeth* (III. vi. 45 seq.). There Lennox, a
Scottish nobleman, expresses the hope that Macduff may
obtain aid from the English Court in the coming attack on
the usurping Macbeth. Lennox's words run:

> Some holy angel
> Fly to the court of England and unfold
> His message ere he come, that a swift blessing
> May soon return to this our suffering country
> Under a hand accursed.

It is uncertain whether the Inquisitor or a member of
the college was responsible for the marginal scoring, which
clearly indicated approval. But the cause of the sign of
emphasis is obvious. The sentiment of Lennox's speech
was readily identifiable with the aspiration which moved
the hearts of the young Englishmen who were preparing
to return as missionaries to their own 'suffering country'
while the penal laws against them were still in full force.

VI

It was long after 1632 that Shakespeare's works circulated on the European Continent. Very few copies seem
to have left England until the eighteenth century was well
advanced. A native of Zurich who visited London in 1614
carried home Quarto editions of *Romeo and Juliet* and
Hamlet, which still survive in the Zurich public library,
but no precedent was thereby created.

The copies of the First and Second Folios which arrived
in Valladolid in very special circumstances, near the date
of publication, remained in Spain isolated specimens of
Shakespearian literature for fully a century and a half.

Another copy of the Second Folio was acquired after 1650 by King Louis XIV's librarian for the Royal Library at Paris—a volume which may still be consulted in the Bibliothèque Nationale.

The discovery of the Second Folio in the English College at Valladolid may best be regarded as proof of Shakespeare's early popularity among his fellow-countrymen, whatever their religious creed. It is scarcely an anticipation of that devotion to Shakespeare which, now universal, was, in Latin countries at any rate, the tardy growth of the late eighteenth or nineteenth century.

III. THE CALL OF THE WEST
AMERICA AND ELIZABETHAN ENGLAND

THE EXAMPLE OF SPAIN [1]

I

IN this series of papers I seek, within the limits of my
capacity, to depict America in the process of revelation
to the sixteenth-century Englishman, and to scan the shifting course of vague hope and conjecture, amid which the
curtain slowly lifted. I hope to define what Shakespeare
and his contemporaries knew of the New World; to track
their information to its source, and to suggest something
of the influence which the knowledge exerted on the current thought and feeling of the Old World. My survey
closes with that *annus mirabilis*, 1607, when an English
settlement in the new hemisphere first took permanent
root at Jamestown, and the shadowy American scene at
length assumed for Englishmen firm outlines, which justified sure hopes of the future.

The human mind is prone to pay closer attention to
results than to causes, to success than to failure. To such
tendency is chiefly attributable the gradual identification
in the popular mind of all American history with the
spread of the Anglo-Saxon race through the northern
continent. Infinite industry has been applied to elucidat-
ing the course of that victorious march, until the details
have come almost exclusively to fill the canvas of popular
pictures of the New World's birth. The decadence of
modern Spain and the long-cherished antipathy to her
religious and political principles have contributed to
obscure the pregnant and pervasive force of her example,
and the dependence of the English pioneers on records of
her teaching and experience. Every year sees smaller
stress laid in popular manuals on fundamental facts which
proclaim the wonder of the Spanish initiative. Even
Columbus, the Genoese pilot of Palos, is at times relegated

[1] This and the following three papers are reprinted from *Scribner's
Magazine*, vols. 41 and 42, May, June, September, November, 1907.

to the middle distance, and his rightful place of predominance bestowed on John Cabot, the Italian pilot of Bristol. It is doubtful if the words which Macaulay penned in 1840—'every schoolboy knows who imprisoned Montezuma, and who strangled Atahualpa'—still retain their axiomatic point. The current educational training seems scarcely destined to familiarize the rising generation with the details or significance of Cortes's conquest of Mexico, of Pizarro's invasion of Peru, and of the numerous expeditions by land and sea whereby Spain with tragic heroism riveted her hold on both northern and southern continents.

Especially has theological bias justified neglect or facilitated misconception of Spain's role in the sixteenth-century drama of American history. Spain's initial adventures in the New World are often consciously or unconsciously overlooked or underrated in order that she may figure on the stage of history as the benighted champion of a false and obsolete faith, who was vanquished under divine providence by English defenders of the true religion. Many are the hostile critics who have painted sixteenth-century Spain as the avaricious accumulator of American gold and silver to which she had no right, as the monopolist of American trade of which she robbed others, and as the oppressor and exterminator of the weak and innocent aborigines of the new continent who deplored her presence among them. Cruelty in all its hideous forms is indeed commonly set forth as Spain's only instrument of rule in her sixteenth-century empire. On the other hand, the English adventurer has been credited by the same pens with a touching humanity, with the purest religious aspirations, with a romantic courage which was always at the disposal of the oppressed native.

No such picture is recognizable when we apply the touchstone of the oral traditions, printed books, maps, and manuscripts concerning America which circulated in Shakespeare's England. There a predilection for romantic adventure is found to sway the Spaniard in even greater degree than it swayed the Elizabethan. Religious zeal is seen to inspirit the Spaniard more constantly and conspicuously than it stimulated his English contemporary. The motives of each nation are barely distinguishable one from another. Neither deserves to be credited with any monopoly of virtue or vice. Above all, the study of contemporary authorities brings into a dazzling light, which illumines every corner of the picture, the commanding fact of the Spaniard's priority as explorer, as scientific navigator, as conqueror, as settler. Not merely is the resourceful Castilian perceived to have explored a great part of the new continent, in face of fearful odds, three quarters of an eventful century before the Englishman even dimly thought of sharing the work with him, but with a rapid prescience which is no less difficult to parallel, the Spaniards are seen to have created and elaborated machinery for governing the great Indian empire of the West the best part of a hundred years before any conception of the kind dawned on the English mind. The briefest study of the course of early colonization of America by Europe reveals Spain as master of a field in which England tardily joined her as a disciple, learning her lesson very slowly and very stubbornly. Little by little the Elizabethan caught from Spain his earliest colonial enthusiasm. It was in Spanish books that he first studied colonial experience. It was in Spanish charts and Spanish treatises of navigation that he sought his first adequate directions for traversing the tracts of ocean which lay between his own country and the New World.

The Elizabethan was a mighty assimilator of foreign ideas. Although he had the faculty of bettering his foreign instruction so that he ultimately outstripped his foreign teachers, yet the harvest that the Elizabethan reaped in almost every field of effort owed much to seeds born of foreign soil. Elizabethan literature is permeated by forms and ideas of foreign origin—from Italy, France, and Spain. Similarly, foreign theory and practice fertilized Elizabethan activity in the New World. To France and Italy

the debt of the Elizabethan adventurer in America was
large, but it was to Spain that he was under the heaviest
obligation. The Atlantic Ocean lay within almost as close
hail of English shores as of Spanish. It was open to England to have sown the seed that Spain first planted in
America. One need not speculate whether, in the absence
of the Spanish initiative, the English would ultimately
have become the dominant people of the New World. It
is sufficient to point out that Shakespeare's countrymen
pursued at a long interval the tracks that Spain had devised, and that Elizabethans, when their vision was clear
of racial and political prejudices, frankly acknowledged the
all-powerful spell of 'the constant travail and valiant mind'
which gave the cue to Spanish effort.

II

A full statement of the Elizabethan debt to the colonizing effort of Spain involves exhaustive study of the one
hundred and fifteen years that separate the discovery by
Columbus of the West Indies in 1492 from the settlement
of Jamestown in 1607. The issue practically involves all
that during that extended period was happening on the
globe's surface from Labrador to the Magellan Straits,
from the Philippine Isles to the Bermudas. No such
survey will be attempted here. I merely invite attention to a few neglected or misapprehended points in
the story which plainly signalize the Spanish inspiration
of Tudor Englishmen.

The first series of episodes which calls for notice has
the negative value of proving England's unreadiness to
appreciate the significance of Spanish energy. There is an
apocryphal story—a late invention—to the effect that
Columbus, when designing his first voyage across the
Atlantic, sent his brother Diego to solicit the aid of King
Henry VII, and that the English king delayed granting
the request until after the sovereigns of Spain had acceded
to it. The earliest authentic incident in the narrative

THE EXAMPLE OF SPAIN

resembles this familiar fable in carrying the moral of a great opportunity missed.

Mystery still overhangs the career and fate of John Cabot, whose exploits are credited with creating England's title in North America. But recent research shows that Spain was responsible alike for the inception of the adventure and for the bestowal on it of a distinctive place in history. It is from the private correspondence or published writing of contemporary Italians and Spaniards, it is from Spanish maps, that John Cabot's precise experiences can alone be gleaned. There he stands revealed as an avowed disciple of Columbus, and a native, too, of Columbus's city of Genoa, whence in early life he migrated to Venice. At Lisbon and Seville he studied those theories of the Atlantic voyage which led Columbus to discover the West Indies in 1492. Cabot shared that great captain's belief that the West Indian islands were stepping-stones to Cathay, the fabled Asiatic empire of gold and spice. The differentiating feature in Cabot's scheme was his choice of a northerly instead of a southerly course. The result of his voyage was the hoisting of the flags of England and of Venice side by side on the ice-bound shore of Labrador. Cabot's triumph lay in touching the inhospitable coast of the North Atlantic eleven months before Columbus, on his third voyage across that ocean, discovered in sunlit Venezuela the terra firma of South America.

The alertness of contemporary Spanish cartographers whose work is extant has alone preserved due record of Cabot's route. The map which he himself drew is lost. Like his Genoese master in the Spanish service, the Italian mariner in the English service imagined that he had reached the gate of golden Cathay. For a moment great hopes of wealth and glory were alive in the country of his adoption. A second expedition on an ampler scale brought Cabot farther south on the coast of the New World, and he scanned from the sea the great expanse of territory which, lying between Newfoundland and Florida, was destined to fall under English sway more than a century later. He vanishes from view while he is glancing from afar at the promised land.

There were none, at the moment, capable of wearing Cabot's mantle. Some Bristol merchants, in the years that followed, sought to pick up his clue; again they relied on foreign co-operation, and took into partnership traders of Portugal, the nation which had already brought West Africa and the islands adjoining within the scope of European civilization. But these Anglo-Portuguese ventures effected nothing.

The next half century is a barren and depressing tract in Anglo-American history. Three small English expeditions set out to explore Labrador or Newfoundland, with results that meant either disaster or futility. During the same period some smacks from English ports fished for cod off the North Atlantic banks. But the fishing fleets of the Normans, Bretons, and Basques were larger and more active than those of the English, and it was French, and not English daring, which first planted a European settlement on North American shores.

In more southerly latitudes it remains to recall the voyages made about 1530 by William Hawkins, of Plymouth. He thought merely to trade with the Portuguese settlers and the aboriginal tribes of the West African coast of Guinea. But, in a spirit of enterprise rare among his English contemporaries, he made a first English essay in that commerce in negro slaves, of which the invention belongs to Portugal, and the initial developments to Spain. Hawkins kidnapped African negroes and, crossing the Atlantic, sold his human cargo among the Spaniards of the West Indies or the Portuguese of Brazil. A century later an immense amount of English energy was absorbed by this commerce, in which Hawkins was the first Englishman to engage. In the first half of the sixteenth century England's incursion into the slave trade of Portugal and Spain alone gave explicit promise of her future intercourse with America.

III

Meanwhile Spain was flying far past all comers in the momentous race. Before England had learned her colonial alphabet, the colossal Spanish empire leaped into being. The barriers of American coasts quickly yielded to the Spanish invasion, and mountains and plains offered the aggressors untouched stores of gold, spice, and pearl. The Isthmus of Panama was soon crossed and Spanish eyes rested on the boundless expanse of the Pacific. The ancient empires of Mexico and Peru, with their mysterious civilizations, extending over areas wider than the whole of Europe, were converted in the twinkling of an eye into provinces of the Iberian Peninsula. With dogged heroism the Spanish conquerors were soon forcing paths across the trackless territories to the north and south of Mexico and Peru, and were planting chains of settlements. Great part of the Central American map was quickly inscribed with the Spanish names of explorers, or of their patron saints, or of their native cities in the home country. An adventurous lover of Spanish romance christened the mysterious sea-girt land to the extreme west of the northern continent California, after the fanciful title of an imaginary island in a popular contemporary work of fiction. On the eastern side of the northern continent, in Florida—named from Pascha Florida, or Palm Sunday, the day of its discovery—a succession of courageous explorers was facing tragedy, while companions of theirs were moving westward to prospect the banks of the Mississippi and view the ridges of the Rocky Mountains.

In the southern continent, north-west of Peru, the newcomers were hunting for the golden city of Eldorado, and meeting death in the foaming torrents of the Orinoco and the Amazon. South of Peru not only did Spain struggle to assert dominion over Chili, but she was marching over the boundless plains of La Plata to the pleasant breezes of the port of Buenos Ayres. Meanwhile, expeditions by sea were surveying the Pacific coasts from California to Tierra del Fuego, and were bringing unsuspected islands within the limits of Spain's empire. Infinite energy and heroic suffering were spent in the search for a trade route to Europe from the western coast of Mexico through the Southern Ocean. Men ready to endure every imaginable peril crowded vessels of all shapes and sizes in both Spanish and American ports, and in growing numbers, year by year, they pushed the quest to remoter bounds.

The incentives to the Spanish conquest were many; some of the conquering host lusted for gold, some for reckless adventure and the practical testing of fancies of romance, others for the exhilaration of change of scene and a larger liberty. But the Church of Rome had blessed the enterprise, and no call to the West sounded more impressively in the Spanish voyager's ear than the appeal of the priest to bring into the true fold the pagan peoples which were known to be scattered over the new-found territory. On numberless hills and headlands fronting both the Atlantic and the Pacific shores pious Spanish hands raised, very early in the sixteenth century, substantial symbols of the Cross, under the shadow of which Spanish priests, monks, and friars preached their faith to the natives. Throughout the bold exploration and masterly settlement of America by Spain, alike during the first and the second half of the sixteenth century, very potent aid was continuously lent by secular and regular clergy, until at length the Church of Rome came to rival the temporal power of the invaders not merely in the great cities, but in the remote villages of the new continent. The whole territory was rapidly distributed into archbishoprics and bishoprics, archdeaconries and parishes. The chief towns had their cathedrals, with their deans and chapters. Every monastic order soon inaugurated its province in the New World and could boast a network of conventual establishments.

Millions of aborigines accepted the teaching of the Christian pilgrims, and if the pagan instinct were rarely crushed altogether the new religion brought in its train much educative influence. Besides churches and monasteries, hospitals and schools spread over the land under the sign of the Cross. Priests, monks, and friars set themselves to stem the devastating epidemics which were always threatening the native peoples. The Roman clergy were enjoined to learn the native languages and, as soon as they could, to preach in tribal tongues. From monastic pens came a long series of native grammars and vocabularies, which bear witness to the Spanish authors' aptitude for their missionary vocation. It was by means of the religious organization of the Roman Church that Spain finally clinched her hold on the American continent.

At the same time a vast machinery was, as if by magic, created at home in the earliest days for the secular government of the new empire. Within ten years of Columbus's landing on a West Indian island a West India House of Trade (*Casa de Contratación*) was established at Seville for the regulation of commerce with the new country; for the issue of passports to settlers; for the orderly accumulation and co-ordination of new geographical knowledge; for the construction of charts and maps; for the education of seamen in the science of ocean travel; for study and research in every department of knowledge which was calculated to improve the art of navigation. The conviction that scientific methods was the key to the earthly paradise of the West quickly conquered the Spanish mind. At Madrid, too, there was formed a Council of the Indies under direct control which framed and executed schemes of colonial administration in its highest branches. The Council instituted an hierarchy of colonial offices, a fiscal system of exceptional intricacy, and a policy for the treatment of natives which accorded on paper with the noblest Christian principles. The Madrid Council of the Indies closely resembled that Council of India which rules from London England's great Asiatic dependency. But the history of the two institutions presents this startling contrast. The London Council was created more than two and a half centuries after English adventurers first set foot on the East Indian continent. The Madrid Council came into being within fifteen years of the first Spanish debarkation on the American coast.

It was under the auspices of this precocious Council of Madrid that both civil and religious institutions of Europe were transplanted to the Gargantuan provinces of Mexico and Peru. Courts of law and ecclesiastical synods, vice-regal palaces and spacious cathedrals, churches and town halls, roads and bridges, public gardens and drainage works, universities and schools, sprang up in 'New Spain' across the ocean at the Council's bidding or with its sanction. The extant municipal records of the City of Mexico begin in 1524. That fact bears significant witness to the method of the Spanish advance.

No instrument of civilization was excluded from the Spanish-American settlements of the sixteenth century. The ceremonial pageantry of the Old World was transferred to the New. The viceregal courts of Lima and Mexico were distinguished by a brilliance only second to that of Madrid. In 1571 'New Spain', or Mexico, celebrated the jubilee of the downfall of the Aztec Empire, and the spectacular display is said to have surpassed any European precedent. Printing-presses were then at work in the chief cities of Mexico and Peru, mainly producing manuals of devotion in the Spanish, Latin, and native languages, but also sending forth codes of legal enactments and some literary prose and poetry. As early as 1551 the University of San Marcos opened its doors at Lima, and was soon afterward installed in an ornate home. In 1553 a university was founded in Mexico on which was bestowed by a royal order the constitution and privileges of the University of Salamanca. Colleges for the higher education of the sons both of settlers and of the better class of natives were afterwards instituted alike in the northern and southern continents. Colleges for sons of Incas at Lima and Cuzco, in Peru, taught the latest developments of European culture. The Spanish conquerors neglected nothing that was likely to guarantee the civilized progress of the New World on the best models known to the Old.

Colonizing and exploring energy on such a scale and method has no parallel in history. It continued without cessation throughout the sixteenth century. It is commonly assumed that with the establishment of the two great viceroyalties of Mexico and Peru within the first half of the century the heroic age of the Spanish conquest of America ends. Daring of an epic type colours the exploring exploits of Spain in America both by land and sea through all the years of Shakespeare's lifetime, while European civilization marched onward without a pause.

There was a dark side to the picture, a blot on the scutcheon, of which the future was to disclose the full significance. But the historical perspective is ruined if the shadows are painted too dense a black. Spain's marvellous triumph over the forces of nature justified a blind faith in her strength, and it is no matter of surprise that she long deemed herself impregnable in the New World. A source of weakness lay in her over-confidence and in her self-sufficiency, which would tolerate no stranger within her gates. She overlooked the dangers inherent in the hugeness of her colonial territory, which rendered barely possible either a well-knit internal government or coasts and frontiers that should be fully defensible from external attack. She neglected the warnings of early raids by Frenchmen. Indeed, the comparative ease with which she repelled French assaults exposed her to the fatal error of underrating the boldness of Elizabethan buccaneers. Yet far into the seventeenth century Spanish America nourished great powers of recuperation. The chief ports, to which Drake and his countrymen set fire, rose from their ashes while the ruins were still smoking. Despite the superior alertness of Elizabethan privateers and their activity in depredation, treasure fleets from the Spanish main long succeeded in crossing the Atlantic Ocean with only occasional loss for two hundred years. Misfortune and misgovernment bred disaster for the mother country in Europe, but it deprived her by slow and at first imperceptible degrees of her predominance in the Western hemisphere. In the result Spain retained her hold on the colonies which she founded at the end of the fifteenth century for a far longer period than England retained her hold on the American colonies which she founded in the seventeenth.

Very various economic and industrial difficulties from the first confronted Spain in the New World, and in view of their complexity the permanence of her hold may well intensify the sense of wonder which her whole experience evokes. Her failure to solve satisfactorily the fiscal and labour problems of her new empire cannot be made merely matter of reproach. No colonizing nation has yet regulated the discovery of immense mineral wealth in a new country so as to obviate tendencies to corruption among both the settlers and their friends at home. It was an inevitable 'dropsy of covetousness' (in the words of Peter Martyr, the first historian of Spanish America) which infected Spanish-American rule, and, with heroic exceptions, contaminated the political hierarchy, from the king at Madrid to the pettiest officers of Mexico and Peru. Official extortion, vexatious taxation, open traffic in fiscal and judicial offices were among the economic evils of the Spanish-American empire for which cure was sought in vain.

The first aim of the conquerors was to secure for themselves absolute possession of the country's treasure, and the only road to this goal lay through the dethronement of the native kings and chieftains, the expropriation of the native occupiers of the land, and the compulsory employment of the native peoples in the mines. A modified feudal land tenure, with its taint of serfdom, was imported in haste from Europe. A vast and heterogeneous native population, of which only a very small portion was physically strong enough to persist in forcible opposition, lay at the mercy of the conquerors. There is little that is unexpected in the hateful incidents of cruelty which marked the Spaniards' subjugation of the natives. Such are invariable features of the association of a race which is high in the scale of civilization with a race which, being low in that scale, is at the same time possessed of property of value to highly civilized life. The normal vice of the situation was exaggerated by the mental or bodily defects of the aborigines, which unfitted them for hard or regular work, and by the inability of the European settlers patiently to tolerate habits or usages which were strange to them and out of harmony with their religious and social traditions.

But the native affairs of Spanish America had a saving grace. The American Indian never lacked Spanish champions, who loudly pleaded for his humane treatment. In the first half of the century the Mexican bishop, Bartolomeo de las Casas, roused in behalf of the natives an agitation which bore fruit in a long series of merciful enactments. Till the end of the century the Council of the Indies impressed on every viceroy of Mexico and Peru the duty of guarding the American Indians from barbarous usage. These Spanish laws for the due protection of the American natives were resented and evaded by a majority of the settlers. But it is an error to deny to the colonial policy of Spain the consciousness of humane obligation.

The Church's imposing claim to bring all the aborigines into her fold failed to procure them a satisfactory social, political, or economic status; yet it served materially to alleviate their hardships. More could hardly have been anticipated of the dominant clerical temper. In spite of the physical courage and spiritual earnestness of the Catholic clergy, their chieftains, with glorious exceptions, cherished corporate interests and ambitions, which exposed them to every worldly temptation. The vices that come of power and wealth infected the ecclesiastical rulers. During the latter part of the century the Church strengthened her position by importing the degenerate and brutal disciplinary machinery of the Inquisition. But it is only right to point out that great as was the suffering inflicted by the Inquisition at Lima and Mexico on European settlers and European captives, the natives were exempted from tortures of the holy office. They were treated as catechumens who were not liable to the rigours of adult discipline. The Inquisition left the native difficulty untouched for good or ill.

It was the intricacy of inevitable conditions which refused the principle of magnanimity free play in the government of the American native. Las Casas, the passionate agitator who sought to redress native suffering, recognized that a vast supply of mechanical labour was essential to the development of the new country, even if the aborigines were unqualified to provide it. His suggested solution is difficult to reconcile with his principles, but it defines the situation. Las Casas recommended the importation of negroes from the west coast of Africa, and the recommendation was adopted. Quite illogically, the black colour and great physical strength of the Africans appeared to justify their enslavement, while the lighter complexions and the weak physique of the native American forbade a state of servility.

The economic and industrial constitution of Spanish America was finally based on Las Casas's foundation of black slavery. Some curious results followed. The native American slowly dwindled in numbers, while the negro rapidly multiplied. Yet the two races freely intermingled and a new racial blend which proved sturdy, although morally unstable, came into being. Similarly, the Spanish settlers themselves lacked that sense of physical repugnance which has restrained the Anglo-Saxon colonist from intermarriage with native races. The Spanish conquerors of Peru of the highest rank wedded from the beginning the daughters of the Incas, and their example was imitated by their humble followers. In all ranks of society racial intermixture produced in course of time new ethnic types of unsteady temperament, and therein lurked fatal seeds of degeneracy.

IV

Well before the sixteenth century reached its meridian Spain was setting Europe an example which might well excite emulation. Yet England, sunk in slumber, gave no sign of emotion. Tidings of the Spanish triumph flooded the European Continent. Not only at Madrid and Seville, but at Rome, Basle, Paris, and Vienna the strange news absorbed attention. Reports of American adventure were penned by versatile Spanish explorers, whose gifts often included vivid power of narration, and their stories were printed almost simultaneously in their author's language, in Latin, French, German, and Italian. At all the leading Continental universities, especially in Germany, geography was restudied and revised in the light of the Western revelations. England alone stood aloof from the stir. The flowing streams of intelligence scarcely touched her shores.

During the early part of the sixteenth century only one English author, Sir Thomas More, bears witness to the intellectual impulse that was generated by the American discovery, and he learned his lesson, not in England, but in the cultured cities of the Low Countries. A visit to Antwerp gave him the suggestion of the 'Utopia', which was written there in Latin, and was published at Louvain. The romance owes its foundation to the Italian letters of Amerigo Vespucci, the Florentine contractor of Cadiz, who crossed the Atlantic many times as Columbus's disciple. It was Vespucci's Christian name, instead of that of his master, which, through the freak of a Lorraine geographer, was permanently inscribed on the new continent. More is the sole Englishman of the period who made specific mention of Vespucci's reports, which were circulating in scores of editions and in half a dozen languages outside impenetrable England. Yet More ignores all other contributions of his time to the budding history of America. The names of Columbus and of his companions were securely enshrined during More's life in the litera-

ture of Spain, Italy, France, and Germany, but he gives
no sign that they had reached his ears.

More wrote of Vespucci and America in Latin. Between 1512 and 1519 three contemporary writers in English (whose work reached the printing-press) made shadowy
allusion to America and the triumphs of Spain, but their
meagre inaccuracies serve to make the English darkness
the more visible. With a confused mention of 'the land
America called after Americus', in a rudimentary English
drama published in 1519, there fell on English literature
a complete silence respecting the New World for four and
thirty years.[1] Portugal, France, Italy, Germany, and the
Low Countries were in that interval eagerly recording the
glorious Spanish advance in books, maps, and globes. Yet
England slumbered on in ignorance or incredulity.

Happily there were English merchants abroad who were
absorbing the foreign enthusiasm and felt shame for their
country's lethargy.

Seville, now the centre of the American trade and the
home of nautical and geographical research, had long harboured an English trading settlement. From Seville came to
England the first direct and reasoned appeal to recognize her
Western opportunities. Robert Thorne, a Seville resident,
who was the son of an enterprising Bristol merchant, forwarded to the English king, Henry VIII, a strongly worded
admonition to take the Spanish example to heart. Even if
South and Central America had permanently passed into
Spanish hands, North America still awaited its conqueror.
But Thorne's stirring message from Seville fell on deaf ears.

Yet productive enlightenment was destined to come at
length out of Seville. An effective pen was at work there
in the interests of England within the very walls of the
Seville House of American Trade, which was a storehouse
of geographical learning. John Cabot had vainly incited
England to adopt Spain's American design when in its
embryonic stage. His son, Sebastian, grown disgusted with
the sloth of his father's adopted country, placed his ser-

[1] [See, however, the *Introduction*, p. xx.]

vices at the disposal of the Spanish pioneers when their
efforts were maturing. Cabot secured a berth in the West
India House at Seville, and finally, in the capacity of
'pilot-major of Spain', controlled, for more than thirty
years, the navigation of the Atlantic. One of his chief
duties was to keep a great standard map of the New World,
called the *Padrón Real*, abreast of returning captains'
reports of American expeditions. On the surface of this
great chart every discovery was entered as soon as it was
attested and every known error erased. Sailing directions
and treatises of navigations were licensed by Cabot and
his colleagues of Seville. He developed a system of naval
instruction. Under his auspices lectures were given to
would-be pilots and sailing officers, and a mode of written
examination was inaugurated. Cabot's curriculum of
study embraced all branches of mathematics, astronomy,
and the use of the globes. Extant syllabuses and examination papers show that his methods of naval education fall
little short of modern standards. The Seville teaching
came to promote naval efficiency throughout Europe.

At length, when Edward VI's reign opened, Cabot,
whose distinction lay in his power of organization and
research, went to London and placed the massive experience, which he had acquired in Spain, at the disposal of
the English Government. The last ten years of his long
life were spent in the English capital, where he preached
unceasingly the priceless value of the Spanish example.

Although he was worn by age and a long life of toil,
Sebastian's persuasive obstinacy caught attention in England. A new 'mystery' or company of London merchants
was formed under his leadership for 'the discovery of
regions, dominions, and places unknown'. The shadowy
paradise of Cathay, which was imagined to lie at the back
of America, was once more the stated goal. But the perils
of the Atlantic, which the Spaniards regarded as their own
waterway, were to be avoided. Cabot advised a north-east
passage to Cathay, which the geographers of southern and
central Europe guessed to exist and to be navigable.

England, after more than half a century's hesitation, was deliberately to join Spain in the exploration of the unknown world. The first-fruits belied expectation. No golden paradise of the West was discovered, but the northern shores of Russia, which none had yet penetrated. Sebastian Cabot's earliest exploring essay under English auspices seemed to founder, like his father's original exploit, amid snow and ice.

None the less the English had begun in earnest to learn the Spanish lesson. Not the least notable feature in Cabot's organization of his North Sea fleet was his official directions to the seamen. They followed models which he brought from Seville. For the first time in English maritime practice strict order was given for the keeping of daily reports of the ship's movements. Immense value was set upon the maintenance of a strict discipline among the sailors and of a lofty standard of piety and morality. Prayers were to be said publicly twice a day; blasphemous language, quarrelling, and, above all, gambling were prohibited under heaviest penalties.

The later history of these directions of 1552 prove to what future purpose Cabot assimilated the method of Spain. Their form and spirit took root in England. Frobisher's regulations for his stirring ventures twenty years later practically repeated them word for word. They were reissued to almost every exploring party that left English shores for the American continent through Elizabeth's reign.

English historians, under the stress of insular prejudice, have often described the official exhortations of the Elizabethan Admiralty to piety, to morality, and to careful record of geographical and nautical data as a peculiar outcome of English Protestantism blended with colonizing aptitude. No misconception could be greater. The piety and religious observances, no less than the scientific study, which were officially enjoined on ocean-going fleets, were institutions of Spain long before England had need of them. The Spaniard made provision for his spiritual welfare in every relation of life, and he was not likely to forgo it when facing the mysterious perils of unknown seas. The solemn injunctions against blasphemy, gambling, or drunkenness aboard Elizabethan ships on the Atlantic were primarily the invention of the devout Iberian.

Meanwhile, Cabot's unquenchable enthusiasm bore richer fruit than North Sea discovery or an improved naval discipline. Amid the stir of preparation for the Arctic expedition a humble clerk in the Treasury at London, by name Richard Eden, caught the infection, and offered his fellow-countrymen for the first time an account, in their own tongue, of the new Spanish cosmography. Eden devised an English rendering of a German professor's description of 'the new found lands and islands of the West'. In an original preface Eden bade sluggish Englishmen mark 'the sudden strangeness or greatness of the thing'. For the first time, albeit vaguely and imperfectly, there was told in English the story of 'Christopherus Columbus, a gentleman of Italy', and of the Portuguese captain, Magellan, who passed through the labyrinthine southern straits. But Eden's German compendium was behind the quickly advancing times. Of Mexico and Peru there was no hint. A mere fringe of the curtain was lifted. Not through Germany, but direct from Spain, could the full news come.

V

An unforeseen alliance of the English and Spanish royal houses lent new and unlooked-for impetus to Cabot's aspiration. The English people were to learn something of the meaning of Spain's American endeavour at their own doors. A mirage of Mexico and Peru was to frame itself in English skies. Through London streets there was to pass a hero of the Mexican empire, and Spanish guards were to draw pledges of Peru's silver harvest.

In Prince Philip's nuptial retinue came to England a little army of Spanish grandees, some of whom had already won fame and fortune in the New World, and were destined to return thither to seek more. The name of Queen Mary's chief Spanish guest conjured up a splendid memory of Spanish achievement in the West. Martin Cortes, Marques de Valle, was part and parcel of the most thrilling episode in recent Spanish-American annals. Born twenty-one years before, in the city of Mexico, he was the son of Hernando Cortes, conqueror of the Mexican kingdom. The father, one of the most heroic figures among the *conquistadores*, had recently died, worn out by bitter rivalries with colleagues. But he had bequeathed to his son, Martin, a princely appanage in the empire of his conquest. The youth was distinguished among his compatriots at Queen Mary's court by his fine physique and the gorgeous pageantry of his equipment. When, a few years later, he returned to his Mexican home, the luxurious magnificence of his household exposed him to the suspicion of aspiring to an independent throne, but after vindicating his innocence he lived quietly in his Mexican palace till his death, just after the Spanish Armada—an event pregnant with ironical comment on the circumstances of his visit to London.

If Martin Cortes's presence at Queen Mary's court first spoke to English ears of the promise of Mexico, another of Don Philip's company was an eloquent representative of recent experience in Peru.

On 2nd October 1554 a Spanish ship unloaded in the Thames a mass of silver bullion valued at £50,000. This was a gift of the Spanish prince to the people of England from the mines of Peru and La Plata. Enclosed in ninety-seven little chests, the treasure was drawn through the streets of the capital to the mint at the Tower in a procession of twenty carts, under the convoy of Spanish halberdiers. Never before had so much silver been seen in London. Tangible proof was offered the London populace of what Spanish adventure in Peru was worth.

Augustin de Zarate, the official in whose charge the metal reached the Tower, proved an efficient missionary in the American cause. A man of versatile accomplishment, he had lately returned from Peru, where his experience was long and varied. There for many years he had superintended the working of the mines. Once more in Spain, he was made auditor of the royal mint at Madrid. Endowed with the literary faculty which was characteristic of the Spanish official, Zarate owed the full scope of his influence on English effort in America to the fact that he devoted his leisure to writing a history of the Spanish discovery of Peru and of the kingdom's subsequent fortunes. The volume was published in Antwerp in the year after his visit to England.

Twenty years later Zarate met an English merchant, settled in Spain, on the highroad outside Toledo, and they fell into familiar discourse. The friendly encounter moved the Englishman, Thomas Nicholas, to turn into his own tongue a great part of Zarate's book, and the translation, which came out in London in 1581, remained for Elizabethans and for a generation of their descendants the sole English source of information concerning Peru.

Such was minor English fruit of the coming of the Spaniards to England when Philip wedded Queen Mary. In America, too, the episode left its mark. News of the marriage quickly crossed the Atlantic Ocean. Philip announced it in an autograph letter to the Viceroy of Mexico, which was read aloud in the council chamber there. In the southern continent a new-born Spanish settlement, now known as Tucuman, near the northern frontier of Argentina, was, in honour of the auspicious event, christened for the time New London. Moreover, by an unhappy coincidence, a crisis in American affairs distracted the attention of the Spaniards in England before the wedding festivities ended. Just before Philip landed in England the hardy natives of Chili—the liberty-loving Araucanians—routed in open fight an invading Spanish army of seasoned troops. General Valdivia and his officers were slain. The disaster threatened Spanish prestige throughout the American empire, and of it Philip first learned during his honeymoon in London.

Without delay, the Spanish prince gave orders for the immediate dispatch of reinforcements. Many of his retinue volunteered for the service, and left Mary's court for the distant seat of war. One of these London volunteers, a royal page, Alonzo de Ercilla, deserves individual mention. Not only did he distinguish himself on Chilian fields during the long-drawn campaign which followed, but he also described the desultory fighting in an epic poem of greater length than Homer's *Iliad*, and in the south of Europe hardly less renowned.

The Araucanian struggle for freedom lasted to the end of the sixteenth century and beyond. It ran its course throughout the period of Shakespeare's career. It is a curious accident that should have associated with English soil Spain's resolute entry into the most persistent of her wars with aboriginal Americans. It was an ordeal which was strangely prophetic of much English experience of the future.

Yet the most effective incitement to English endeavour in America which sprang from Philip's marriage remains to be told. Richard Eden, the humble treasury clerk, who had already translated a half-informed German compendium of the new cosmography, comes anew upon the scene as a bearer of the light. He sought intercourse with the Spanish visitors. Encouraged by old Cabot, he sent to press, in readable English, an encyclopaedia of the recent Spanish record of America. The bulkiness of his manuscript appalled the London printers, who put it into type under protest. Germany and Italy had already set the pattern of such ample historical reports of the opening act of the New World drama. Eden's originality solely lay in his naturalization of a foreign type in England.

Eden's effort gave the English people in their own tongue information of America, which they alone among civilized European nations had lacked hitherto. In a dedication addressed to Prince Philip Eden took a just, if somewhat highly-coloured, view of Spanish effort. He extolled the *conquistadores*, likening them to Hercules and

Saturn, 'and such other which for their glorious enterprises were accounted as gods among men'.

Henceforth the Spanish histories of Peter Martyr, the
friend and patron of Columbus, Oviedo, the first official
chronicler of the Indies, and Gomara, the secretary of
Cortes, were recognized as treasuries of argument and
information for English no less than for Spanish projectors
of settlements in the new continent. English versions of
them all won popularity in Shakespeare's youth. Eden's
book was the precursor and the model of the more
exhaustive collections of Hakluyt and Purchas, which
repeated his impressive appeal to England to emulate the
Spanish example. A disciple of Hakluyt, Michael Lok, by
profession and descent a foreign merchant, rendered
Martyr's inspiring *Decades of the Ocean* at full length
from the Latin into English. Addressing the English
reader, the merchant-author bore witness to the stimulus
which the Spanish record exerted on Elizabethan effort
in these pregnant words of advice: 'We Englishmen', runs
the suggestive counsel, 'are chiefly to consider the industry
and travails of the Spaniards, their exceeding charge in
furnishing so many ships, their continual supplies to
further their attempts, their active and undaunted spirits
in executing matters of that quality and difficulty, and
lastly, their constant resolution of Plantation. All which
may be exemplary unto us to form the like in our Virginia.'

VI

Thus the demons of ignorance and blindness which
withheld the English from the American quest seem to
have been exorcised by the presence of Philip of Spain and
his friends at Mary's court, by Sebastian Cabot's persistent
advocacy in England of the maritime methods of Spain,
and finally by Eden's English presentation of the Spanish
histories. Yet England still hung back, and not before the
course of secular and religious politics in Europe had sown
an implacable enmity between England and Spain in the
Eastern hemisphere did the former country give active

proofs of any fixed resolve to adopt the aspirations and methods of Spain. The boldest Elizabethan might well quail at the thought of matching what Spain had achieved, not merely in the early years of the sixteenth century, but in the period which lies between the dates of Philip's marriage to Queen Mary and the end of Elizabeth's reign, when Elizabethan energy was at its zenith. Year by year, church and state on the Old World model were taking firmer root in the Spanish-American empire. Year by year, the limits of Spain's settled rule in the New World were expanding. Callao, the port of Lima, the capital of Peru, and Vera Cruz, the port of the city of Mexico, had become the richest and the busiest ports of the world. Mexico and Peru were ringed about by prosperous provinces. Failures of the past had been retrieved. A first plantation at Buenos Ayres, which came to nothing, was in 1580 replaced by another, which flourished and was lasting. The bay and county of Monterey preserve the name of the Spanish Viceroy of Mexico, who early in the seventeenth century specially distinguished himself by his confirmation of Spain's hold on California. In the seas of the far north and of the far south Spain was continually pressing forward. Her fishing fleets now sailed year by year to the Newfoundland coast, and the Basques of San Sebastian were inaugurating the whaling industry off Greenland and Iceland. The Pacific islands, called after the king of Spain the Philippines, were a flourishing Spanish settlement; the foundations of Manila, the capital city, were laid in 1564. The South Seas were threaded in 1567, and a landing effected on the Solomon Islands, where the ruins of the Jewish temple were located by fanciful theologians. Three daring expeditions within the next forty years pursued the like course and came near bringing Australia under the Spanish flag. The familiar name of Torres Straits, between the most northerly point of Australia and the island of New Guinea, preserves the memory of a Spanish mariner who sought to proclaim in the early years of the seventeenth century Spain's domination of the south pole. Very puny seem even the most imposing achievements of Elizabethan England compared with those wherewith her chief teacher was putting the finishing touches to her mighty work.

Gradually Elizabethan literature on the subject of America grew voluminous. For the most part it consisted of translations from foreign languages, in which French held a place only less prominent than Spanish. But the Spanish books had a far larger experience to divulge than those in any other tongue. Full accounts of the marvellous triumphs of Mexico and Peru were extracted from the authentic works of Gomara and Zarate. Las Casas's piteous appeal on behalf of the American Indian stimulated hostility to Spain. The long series of original English tracts advocating earnest pursuit of American colonization, which was initiated by Sir Humphrey Gilbert, was liberal in reference to foreign authors like these.

But more serviceable was Spain's scientific literature concerning America, which was now also made available for Elizabethans in their own tongue. Of the English versions of Spanish manuals of navigation the earliest was the industrious Eden's rendering of the standard work by Martin Cortes, which was carried out at the suggestion of an English sailing-master. There were at least ten English editions of the book in Shakespeare's lifetime, and it was only one of a series of Spanish books of the kind with which Elizabethan seamen were familiar. Sir Martin Frobisher carried with him on his first expedition to Labrador the 'Arte de Navegación' of Pedro de Medina in the original Spanish; the first English translation appeared five years later. By that time Englishmen had begun to write navigation manuals for themselves. But it was not till the extreme end of the century that men of the mathematical acumen of Edward Wright and John Davis advanced on what the foreigner had done. Even when the Elizabethans were bettering the instructions that the Spaniards had given them, they liberally acknowledged the services that their masters had rendered them. John

Davis, whose name is writ large in the map of the world in Davis's Straits, between Labrador and Greenland, expressed a universal sentiment when he remarked in his 'Seamen's Secrets', the greatest of all Elizabethan contributions to nautical science: 'For what hath made the Spaniard to be so great a monarch, the commander of both the Indies, to abound in wealth and all nature's benefits, but only by the painful industry of his subjects by [study of] navigation.'

Richard Hakluyt laid fully as much stress as John Davis on the need of studying the scientific methods of navigation which prevailed abroad. He urged the English Government to establish lectureships at Oxford and London on the model of those at Paris and Seville. On all foreign teaching he set a high value, on that of France and Italy as well as of Spain. But he frankly avowed that he learned most from 'his extreme travail in the history of the Spaniards'. He eagerly purchased Spanish manuscripts, Spanish charts, and Spanish sailing directions. He interrogated Spanish sailors who were brought to England as prisoners by the Elizabethan fleets, and closely scanned the papers and letters which were found in Spanish prizes. Scarcely a printed book in the Spanish tongue which dealt with the geography or natural history of any part of the New World escaped his eager eye, and every piece of information that he himself acquired he freely placed at the disposal of those of his countrymen who were bent on an Atlantic voyage.

VII

The full history of Elizabethan exploration of America or of Elizabethan navigation in American waters falls outside the scope of this paper. For my present purpose it is hardly necessary to distinguish between the two kinds of Elizabethan exploits in America—between the expeditions which were undertaken as acts of war against Spain, and sought the destruction of Spanish shipping, or the capture of Spanish treasure, and the expeditions which were dispatched for purposes of discovery or colonization. With the former endeavours the names of Sir John Hawkins, Sir Francis Drake, and Thomas Cavendish are chiefly to be associated; with the latter the names of Sir Martin Frobisher, Sir Humphrey Gilbert, John Davis, and, above all, Sir Walter Raleigh. But all these men have this in common that they acknowledge in word or deed the value of Spanish example. All studied Spanish charts before embarking on the Atlantic Ocean, and most of them sought the services of foreign pilots. It was a Portuguese pilot who accompanied Drake on the most difficult part of his voyage round the South American continent, and it was his capture of a rich collection of Spanish charts in a Spanish ship off Peru which encouraged him to shape his course homeward across Spanish tracks in the Pacific, and thus to complete his circumnavigation of the globe. The chief distinction between Elizabethan attempts at colonization and those of Spanish predecessors or contemporaries lay in the many failures of the English before a permanent lodgement on any part of the American continent was effected. Where there was greatest originality there was least practical fruit. Sir Martin Frobisher's three voyages to Labrador, which he called *Meta Incognita*, brought him to lands and seas which the Spaniards had not visited. His design of reaching Cathay by a north-west passage through the Arctic Ocean was familiar to French mariners, but no Frenchman gave the scheme so thorough a trial as he. John Davis, another Elizabethan, pushed Frobisher's exploration to farther limits. Frobisher's and Davis's original contributions to geographical knowledge rank them with the heroes of the world. But their resolve to plant an English colony on the northern road to the fabulous empire came to nothing. They named bays and straits and headlands after English persons or places. Frobisher christened a Greenland cliff Charing Cross, but this terminology, which followed Spanish precedent, carried with it no practical fulfilment of colonial aspiration.

Sir Humphrey Gilbert's succeeding adventures in the

more southerly regions of Newfoundland led to little more substantial result. Although Spanish ships were regularly visiting Newfoundland coasts, Spain had planted no settlement there. France, however, had secured a firm foothold. She surmounted difficulties which the Elizabethans found insuperable.

A somewhat larger measure of success attended the Elizabethan endeavours in the more southerly districts of the northern continent. There Spanish adventurers had been before them and they had set their experiences on record; Florida, or Terra Florida, the name conferred by the Spaniards on an indeterminate region in the south-east corner of North America, had been the scene since 1512 of some of the most desperate exploits of Spanish explorers. The beauty of the scenery, the fineness of the climate, the richness of the soil, had fascinated the earliest European visitors. Very early in Queen Elizabeth's reign English soldiers of fortune had played with the fancy of emigrating to this paradise. But nothing came then of the aspiration. The barbarity with which the Spaniards expelled from the country French Huguenot settlers illustrated the value Spaniards set on their exclusive ownership, and seemed to promise little scope for English ambition. But as the Spanish and French descriptions of the fascinating country were more closely studied by Elizabethan Englishmen, the conviction grew that some part of it lay beyond the practical range of Spanish influence and might well be destined for English occupation. Hakluyt, in the early days of his geographical researches, strongly urged his fellow-countrymen, on the faith of French and Spanish testimony, to make a colonial experiment on the luxuriant soil of Florida. Sir Walter Raleigh caught the enthusiasm, and he organized the costly series of expeditions to that section of the Spaniards' vaguely bounded 'flowery land' which he christened Virginia. For a time there seemed a likelihood that the Elizabethans whom Raleigh sent thither might plant there the seeds of an English empire. But the settlers were unable to hold their own. Those who voyaged forth to dwell there disappeared and eluded all efforts to rescue them. Thus far the Spanish lesson had been imperfectly learned. Yet the Virginian scheme was never completely abandoned, and there issued from it, after many failures, the final triumph of Jamestown. There at length, in 1607, arose an English settlement which bore lasting fruit. But as often as that fact is recalled, the philosopher should remember that the courage which enabled the Elizabethans to persevere in the Virginian design was fostered by close study in Spanish books of the reports and experiences of the Spanish explorers of Florida. In order to maintain the spirit of his countrymen in their Virginian endeavours, Hakluyt rendered into English a Spanish volume which he significantly named *Virginia richly valued, by the description of the mainland of Florida, her next neighbour.* The book was a full description of the Spanish discovery of Florida and of 'the comodities of the said country' according to Spanish testimony.

Sir Walter Raleigh, the virtual founder of Virginia, is the presiding genius of the embryonic English empire on American shores. Politically, he was Spain's relentless foe. He was ambitious for his own country to share, if not to crush, Spanish dominion of the New World. The indifference of his fellow-countrymen to the opportunities which America offered them roused in him an angry disdain. Raleigh's nature was a mingled yarn. Intellectual strength was intertwined with lawless passion. A genuine love of learning and speculation kept his powerful prejudices within bounds. Jealousy of Spanish power and of Spanish wealth never blinded him to the significance of Spanish methods in the spheres of exploration and colonization. No Elizabethan studied Spanish-American experience with greater zeal, and none admitted less equivocally the value of its example.

As a schoolboy Raleigh had eagerly imbibed tales of Columbus and his companions, of Cortes and of Pizarro. As a young man he had interested himself in the first researches of Hakluyt, and purchased Spanish manuscripts for him at a high rate. His organization of the Virginia expeditions from 1584 onward were the first fruits of his Spanish studies.

His interest in Spanish effort was signally stimulated by a curious experience which befell him in the year 1586, the year, as it happened, when Shakespeare in all probability first came to London. The episode brought home to Raleigh, and through him to many another Elizabethan, the meaning of Spanish methods of explanation.

On 11 September 1586 Raleigh's cousin, Sir Richard Grenville, who shared many of his colonial aspirations, arrived at Plymouth after an Atlantic voyage. He had been sent out to Virginia at Sir Walter Raleigh's expense on one of those many expeditions which accomplished nothing. On the return voyage he seized a Spanish ship off the Azores, and brought home her officers and cargo. Chief among Grenville's prisoners was Don Sarmiento de Gamboa, who deserves to rank with the Spanish heroes of the New World. He was of the school of Columbus and Cortes. Raleigh claimed the right of guarding him, and for seven weeks the two men, whose aims and temperament were nearly allied, were in continuous amiable intercourse with one another. The jailer became the eager pupil of 'the worthy Spanish gentleman' who was his prisoner.

Sarmiento's career and experience fitted him to be an efficient instructor. Now well over fifty, he migrated, when about twenty-three, to Mexico. Soon settling in Peru, he travelled up and down the country seeking information of the dispossessed native peoples. Of the expedition to the Pacific Ocean which resulted in the discovery of the Solomon Isles, Sarmiento was the moving spirit. His main energies were thenceforth devoted to the observation of coasts and oceans and to the making of maps. His maps and chart betray a mathematical accuracy and artistic skill which won the admiration of all subsequent navigators of scientific aptitude.

It was in the Straits of Magellan that Sarmiento ren-

dered his chief service to nautical knowledge. Sir Francis
Drake's heroic voyage through the straits had excited
Spanish fears. Only expeditions in the Spanish service had
accomplished or attempted that perilous passage before.
The Englishman's triumph led the Viceroy of Peru to
proclaim that the safety of the American empire required
the future exclusion of all foreigners from the waterway
between the Atlantic and the Southern Seas. Thereupon
Sarmiento undertook to fortify the straits. With that end
in view, he for the first time surveyed and described them
in a narrative that enjoys standard rank in geographical
literature, and his memory still justly survives on the
shore of the straits in Mount Sarmiento. But Sarmiento
was not content with these scientific triumphs. He induced the authorities at Madrid to entrust him with a
share in the planting of a colony of Spaniards within the
straits. That design ended in disaster, and it was while on
his way to Spain in search of help that he fell in with
Sir Richard Grenville, and became Raleigh's captive
in England. In sociable intercourse with Raleigh he
communicated much of his knowledge, and deepened
Raleigh's conviction that precise cartography and scientific
navigation were indispensable implements for empire
builders.

Encouraged by Sarmiento's genial teaching, Raleigh
continued his studies of Spanish exploration. It was under
their influence that he had conceived his earlier design on
the northern continent. Now he turned to emulate more
precisely Spanish efforts in the South. The expedition to
Guiana was an exact counterpart of Spanish experience.
The spirited narrative of this enterprise, which Raleigh
published on his return, was introduced by a full and
particular account drawn from Spanish sources of the
whole history of Spanish exploration of the country
about the Amazon and the Orinoco throughout the
sixteenth century. In this first English attempt to gain
a foothold in South America, Raleigh relied on personal intercourse with Spaniards as well as on his reading

in Spanish books and manuscripts. His relations with Don Antonio de Berreo, governor of Trinidad, who was his prisoner while he refitted his fleet at that island on his outward journey, were almost identical with those he had already enjoyed with Sarmiento in London. Don Antonio had seen much exploring service both in the north-east and north-west of South America, and he had married into the family of one of the *conquistadores*. From Don Antonio's lips Raleigh learned of his 'proceedings past and purposed', and the information gave Raleigh invaluable guidance.

Raleigh failed in the attempt to plant an English settlement in Guiana. But his arguments and experience lent new impulse to the nation's growing conception of the meaning of Spanish achievements. Raleigh's friend and companion, Laurence Keymis, bore witness to the force of Spanish example with even greater plainness of speech than Raleigh himself. Englishmen had long suffered, he averred, for their refusal to believe the story of Spain's discoveries. Let them at the eleventh hour acknowledge the truth, and perceive that labour and industry had given the bare-legged mountaineers of Castile command of an empire which their ingenuity had first brought to light. Well might England pray Heaven to grant her the sagacity and the energy which should impel her to follow in the footsteps of Spain.

When in the days of his adversity Raleigh surveyed the history of the world, and was narrating the wondrous fortunes of the ancient empires of the East, he glanced involuntarily at the victorious march of Spain through America, and with a philosophic calm, which was purified of prejudice and rancour, recalled the persistent purpose, the scientific curiosity, the heroic suffering, on which Spain's triumphs were built.

'I cannot forbear', he wrote, 'to commend the patient virtue of the Spaniards; we seldom or never find that any nation hath endured so many misadventures and miseries as the Spaniards have done in their Indian discoveries; yet, persisting in their enterprises with an invincible constancy, they have annexed to their kingdom so many goodly provinces as bury the remembrance of all dangers past. Tempests and shipwrecks, famine, overthrows, mutinies, heat and cold, pestilence and all manner of diseases, both old and new, together with extreme poverty and want of all things needful, have been the enemies which everyone of their most noble discoverers at one time or another hath encountered. Many years have passed over some of their heads in the search of not so many leagues. . . . Surely they are worthily rewarded with those treasuries and paradises which they enjoy, and well they deserve to hold them quietly, if they hinder not the like virtue in others, which perhaps will not be found.'

Raleigh's concluding expressions of doubt whether the Spaniard would willingly suffer others to share the profits of their labours were well justified, but he offers the best excuse that could be suggested for a policy of exclusion. The Spaniards had honestly earned their reward. Raleigh's eloquence enshrines the impression which the occupation of America by Spain was calculated to make on the intelligent, dispassionate Elizabethan observer. The statement imputes to Tudor Englishmen the reproach of tardiness in realizing their destiny. The Spanish example was, in its broad features, no unworthy one to follow, and it is to the credit of the Elizabethans, and to the advantage of their descendants, that, late as was the hour, they came to recognize its true value.

THE TEACHING OF THE HUGUENOTS

I

IT is hard to state precisely when mariners of France first obeyed the call which drove seafarers of Europe across the veiled ocean of the West. There is a likelihood that while Columbus was still a humble pilot of the Mediterranean a sailor of Dieppe found his way from a West Indian island to the mainland of Brazil, and, making an inland expedition there, came home with supplies of dye-wood, monkeys, and parrots. It is unquestioned that at the opening of the sixteenth century the ports of Dieppe, Honfleur, St. Malo, and St. Jean de Luz dispatched fleet after fleet of tiny craft in the vain hope of sharing with the captains of Cadiz, Palos, and Huelva the profits and perils of the American venture. Throughout the sixteenth century French sagacity lagged behind Spain, quite as far as English sagacity, in formulating and executing successful plans of exploration or occupation. But, in the early decades of the Spanish triumph, Normans, Bretons, and French Basques, with a persistency unknown at the date to Englishmen, repeatedly challenged adventure in both the northern and southern continents of the New World.

The colonial methods and motives of France may seem, at a first rapid glance, merely to reflect Spanish endeavour with pale and ineffectual fire. The earliest French explorers of America shared Spain's enthusiasm for bringing the heathen natives of the New World within the ecclesiastical fold of the Old. The French adventurers, like their Spanish compeers, marked their landing-places on the new continent by the erection of wooden crosses and of pillars surmounted by the arms of the sovereign of France. Such symbols implied that the French explorers, no less than the Spanish discoverers, claimed to be European missionaries of the settled order of things at home, both in Church and State. In point of fact, the French explorers were soon moved by quite other hopes; it was small part of their ultimate ambition slavishly to reproduce on American soil the institutions of their mother-country. Yet the material results of the colonial aspirations of France through the wonderful century look so puny, when they are compared with the triumphal issue of the Spanish effort, that the superficial observer might well be pardoned for treating the whole series of early French experiments as futilities signifying nothing.

Closer investigation throws another light on the story of French endeavour. Sixteenth-century Frenchmen never acquired the priceless practical arts of colonial organization of which the sixteenth-century Spaniard enjoyed the mastery as if by intuition. But the French mind was then, as always, more accessible than the Spanish to broad original ideas. Out of the early sporadic expeditions across the Atlantic of Norman, Breton, and French-Basque mariners, there gradually grew a series of conceptions about America which were quite alien to the Spanish spirit, and were as big with meaning for after ages as the material spoils of Spain. Fot the moment French aspirations either found no record on the American map or were inscribed there very faintly, but French ideas about America proved in the long run hardly less memorable than the consummated conquest of Spain.

French minds first matured the notion of colonizing with Europeans the wintry latitudes of the northern continent which lay beyond the sunlit range of Spanish ambition. The vision had already flitted across English and Portuguese brains; English aspiration was subsequently to make it a permanent and an imposing reality, but France first gave the fancy definite shape. Other conceptions which French intelligence especially cherished and developed were cast in more philosophic or speculative moulds. Frenchmen eagerly credited native American society with simplicity of life and strict adherence to natural law; the culture of the Old World was seething with corruption, and its only chance of cure lay in assimilating the purity of the New World. An even more stimulating French conception breathed the confident faith that the thinly peopled paradises of the West were destined to give asylum to those who were yearning at home for a liberty of thought or action which the existing polity of Europe denied them. Such ideas of life and liberty reflected more or less distinctly phases of enlightenment which were peculiarly characteristic of the liberality of the French Renaissance. Something of their inception may be traced to foreign suggestion. More's *Utopia* enshrines cognate speculation. But France contrived to stamp her American ideas with her own individuality, and England learned of French teachers the crowning conception of the New World as the unfettered land of freedom.

The French endeavoured during the sixteenth century to give practical effect to this trinity of conceptions. They sought to prove by experiment the capacity of Europeans to live in the frozen zone; they taught by active example faith in the innocence of native America, and in the boundless opportunity of liberty on American soil. It was such notions which brightened French colonial philosophy alike in its infancy and its manhood. At the outset the attempts to put these ideas into practice reaped only tragedy. The record is permeated by frustrated hopes. But in spite of the chill of early disappointment, none of the aspirations which America bred in the French mind perished altogether. All in due time blossomed into flower, ripened, indeed, into rich fruit. The French conception of the 'simple life' of America and of the beneficence of nature's reign there bore the least opulent harvest; yet it excited that fruitful kind of scepticism regarding the meaning of civilized progress which Rousseau was to systematize in the eighteenth century; it generated a rational interest in aboriginal history, and a humanity in the treatment of the natives which lay beyond the mental range of most of the conquering Spaniards. The fertility of the other two conceptions is more obvious.

The hope of a vast European settlement amid North American snows issued in the imposing settlement of Canada; while the French vision of America as a limitless expanse of liberty, although it merely flashed like an insubstantial pageant over the early colonial history of France, acquired lasting substance in the momentous colonial ventures of Puritan England.

II

It is my main aim to sketch here the conception of liberty which Frenchmen came to reckon indigenous to American soil, and to indicate the effects which that conception worked on the Elizabethan spirit. In the middle distance of the picture there gleams the allied fancy of the golden age of innocence which glorified native America in French eyes. In the background there looms French adventure in the extreme north of the American continent which preceded the birth of both the emancipatory and the Utopian ideals, and, after a brief period of suspense, marched onward to effective victory. The perspective of history requires brief preliminary notice of these impressive features of the scene, amid which the French notion of New-World freedom grew to maturity.

Frenchmen's attention was first drawn to the northern territories of America by very prosaic motives—by the expectation of finding new fishing grounds, for which their scent was keener than that of the other maritime peoples of Europe. The early predominance of Breton and French Basque in the North American fisheries is indicated on the earliest American maps by the title of Cape Breton, which was crudely bestowed for all time on an island off the Nova Scotian coast, and by the Basque appellation of Baccalaos (i.e. codfish), which was borne by the sea-girt territory of Canada through the early years of the sixteenth century. But the exploits of French fishermen off Newfoundland and Labrador quickly generated in France the larger hope of a north-west waterway, which should conduct French enterprise to the imaginary empire of Cathay. English and Portuguese pilots, Italian and German geographers, had long vaguely suggested a north-west passage to the fabled treasury of the East. It was French mariners who first put the theory to a sustained test. South America had already aroused their curiosity, but it was in North America that they achieved their first genuine triumphs of exploration.

Francis I, who absorbed the venturesome spirit of the French Renaissance, was ambitious of extending French power at sea. When he was warned that Spain and Portugal had already divided the New World among themselves, he replied by asking to see Adam's will in order to acquaint himself with the original terms of the bequest. Under the French king's patronage, the Italian pilot, Giovanni de Verrazano, surveyed, at close quarters, the North American coast. He passed from Florida to Newfoundland in the vain quest of a north-west avenue to wealth. He succeeded in outlining North American territory on map and globe with a precision that had no precedent. By his pencil for the first time the title of Nova Gallia or New France was written on the American continent, and places so familiar under their subsequent designations as Charleston (South Carolina), Newport (Rhode Island), and Portsmouth (New Hampshire), were given a 'local habitation'. Six decades afterward the records of Verrazano's experiences helped to fire belated endeavour in Elizabethan England.

This Franco-Italian achievement was quickly surpassed in its own sphere of activity by the experiment of a mariner of pure Breton blood. Jacques Cartier, of St. Malo, first crossed the Atlantic in 1534 in a fixed resolve to sail the north-west passage. For eight years he clung persistently to hopes of triumph. The outcome of his efforts belied his expectations. Something better than he anticipated was achieved. A great tract of Canadian territory was explored and described, The first foundations were laid within the zone of snow and ice of a spacious and prosperous French colony under the established law and religion of France. In his second, and again in his third expedition Cartier spent more than a year on Canadian soil. He learned by experience the rigours of the wintry climate. Yet he pronounced the country capable of conquest and settlement by the French. On the shores of the Gulf of St. Lawrence he set up, in the presence of a great assembly of natives, the heraldic symbol of the *fleur-de-lis*, and he entered into friendly relations with the tribes who occupied the sites of Quebec and Montreal. His courteous attitude to the natives inaugurates a new tradition on the North American continent. His disinterested curiosity regarding their language and customs renders his narratives of travel the most enlightened of all early records of American exploration, and well fitted them to become text-books of Elizabethan enterprise.

The communistic ideal of the simple native life roused in Cartier keen admiration, and he brought home from his first expedition ten of the aborigines to teach his enlightened sovereign and fellow-countrymen new views of social conduct. Yet it was as a work of orthodox piety that Cartier mainly recommended the Canadian venture to his fellow-countrymen. He lost no opportunity of testifying his loyalty to his faith. His ambition was to spread among the American Indians the light of Rome, and he solemnly assured his sovereign, Francis I, that it was the will of God that he should teach them his religion. He adopted the Spanish custom of naming the places he discovered after saints or festivals of the Roman Church. The great island at the mouth of St. Lawrence's Gulf he called Assumption, because he descried it on the day consecrated to the Assumption of the Blessed Virgin. The Gulf of St. Lawrence he so designated because he entered it on the day of St. Lawrence, the Roman deacon and martyr.

Intense as was Cartier's spiritual ardour, sincere as was his sympathetic attitude to the natives, it was his persevering adherence to the northern trails which most boldly differentiated his achievement from that of the Spaniards, and gave it its importance in the future. The third and last expedition to North America, in which Cartier engaged, was not destined at the moment to fulfil his plan of establishing 'New France' in the north of the western hemisphere as firmly as 'New Spain' was rooted in the south. Cartier was not to blame for the want of success. A miscellaneous band of colonists sailed under the command of a lord of Picardy, Le Sieur de Roberval. The noble leader was formally appointed by the French Crown the first viceroy and lieutenant-general of Canada, and was also decorated with other titles drawn from native place-names of the region. Cartier, the pioneer, now filled a subordinate post. His noble chief proved unequal to his exalted office. The viceroy's chosen pilot, a heroic mariner of southern France, Jean Alphonse de Saintonge, had only enjoyed experience of Eastern and tropical seas. The French colonists' knowledge and equipment yielded for the time to the strain of the climatic conditions, and Cartier failed to retrieve the situation.

The last ambitious attempt of Cartier and his companions to erect a Canadian viceroyalty thus ended in apparent failure. But there were pregnant compensations. The country was never again completely shut to French trade. Thenceforward French merchants fetched from North America year by year rich skins and furs. The French fishing fleets off the coast grew larger annually and returned home with heavier spoils. More than half a century was still to pass away while individual Frenchmen, fired by commercial ambition, made inland excursions summer after summer. But at the end of the period of probation French dominion over Canada was to emerge full-fledged.

III

Great French literature always kept in close touch with French colonial effort and spurred it onward. The magnetic attraction which the American North possessed for Cartier and his fellow-sailors found an echo in the later pages of Rabelais. That master comedian expounded fantastically the whole spirit of the age, and kept the essence of it alive through many generations. It is a strange medley of current maritime experience which Pantagruel undergoes on his voyage from the port of Thalasse to the country of Bacbuc, where lies the shrine of the Divine Bottle. But the author crudely fuses with his heterogeneous news from East and West the current story of North American exploration. Rabelais's Thalasse is Cartier's St. Malo; Rabelais's Captain Brayer is the hero himself. Many grotesque sounds and sights which afflict Pantagruel distort very slightly the records of Cartier's experience off Newfoundland or Labrador. So, too, the adventures which Rabelais puts to the credit of Xenomanes, Pantagruel's strangely learned hydrographer, reflect the moving accidents which befell Cartier's rival, Jean Alphonse of Saintonge, who piloted to Canada Le Sieur de Roberval, the first French viceroy of Canada.

Jean Alphonse, although a somewhat shadowy figure in the history of exploration, left as marked an impression as Cartier himself on the French literature of his epoch. He penned his own gallant story, in which a great poet of the time, Mellin de St. Gelais, betrayed an even deeper interest than Rabelais acknowledged. Not merely did St. Gelais defray the expenses of publishing Jean Alphonse's record, but he commended in original prefatory verse the seamanship which disclosed unsuspected marvels of ocean, heaven, and earth. It was such sort of literary fuel which ministered to the flame of French maritime energy in North America.

The work of Rabelais and St. Gelais lived long, but the authors passed away long before Cartier's mantle found a fit wearer. Samuel de Champlain, who came, like Roberval's pilot, Jean Alphonse, from the neighbourhood of La Rochelle, ultimately proved to be the most successful of all French explorers or colonists of North America. It was in cruises along the West Indies and Mexico, at the extreme end of the sixteenth century, that he won his spurs. There he gave earnest of his sagacity by suggesting the formation of a canal through the Isthmus of Panama. That project, which had already occurred to a Biscayan pilot, has waited long for realization. Subsequently Champlain faced the more familiar problem of a short way to Asia by a north-west passage. But he did not set a foot on North American soil until the year of Queen Elizabeth's death, when England, at length dimly conscious of her colonial destiny, had commenced her own gallant attack on the geographical puzzle. Then Champlain's companions set out to enforce a trade monopoly which the Crown of France had granted them over the natural products of Canada. But Champlain subordinated mercantile hopes to his passion for discovery. He pursued an original inland clue. His bold endeavours first brought within the ken of Europeans the mighty chain of Canadian lakes. The existing town of Quebec was his foundation. His quest well served the assertion of French sovereignty over Canada. Although British political rivalry for a time rendered the issue doubtful, the French claim was formally admitted before Champlain's death. When he breathed his last in Quebec in 1637, he knew that genuine fruit had come of the aspirations which Cartier formulated, and he and his companions revived and developed. At length a French province was established, with boundless possibilities of expansion, about the mysterious oceans and lakes of the far north. French maritime energy had aimed first at new fishing grounds in the north, and then at a rapid seaway to Eastern opulence. Finally, its scope broadened, under stress of commercial instinct, into a colonial empire. The victory had been won over snow and ice which looked impenetrable.

IV

The French attack on North America in the sixteenth century consisted of a series of brilliant reconnaissances. It was no continuous campaign and never absorbed the whole of French colonial effort. American territory lying farther to the south from the outset divided French colonial aspirations. Through the early, and especially through the middle, years of the century, it was to Brazil or to Florida that philosophic and religious speculation drew some of the most enlightened hopes of France.

The early associations of France and Brazil form a somewhat obscure episode in the history of the New World. Their beginnings can be vaguely traced to a period anterior to the first Spanish landing in South America. But certainty is only reached after the Spanish monopolists of empire abandoned Brazil to Portuguese rivals in the first year of the sixteenth century. That measureless region was sixteen times the size of France, and not very much smaller than the whole of Europe. The Portuguese long exerted mere nominal control of their unwieldy American province. The restricted scope of the organized government of Portugal gave opportunity for unlicensed invasion, of which French adventurers took much advantage, both before and after they had turned their attention to the less tractable north.

No sooner had the Portuguese set up their first outpost at San Salvador (Bahia de Todos or Santos), the midmost point of the long, winding Brazilian coast, than a brave Norman adventurer, Captain de Gonneville, of Honfleur, was driven by adverse winds from the African passage to a distant point on the expansive Brazilian main. There, in accord with Spanish ritual, he planted, in view of the sea, on Easter Day, 1504, amid beating of drums, blowing of trumpets, firing of guns, and intoning of prayer, a cross thirty-five feet high, on which he carved the names of the Pope, Julius II, and of his sovereign, King Louis XII of France.

French sovereignty in the New World was asserted with the accepted formalities on Brazilian soil for the first time. Cartier's like ceremonial procedure in the north was anticipated by De Gonneville. The captain of Honfleur himself stayed in Brazil only six months, and never revisited the land; but his experience and spoils stimulated French hopes of the future. He brought home with him red dye-wood and brilliantly plumed birds. His cargo appealed to his countrymen's sense of colour, and sharpened French interest in the New World. There also accompanied De Gonneville the son of a Brazilian chieftain, who was the first of a long line of American natives to visit sixteenth-century France. His presence excited vast curiosity about an unsuspected phase of human life. The Catholic Church was quick to claim the captive's soul, and he was baptized. The geniality of his French host's temperament and the pliancy of his own reconciled him to his new environment. He soon married his captor's daughter, and founded a family which long flourished in France. Such a precedent had no precise sequel. But it challenged ancient prejudice and tended to broaden sympathy.

Until the sixteenth century well rounded its meridian France displayed no small zest in maintaining association with Brazil and the Brazilians. Cartier schooled himself for his passage northward by engaging in an expedition to Brazil. Ships from St. Malo, Dieppe, and La Rochelle constantly challenged the artillery of Spanish fleets in order to fetch home from the Brazilian forests rich wood and birds, rare fruits and plants, which found a ready market among fashionable purveyors of Paris. Natives, in small numbers, invariably returned in the train of the voyagers, and were warmly welcomed by clergy and laity. Cartier, in bringing Eskimos from the north, was conforming to a custom which was in force already among those sailing to southern seas. In the Cathedral of Rouen and the chief church of St. Malo Brazilians received from time to time rites of baptism. An early sixteenth-century *bas relief*, which may still be seen in the Church of St. Jacques, at Dieppe, shows a group of Brazilian natives, their heads decorated with plumes of feathers. The carved stone was the gift of a rich merchant of the port, who organized much maritime exploration. The highest ranks of society showed active interest in the native visitors. In the middle of the century members of a Brazilian tribe called Tupinamba took prominent part in the pageants which

celebrated the entry of the King of France (Henri II) and
Catherine de Medici into Rouen. The scenery of Brazil
was artificially reproduced on the banks of the Seine. In a
mimic forest the Brazilian chief addressed his followers in
their own tongue, and the savages gave an imitation of
native modes of warfare. Twice in the following year did
American aborigines play a like part in the ceremonials of
the French court, and on the latest of these occasions the
most enlightened Frenchman of his epoch, Montaigne,
was moved to inquire of one of the strangers his impressions of civilized France. The American confided to the
French philosopher his difficulty in accounting for the
presence of rich and poor, of well-fed and ill-fed, side by
side. He wondered at the respect which was paid by
strong, bearded men to weak, beardless youths on grounds
of high hereditary rank.

In his romance of *Utopia* Sir Thomas More pictured
the ideal polity and economy of a primal age of golden
purity, which he located in an imaginary island near
Brazil. Rabelais borrowed literally some of More's invented topography of the New World. The direct intercourse of Frenchmen with their Brazilian guests reani-
mated in France More's beatific vision of an American
Utopia, and gave it new strength and reality. Montaigne's
conversation with the Brazilian suggested to him an half-
ironic eulogy of the natural state of man and a new social
philosophy.

In this region of speculation Montaigne had many
companions. The most melodious and thoughtful poet of
the French Renaissance, Ronsard, versified the theory of
uncivilized man's purity. Free from sin or fear of law,
ignorant of the names of virtue or vice, of senate or king,
the natives, according to Ronsard's verse, pursued a life
of unsullied pleasure, cherishing their own idiosyncrasies
and exercising a rare faculty of self-control (*seul maistre
de soi*). The perfection of social order was reached in the
communistic ideal of savage Brazil, where possession of the
earth was no more restricted than ownership of the air or

the water of the sea. The aboriginal American was no degenerate. He still cultivated the Garden of Eden. It was not the European who could teach the American how to live; the European must crave that instruction of the American.

> Ils vivent maintenant en leur âge doré. . . .
> Vivez, heureuse gent, sans peine et sans souci,
> Vivez ioyeusement, ie voudrais vivre ainsi.

The poetic fancy long scorned all scientific refutation, and fostered a spirit of criticism which touched the oldest of religious, social, and political institutions in France. Elizabethan thought and literature showed traces of the conception, which travelled far beyond French boundaries. The powerful impulse which Montaigne's argumentative presentation gave the theory coloured some of Bacon's speculation, and found a faint echo in the work of Shakespeare.

V

Meanwhile religious revolution threatened France, and her social and civil equilibrium tottered. The claims of the Church of Rome to the allegiance of Christians were called in question throughout Europe. The new model of Christianity, which Luther had devised in Germany, was welcomed with enthusiasm by masses of Frenchmen, and was carried even further from the original pattern by the zeal of a Frenchman, Calvin. The French reformers of religion, who adopted the designation of Huguenot from the German word *Eidgenossen* (i. e. confederate), were soon to acknowledge discipleship to none but Calvin. In north, south, and west bands of Frenchmen abjured the old papal traditions. A Presbyterian form of church government was adopted, and congregations which lacked neither rank, nor wealth, nor intelligence multiplied in the great centres of population. The Catholic Church appealed to the French king to crush by physical force this rebellion of the spirit which stirred thought of change in the political as well as in the religious sphere. A furious persecution of the Huguenots was initiated. The Church denounced the apostates as pestilent heretics, and not obscurely recommended to the secular power a policy of massacre. The law of the land soon prohibited the Huguenots' form of worship, made it a penal offence to acknowledge or publish their opinions, questioned their title to property, banished them from public employment, overwhelmed with heavy penalties any who harboured them, and bribed informers to bring forward damnatory evidence. Neither the Protestants in England under Queen Mary nor the Catholics there under Queen Elizabeth were exposed to so merciless a storm of penal legislation as the Huguenots of France endured in the middle of the sixteenth century. But neither fire nor sword, neither fine nor imprisonment, killed the new creed. Its growth was very slightly retarded. So far from dying, it developed new means of life.

The poetic theory of the persistence in America of the primeval age of innocence seems first to have moved a section of the Huguenots, when the persecution was nearing its full tide, to look across the Atlantic for relief from immediate torment and for opportunity of final enfranchisement. The New World, which was imagined to preserve human nature in its primordial simplicity, might well serve as an asylum for the Christian faith, which had at length been restored to its original purity. The persecuted Huguenots were easily persuaded to identify the uncorrupted evil of America with their land of promise. Many of them proclaimed it their mission to rebuild God's violated temple in the Far West. Their hope of enjoying free scope for their own spiritual development was sustained and strengthened by the consolation that they would be spreading spiritual salvation among the innocent heathen, who did not yet number among their felicities true knowledge of Christ. The Catholic invaders had infected large numbers of the aborigines of the new continent with their erroneous teaching, and their missionary triumphs provoked loud exultation among the servants of Rome. It was the destined duty of a Protestant immigration to provide an antidote in the recovered Christian truth.

In the highest quarters of the state the French conception of America as the future home of Protestant freedom first found substantial encouragement. Coligny, the admiral of France, and a statesman of sagacity, long cherished sympathy with the Huguenot faith before he openly declared himself the militant chief of the Huguenot movement. It was, when Coligny's relations with his Protestant fellow-countrymen were still in doubt, that he lent the weight of his great name to a scheme for founding a Protestant empire of liberty on the other side of the Atlantic. A man of paradoxical character came forward to put the aspiration to practical tests. Nicholas Durand, Seigneur de Villegagnon, had, a quarter of a century before, been one of Calvin's fellow-students at the University of Paris. He had since seen both naval and military service in many parts of Europe, and had risen to the position of vice-admiral of Brittany. Acquiring a taste for theological controversy, he acknowledged the force of the Huguenot argument. But abnormal vanity played a prominent part in his visionary and mystical temperament, and the event proved that his religious convictions rested on shifting foundations. As a bold and efficient naval officer, he attracted the favour of Coligny, and his patron approved a scheme of his propounding to raise the Huguenot flag in South America.

Brazil, the spacious province of South America, whither a long succession of French mariners had already voyaged, was Villegagnon's chosen haven. In the summer of 1555 a little fleet of three vessels, under his command, brought from Havre and Dieppe to the beautiful bay of Rio de Janeiro a hundred Protestant Frenchmen, after a four months' voyage. Christening the land 'La France Antarctique', Villegagnon formed, on a palm-clad island in the bay, a settlement which was named by him Coligny, but is now called after himself. The tropical vegetation and the strange splendour of the flowers and birds satisfied him and his fellow-voyagers for a moment that they had reached the heavenly paradise. But the expedition was ill-equipped for the practical needs of colonial life. A library of theological books, which Villegagnon brought with him, proved a poor substitute for stores and implements of building and agriculture which he left behind. In a few months Villegagnon sent most of his companions home to crave of Coligny adequate supplies and reinforcements of Protestant enthusiasm.

The most significant message that Villegagnon's envoys carried to Europe was addressed not to French laymen, but to the spiritual chief of the Huguenot faith. It was of Calvin in Geneva, whither the reformer had been driven by persecution in France, that Villegagnon begged help in building a Protestant empire in Brazil. Calvin was by accident absent when Villegagnon's messengers arrived in Switzerland. But French and Swiss ministers and magistrates welcomed them to Geneva, and at a special service in the Church of St. Pierre, there was preached the obligation to plant in Brazil a free community of Calvinists. Fervent thanks were offered to God for having given French lovers of the true doctrine a home where threats of suppression lost significance and where God's saints might reign in peace.

A large band of Genevans offered themselves as colonists, and two ministers of Calvin's Church, Pierre Richer and Guillaume Chartier, accepted the posts of chaplains. These two men were the earliest ordained ministers of the Reformed Church who reached the American continent. Calvin, dreaming of the day when priests should fill the places of kings, gave the enterprise his blessing. Coligny invited the leader of the Genevan contingent to visit him on his way through France, and dismissed him with encouraging courtesies. Hundreds of Huguenot enthusiasts, including students and mechanics, flocked to Honfleur, where the embarkation took place. On the eve of their departure the emigrants suffered a cruel reminder of the murderous rancour which their new faith bred. While a party of them was celebrating the Lord's Supper in their lodgings, an angry Catholic mob broke in, and one of their number was slain. But at length, on the 20th of November 1556, three vessels, crowded with the Protestant zealots, put out to sea. The pure Christian faith was openly crossing the Atlantic to expand and fructify under new skies. With the emigrants and their preachers and teachers there sailed six French boys and six French girls, who were to learn the native language and were in due course to interpret the faith to the aborigines. No Frenchwomen had previously ventured on the American continent. Every hope of the Pilgrim Fathers was stirring in these French adventurers of 1556, although sixty years and more were to elapse before the *Mayflower* left Plymouth Sound.

A four month's voyage brought the Calvinist zealots to Villegagnon's settlement on Coligny Island, off Rio de Janeiro (in the spring of 1557). Villegagnon gave the new-comers a fitting Puritan welcome. He warned them against vice and bade them flinch not from the simple life. He promised a refuge to all persecuted believers in a land which was free from fear of king, emperor, or potentate. Leading the newcomers to a chapel fashioned on a Gene-van model in the centre of the island, he bade all sing in unison (in the version of the French Protestant poet, Clement Marot) one of David's psalms of exile (Psalm v):

> Mon Dieu, guide moy et convoye
> Par ta bonté, que ne soys mis
> Soubz la main de mes ennemis,
> Et dresse devant moy ta voye,
> Que ne fourvoye.

Then the Genevan minister, Richer, preached with fervour from Psalm xxviii, verse 4: 'One thing have I desired of the Lord, that will I seek after; that I may dwell in the house of the Lord all the days of my life.'

The hope that the pathless Brazilian forests would provide the vanguard of Christianity with the security that Europe denied it seemed for a time on the road to realization. Ministers soon wrote home to Calvin that the colony resembled the Christian household which Nymphas founded in the time of the apostles (Colossians iv. 15). They assured friends at home that Calvinism was destined to be the religion of America. But the perversity of the chieftain, Villegagnon, stirred clouds on this sunlit horizon. Liberally interpreting Calvin's theocratic theory of government, he constituted himself high priest and chief magistrate. In all that pertained to morality or theology he declared himself sole arbiter. Extravagance in dress or diet became a criminal offence. He revised the ritual of worship, and suffered no religious service to conclude without a sermon of an hour's duration. He himself cultivated a gift for extemporaneous prayer, which he exercised mercilessly.

The only recreation in which Villegagnon suffered any to indulge was discussion of recondite points of dogmatic theology. Thence came grievous peril to the whole colonial fabric which had been raised under tropical skies. The theological debates led to dissensions which spread from minutiæ to fundamentals. The despotic ruler began an inquiry into the fitness of American corn for use in the manufacture of sacramental bread, and then challenged the mysterious problem of transubstantiation. Villegagnon himself grew distracted by perplexities, and Pastor Chartier was ordered home to invite Calvin's judgement. The minister took with him an incongruous gift of ten Brazilian natives for the French king. Meanwhile a young colonist from the Paris Sorbonne, who was no mean dialectician, acquired a singular influence over Villegagnon, and the despot's Calvinist convictions showed signs of weakening. The poison spread quickly. Villegagnon renounced allegiance to Calvin and pronounced him a heretic.

Staunch Calvinists made an attempt to depose the

erratic and despotic governor, and when they failed, sought a new asylum on the mainland. There the natives welcomed them with warmth, and the loyal Huguenots consoled themselves for their companions' apostasy by missionary energy. The natives delighted in the Frenchmen's psalmody, and heard sermons in an unknown tongue with exemplary patience. Villegagnon meanwhile passed beyond redemption. Four rebellious Protestants who approached him with an appeal for peace he condemned to death. They were flung by his order into the sea. In such paradoxical circumstances was the martyrdom of Protestants inaugurated on the American continent.

Finally, almost all the settlers returned to Brittany, after a voyage which exposed them to tragic hardships. Villegagnon followed in their train, and a handful of adherents whom he left behind on Coligny Island, fell a prey to Portuguese vengeance three years later (1560). The Portuguese tardily awoke to the trespass of Frenchmen on their territory and, swooping down on the survivors of Villegagnon's colony, killed or imprisoned them all. Amid massacre and theological broils the first endeavour to settle the Reformed Church in America came to a violent end.

Not that Huguenot hopes of Brazil were thereby quenched. Huguenot sailors of Normandy were ill-content to abandon to the sway of Romanist Portugal the land which had been watered with Calvinist blood, but they adopted methods of asserting their pretensions which hardly entitled them to success. Religious scruples did not deter Huguenot enthusiasts from overhauling unprotected Portuguese ships on the Brazilian voyage in order to kill or drive into the sea priests or Jesuits who were found aboard. Guns and ammunition were regularly sold by Huguenot buccaneers to Brazilian natives. The desperate policy was pursued to the end of the century. But it failed to retrieve the situation that Villegagnon's perverseness was thought to have flung away.

Yet there remains to mention one pleasant trace of the

Huguenots' association with Brazil. The natives long cherished tender memories of their guests. Near the close of the century, fortune condemned an English sailor, Anthony Knivet, to many years' wanderings among the aborigines of South America; and when he fell in with a Brazilian tribe, a self-protecting instinct led him to feign to be a Frenchman. Before his eyes his native hosts slew his Portuguese companions, but they gave him kindly hospitality in the belief that he belonged to a nation whom they loved.

VI

The tragedy of Villegagnon in Brazil had not dismayed Coligny, whose Huguenot sympathies were no longer disguised. When those who had remained steadfast to Calvinism came back from Brazil, they found eight hundred sympathizers ready to carry on the great Huguenot mission across the Atlantic, while it was estimated that ten thousand more were willing, at need, to risk in the cause their lives and property. Such widespread zeal was not easily balked, and, within five years of Villegagnon's failure, the old hope of a Huguenot empire of the West was flaming more brightly than before. But it was not to Brazil, where the Portuguese were now active against intruders, that Coligny and the projectors of a second Huguenot colony turned their gaze.

News recently spread through France that a tract of country in the northern continent excelled in luxuriance and fragrance the fields and forests of Brazil. The territory was known as Florida, because the Spaniards had discovered it on Palm Sunday (Pascha Florida), and not, as the word was often interpreted, because of the region's wealth of flowers. Florida then included within its ill-defined boundaries, in addition to the Southern State of the American Union which now alone bears the appellation, an expanse of land reaching as far north as Maryland, if not beyond. Many events which contemporary writers of the sixteenth century locate in Florida really took place in what are now the States of North or South Carolina, or Virginia. Spaniards had made many spasmodic attempts to occupy this vague country which they had very partially explored. In 1560 the smiling pastures were still in undisputed possession of sparse native tribes, and were believed in Europe to lie open to all comers. Many Frenchmen were prone to identify the rumoured beauty of the scenery and the reputed mineral wealth with the Garden of Eden or the Land of Ophir. The Huguenots were easily brought to imagine that there a final refuge had been divinely appointed for their spotless faith. At the same time Frenchmen, who were not Huguenots, moved by jealousy of Spanish predominance, favoured a project of peaceful conquest which gave promise of a colonial empire of rare natural fertility.

Jean Ribaut, of a good family of Dieppe, that nursery of expert sailors, made the first step forward. He was a master of seacraft, and had fully identified himself with the Huguenot movement. To him Coligny entrusted the command of the first Huguenot expedition to Florida. Joined by Calvinists of all walks in life, he steered his fleet on an original course which avoided the West Indian islands. Without sighting land, he reached, in little more than two months, the shores of North America near the present town of St. Augustine in Florida. The adjacent St. John's River, which Ribaut, like some Spanish predecessors, confusedly took to be the Jordan, he christened the River of May, because on May day he discovered it. On its bank he set up, with accustomed ceremonies, a stone pillar inscribed with the insignia of the French monarch, Charles IX; the pillar was soon worshipped by the natives as an idol. Thus the French occupation of Florida was inaugurated.

Travelling a little to the north, Ribaut reached a spot on the South Carolina coast, which he called Port Royal, and it is still so called on many maps. On a neighbouring island he finally placed his Huguenot settlement, naming it Charles Fort, after his sovereign. That site is now occupied by the town of Beaufort. As soon as the foundations of the colony were laid, Ribaut and his chief officers took leave of their companions and sailed home to consult Protestant friends about large plans of future developments.

In France the Huguenot strife had developed into a furious civil war in which the Catholic forces were gaining the upper hand. It was no time to pursue a visionary project across the Atlantic. Ribaut, in despair, retired to England, and there published a spirited account of his hopes and experiences in Florida, which stirred the emulation of Protestant Englishmen. For a time Ribaut abandoned active colonial endeavour.

The trouble at home gave small opportunity of sending out assistance to those whom Ribaut had left behind in South Carolina. But after two years the domestic strife subsided, and Coligny then equipped a larger fleet than any that went before to relieve and extend the Florida colony. Ribaut was still absent from France, and the chief command was bestowed on his chief companion in the first expedition, René de Laudonnière, a pious Huguenot nobleman, who had seen service at sea, and had the merits and defects of a confident and religious naval officer. He was bidden take with him none but God-fearing Calvinists. Small attention was paid to the more useful characteristics of prospective colonists. An artist, Le Moyne, was of the company, together with noblemen, soldiers, lawyers, and artisans. Practical agriculturists were not invited. Amid psalmody the expedition left Havre, and to the like accompaniment it disembarked in Florida near St. John's River. Ribaut and Laudonnière had landed on the same spot two years before, but had not tarried there. Now Laudonnière laid there the site of a new settlement, which he christened La Caroline. That title was an accidental anticipation of the name of Carolina, which English occupiers a century later bestowed on the adjacent territory in honour of their king, Charles II of England.

Of the older Huguenot settlers in South Carolina no

trace was found. They had rebelled against their leader, and through ignorance of colonizing arts, had been reduced to helpless starvation, which they tried to alleviate by eating one another. A few survivors built a pinnace, on which they ventured out to sea, to be rescued by an English vessel and to be landed at an English port. Unknowingly Laudonnière had crossed the path of these colonial derelicts on his recent outward voyage.

Laudonnière's colony suffered most of the torments of its predecessor. His companions despised manual labour, and, when supplies were exhausted, threatening famine bred mutiny. The malcontents were expelled, and sailed away to excite, by acts of piracy off the West Indian islands, the perilous resentment of Spain. Laudonnière's loyal adherents sought comfort in their sufferings in prayer and psalmody. The land echoed with Marot's pious verse, and friendly natives, catching the sacred tunes, adapted them to their pagan rites. For a generation afterward, Protestant melody haunted the aboriginal habitations of the land. With the natives in his near neighbourhood Laudonnière cultivated cordial relations. But he challenged disaster by taking their side in warfare with more distant tribes.

After a year the prospect of the Huguenot settlers looked black. Cut off from home, they grew sullen and listless. Suddenly relief offered from an unexpected quarter. An English expedition under Sir John Hawkins, which was returning from a slave-trading errand in the West Indies, coasted along Florida. On one of the English ships was a Dieppe pilot, who had brought Ribaut out two years before. Communications were easily opened with his compatriots on shore. Laudonnière welcomed Hawkins with eagerness, and declared him to be 'a good and charitable man.' But, to the dismay of his companions, he declined the English captain's offer to carry him and his colonists home. He was content with purchasing of his visitor a small ship, some foodstuffs, and wax for the making of candles; he gave in exchange guns and ammunition, of which he blindly thought that he had no need.

Within three weeks of Hawkins's departure the scene suffered further change. Reports of Laudonnière's misgovernment had reached France. It was said that he was playing the tyrant, and was counterfeiting royal power. Ribaut, recalled from exile in England, was ordered out as the king's lieutenant, at the head of a large company of new settlers, to supersede the alleged pretender. After leaving Dieppe, one of Ribaut's ships spent three weeks on repairs off the Isle of Wight and spread intelligence of the venture in England. Ribaut crossed the ocean without adventure. Laudonnière received him with natural misgiving. But the days of the Huguenot colony were numbered. Spain was preparing to strike a fatal blow at the heretic invasion of her imperial sphere of dominion.

Five days after Ribaut's arrival in Florida, fifteen Spanish vessels, carrying 2,600 men, hove in sight of the luckless Huguenots, under the command of a fanatical Catholic, Don Pedro Menendez de Avila. Laudonnière wrangled with Ribaut over lines of defence, but possibilities of resistance were negligible. With a revolting brutality, which has few parallels in history, all but a score of the Huguenot colonists were massacred by the Spaniards. Not as Frenchmen, but as heretics, wrote the Spanish leader, were they done to death. Ribaut cheerfully marched to his doom chanting a psalm.

Laudonnière, with a score of Frenchmen, succeeded in escaping the barbarous slaughter of his compatriots and co-religionists. They safely emerged from the peril of an Atlantic voyage in a small boat. By error the distressed mariners landed on the coast of Wales. From Swansea they made their way to London. Laudonnière gratefully acknowledged hospitalities on the road, and received assistance which enabled him finally to reach his native land. One of his companions, the artist, Jacques le Moyne, who brought from Florida a valuable collection of sketches and maps, was befriended by the English Puritans and set up a studio in Blackfriars.

Meanwhile, the French Government vainly sought

through diplomatic channels some redress of the cruel wrong which Spain's agents had wrought on the Frenchmen in Florida. Private patriotism devised cruder but more effective means of vengeance. Le Sieur Dominique de Gourgues, a passionate Gascon, enlisted a troop of desperadoes, and, convoying them in three small vessels from La Rochelle to La Caroline, surprised the Spanish occupants. Relentlessly there was meted out to them the same barbarous penalties which they had already exacted of Ribaut and his men. The natives welcomed the avenging host with snatches of the psalm tunes which the slaughtered Huguenots had taught them, and showed active sympathy with the work of French retaliation. 'Not as Spaniards, nor as mariners, but as murderers, robbers, and traitors, did the Spanish conquerors suffer,' declared Gourgues, in grim mockery of the words which the Spaniards had applied to their Huguenot victims. Though Gourgues was himself no Protestant, he had punished Spain's murderous assault on the Huguenot settlement. The Huguenot town of La Rochelle gave him a triumphant reception on his return from his deed of blood.

Huguenot statesmen subsequently meditated a further experiment in Florida on the old pattern. But little came of such design save lawless buccaneering, which lacked official sanction. Among the crews of the French privateers, Calvinists commonly predominated, and they gave short shrift to Spanish priests and monks who fell into their clutches. But the formal settlement of the Huguenot colonist was stayed almost as effectually in Florida by Ribaut's murder as in Brazil by Villegagnon's apostasy.

The last of the early Huguenot efforts in America took a different direction and need not detain us here. By the end of the century the Huguenots had won toleration in France, and were exhibiting rare commercial aptitude. It was their mercantile ambition rather than their old ideal of liberty of faith which opened a new chapter in the history of their colonial endeavour. Abandoning past

hopes of Southern settlements in America, they revived,
mainly with a view to increase of trade, the earlier hopes
of a French empire in Canada. In 1603, when England
was at length turning to solve colonial problems for herself, a Huguenot leader of La Rochelle obtained a royal
charter granting him a monopoly of North American
commerce. The exclusive privilege excited the hostility
of private traders of Brittany and Normandy and it roused
resentment among Catholics. By sale or regrant the charter passed from hand to hand, and its successive holders,
aided by the contemporary discoveries of the heroic explorer, Champlain, gradually brought Canada under
French sway. Experience revealed practical difficulty in
keeping French colonial endeavour under Calvinist control. For a few years Protestants maintained the upper
hand. Then for a brief season toleration of Calvinist and
Catholic was enjoined on those who were responsible for
the Canadian government. But neither Protestant nor
Catholic took kindly in colonial life to that principle of
enlightenment. Between the two creeds there raged on
American soil a furious strife, which perplexed the natives,
whom both parties sought to bring into the Christian fold.
Huguenot captains were reluctant to release Catholic seamen from the psalm-singing and exercises in prayer which
were part of the Huguenot discipline both at sea and on
land. Catholics retaliated by obstructing Protestant worship. Finally, supreme power over Canada was acquired
by a patroness of the Jesuits, and her protégés converted
the North American colonies of France into outposts of
rigid Catholicism.

VII

Before this consummation was reached, England had
assimilated the colonial teaching of the Huguenots in
its early and most enlightened phase. At first the Elizabethans studied the Huguenot lesson listlessly, but, as the
colonial spirit gained robustness among them, they paid
it an earnest attention, which led to momentous con-

sequences. In the event Protestant England fully avenged in the seventeenth century all the injuries and rebuffs which Protestant France endured in the New World during the sixteenth.

The colonial teaching of the Huguenots reached the Elizabethans through many channels. Englishmen enjoyed opportunities of personal intercourse with some who had actively engaged in the French enterprises across the Atlantic, while the voluminous French literature, which reported at first hand the whole course of the moving Huguenot story, was rendered with singular promptness into English.

Elizabethan Englishmen came into close touch with the Huguenot colonists of Forida. Survivors of the first settlement were rescued from shipwreck by English mariners. Survivors of the second settlement landed at Swansea, and, trudging through the heart of England to London, were relieved in their destitution by English sympathizers. The martyred Ribaut spent in exile in the English capital nearly the whole of the two years which intervened between his first and his second voyage to Florida. Part of his time there he devoted to describing from his own experience 'the wonderful strange natures and manners of the people [of Florida], with the marvellous commodities and treasures of the country, as also the pleasant ports, havens, and ways thereunto, never found out before'. Though he wrote in French, his original narrative is now only extant in the English translation, which came out in 1563 with a dedication to the chief goldsmith of London, a leading alderman of the corporation, Sir Martin Bowes. Another actor on the Florida scene, who was hardly less imposing than Ribaut, figured, too, for a season on the English stage. The Gascon Gourgues's deed of vengeance was loudly acclaimed in England. Queen Elizabeth, responding to popular sentiment, invited him to her court, where he was regally entertained and consulted as to further assaults on Spanish prestige.

News of Ribaut's tragic fate spread through Elizabethan

England with lightning speed. A vivacious report of the massacre was quickly published in Paris by one of Ribaut's few surviving companions, Nicholas le Challeux, a Huguenot carpenter. Le Challeux's statement achieved instant popularity in an English translation. The humble author, on his journey out to Florida, had spent nearly three weeks in the Isle of Wight, and had made English friends there. Le Moyne, a second Huguenot survivor of the Spanish outrage, returned to Europe by way of England, and never left the country again. He was long a picturesque figure in the Huguenot colony of Blackfriars and enjoyed the patronage of Sir Walter Raleigh and Sir Philip Sidney. To Sidney's wife he dedicated a curious publication of drawings of beasts, birds, flowers, and fruits, and at Raleigh's expense he executed in colours a pictorial account of his American experience. When De Bry, the great Frankfort publisher, came to London to bargain with him for the purchase of his rich portfolio of sketches of Florida life and nature, the refugee declined to sell from a sense of loyalty to his English friends. But after his death his widow, ignoring his scruples, made over his artistic relics to the German dealer, who at once gave them to the cultured world of Continental Europe.

A complementary link between Huguenot and English colonial hopes was forged by the visits to Paris of Englishmen to whom the Huguenot adventures appealed very directly and who thirsted for precise knowledge of them. Richard Eden, the earliest English compiler of the foreign literature of New World travel, was, early in Elizabeth's reign, for no less than ten years secretary to a chieftain of the Huguenots, the Vidâme de Chartres. The Vidâme lived in Paris, although he often visited England to beg help for his persecuted sect, and he finally fled thither for good after the St. Bartholomew Massacre. Through nearly the whole period of the Florida adventure Eden was watching its ebb and flow at the headquarters of the Huguenot movement in France, while in the Vidâme's service. Other Englishmen emulated Eden's example.

Sir Humphrey Gilbert, when preparing his spirited plea for the settlement of North America by Englishmen, consulted in Paris the aged geographer, André Thevet, who had written a fanciful account of Villegagnon's strange exploits in Brazil. Thevet, who had been a friend of Rabelais, claimed to have visited Villegagnon in Brazil. His story, which betrayed a whimsical credulity, circulated in an English translation. A few years later a greater colonial propagandist of English race than Eden or even Gilbert, Richard Hakluyt, also spent five years in Paris as chaplain to the English embassy there. With infinite zeal he cultivated personal intercourse with all who could instruct him in the French experience of America. He corresponded with Cartier's kindred, he visited Thevet and reprinted the English version of Ribaut's record. The pettiness of the advances, which Protestantism, despite the Huguenot sacrifices, had made in America, compared ill in Hakluyt's mind with the triumphal progress of Catholicism under the protection of Spain. His Parisian sojourn served to excite the passionate energy with which he urged on Protestant England the duty of retrieving the Huguenot defeat. Sir Walter Raleigh's persevering attempt to colonize Virginia, which formed part of the vaguely defined territory then bearing the name of Florida, was a reply to Hakluyt's summons.

Great as was Sir Walter Raleigh's debt to Spanish example, the teaching of the Huguenots left on his mind abiding and fruitful traces. Hakluyt spread in France the notion that Raleigh was the hope of the Protestant cause in America. In 1586 there came out in Paris, in the French tongue, a collection of all the records of the Florida settlement, including not only Ribaut's narrative, but the reports of Laudonnière and of Gourgues, the avenger of the Huguenot massacre. The Huguenot editor dedicated the book to Raleigh, as the hero of colonial Protestantism. There mingled in those pages tales of adventurous exploits with pregnant comments on the theory and practice of colonization from religious, moral, and economic points of view. A year later Hakluyt published in London his own English translation of this 'notable history'. Again the dedication was addressed to Raleigh, who was adjured to redress in Virginia the Huguenot failure in Florida.

Meanwhile the Huguenot teaching acquired additional force from chance meetings of Huguenot sailors with Elizabethan adventurers in remote corners of South America. The mutual relations were invariably as cordial as those which distinguished the intercourse of Laudonnière and Sir John Hawkins in Florida in 1564. It was off the Isthmus of Panama that Francis Drake fell in with a Huguenot ship of Havre, whose captain brought him the first pathetic tidings of the St. Bartholomew Massacre, and gave him as proof of friendship a pair of pistols and a fair gilt scimitar. At Drake's invitation the Huguenot mariner joined him in an inland exploring raid through the Isthmus of Panama, so unreservedly did French and English Protestants acknowledge the unity of their cause. A quarter of a century later courtesies of like character were exchanged off Brazil by Sir James Lancaster, the adventurous voyager of London, and Captain Noyer, a merchant seaman of Dieppe, both of whom were raiding with Protestant zeal the Portuguese stations of the Brazilian coast. Through the same period Norman pilots of Calvinist sentiment readily found berths on Elizabethan fleets which were bound for the Spanish main. A pilot of Dieppe sailed with Sir John Hawkins in 1565. A pilot of Havre accompanied Sir Walter Raleigh to Guiana thirty years later. The Huguenot message repeatedly passed to the Elizabethan sailor by word of mouth.

It was in the Huguenot spirit that the Puritans of England, when penal legislation drove them from their homes, looked to America for protection and salvation. The vision of religious liberty in the New World was a Huguenot creation. It was slow to acquire stern enough sway over the minds of Englishmen to move them to action. But under stress of events the experiences of English Puritans fell into closer and closer agreement with those of the French Huguenots. Then the word written and spoken in France of the Calvinist colonies did penetrating work in England. The beginnings of New England were cast in the Huguenot mould. The great American project of Puritan England differed from the French schemes in Brazil and Florida neither in motive nor in principle, but in practical achievement and enduring triumph. From the colonial failures of Protestant France flowed the colonial successes of Protestant England.

THE AMERICAN INDIAN IN ELIZABETHAN ENGLAND

I

OF all the puzzles which the discovery of America offered Europe the riddle of the aborigines kindled profoundest perplexity. The secret is still well kept. The question whence the native races sprang has elicited, since its first propounding, a multiplicity of answers. But no response has enjoyed universal credit.

At the outset, the existence of an American people seemed hardly reconcilable with Holy Writ. Christian doctrine had never seriously challenged the popular notion that there flourished in remote corners of the earth fabulous monsters, which either combined in the same corporeal frame outward characteristics of man and beast, or were distinguished by hideous malformation or distortion of the normal human form. Pliny had handed down to the pretended medieval traveller, Sir John Mandeville, records, whose truth went unquestioned, of dog-headed and headless men, of giants and dwarfs, who dwelt in inaccessible fastnesses of Asia or Africa. But the American races confused counsel by their superficial resemblance in stature, complexion, and bodily structure to the normal population of the Old World. The colour of their skin increased the complexity of the problem. It was neither black like that of the African, nor dusky yellow like that of the Oriental. It was, as a rule, of russet or cinnamon hue, which was barely distinguishable from that of many inhabitants of Northern or Middle Europe. The tint of American complexion, indeed, often approximated much more closely to the so-called whitish tones of the English countenance than to the olive tinge of the Spanish. But in spite of the aboriginal American's apparent physiological affinity to Christian peoples, the Scriptures, which claimed to hold the key to all human history, wholly ignored him, and offered no manner of clue to his origin or development.

Theologians helplessly acknowledged the difficulty. The Bible pronounced Noah to be progenitor of all the normally proportioned human race, of every variety of colour. But the patriarch's sons, who were no more than three in number, were implicitly denied the fatherhood of the American people. From Shem, according to the Scriptures, descended all Asiatics, from Ham all Africans, and from Japhet all Europeans. No son of Noah was the avowed forefather of the Americans. Some cataclysmic migration from Europe, Asia, or Africa could alone account, if Noah's universal paternity were to go unassailed, for the peopling of the vast continent of the West. But no satisfactory record of any vast migration from the Old World to the New by way of either Atlantic or Pacific Ocean was known to divine or secular chronicles. Legendary wanderings of the lost tribes of Israel, or of the Trojans under Brutus, after the fall of Troy, were recalled by sixteenth-century inquirers. But these traditions failed to lighten the darkness.

Again, from the time of the first discoveries, there was inevitable doubt whether the American races, despite specious physiological affinities, came all of a single stock. They were seen to differ among themselves in custom, if not in speech, to an extent that lacked parallel, at any rate, among the nations of Europe. What kinship could be rationally suggested between Incas of Peru or Aztecs of Mexico, with their strange skill as mathematicians, potters, weavers of silk, and workers in metal, and the Amazonian tribes, who could not count above five, or the naked Patagonians, who lived on human flesh, or the Californians, whose notion of pleasure expressed itself in horrible self-mutilation. Then there was a widely scattered middle type, which was as far removed from the culture of Peru or Mexico as from the barbarism of Patagonia or California. There were innumerable peoples, neither genuinely civilized nor wholly and frankly savage, who showed no sign of psychological and ethnological relationship either with those American nations who cherished a definite tradition of elevated social culture or with those who wallowed in unmitigated savagery.

Work of human hands on the American continent tended at the same time to encourage questionings of the scriptural records of human experience. Cyclopean buildings, which lay scattered over the central provinces of the new continent, had their foundations hidden in the 'dark backward and abysm of time'. They existed, according to reasonable calculation, before the scriptural date of the creation; they were older, at any rate, than the biblical deluge. The possibility suggested itself that human life was of older standing in America than in Asia or Europe, and had undergone far-off developments, wholly independent of human vicissitudes elsewhere. The orthodox monogenic creed which traced mankind's descent through Noah from a single pair of human beings, was seriously challenged as soon as there floated within the range of Christian vision a conglomeration of peoples of untraceable and enigmatic pedigree. No American nation claimed descent from Ham, Shem, or Japhet. Almost all were alien in mental, moral, and spiritual calibre from the races whose experience was recorded in sacred or profane history. American ethnology was destined to startle and unsettle orthodox European beliefs in a greater degree than any marvels of inanimate nature in the New World.

II

During the greater part of the sixteenth century England made small effort to emulate either the exploring and colonizing successes of Spain or the comparative failures of France on the American continent. Occasional voyages of English merchant seamen across the Atlantic gave small or no hope of future English conquests, and added little to the existing sum of geographical knowledge. Yet England came under the spell of the aboriginal mystery almost as early and almost as completely as the nations of Europe who long preceded her in establishing themselves on American soil. At the very dawn of the century natives of both North and South America were brought home by English mariners on their fruitless expeditions to American shores, and the strange visitors were eagerly welcomed by the highest in the land. Eskimos were guests at the court of Henry VII; a Brazilian cacique enjoyed the hospitality of Henry VIII. During Queen Mary's reign public attention was for a time diverted to aboriginal visitors of darker hue from the west coast of Africa. But with the new outburst of exploring activity, which began in the second decade of Queen Elizabeth's reign and thenceforward grew in volume year by year, the American Indians reappeared in their mysterious remoteness on English shores. Through the greater part of Shakespeare's manhood all ranks of the nation were deeply stirred by a constant succession of small bands of savage immigrants from both the northern and southern continents of America.

The strangers came to sixteenth-century England, it should be noticed, from regions of the Western hemisphere which were yoked loosely, if at all, to Spain's colonial empire. Of the advanced civilization which prevailed in Mexico and Peru, the central provinces of Spanish dominion, no representatives were suffered by Spanish policy to seek asylum in sixteenth-century England. All the native Americans who were guests of Tudor Englishmen came from districts lying outside the pale of Mexican or Peruvian culture. They were of that widespread aboriginal type which was gifted with an intelligence amply sufficient to enable them to adapt to human purposes the simple forces of nature, although they lacked all but the most rudimentary powers of intellectual perception. They were experts in the arts of hunting and fishing. They were skilled makers of instruments of sport or war, like bows and arrows, spears, and fishing nets. Their boats were ingeniously contrived, and many implements of domestic use, often of earthenware, bore further witness to mechanical aptitudes. Arts of agriculture were familiar to them, and their wide fields of maize were cultivated with assiduous care. Nor did they lack culinary skill; their meat and fish were invariably roasted or broiled. They adorned their faces and bodies with coloured pigments arranged in elaborate patterns, and though their clothing was for the most part scanty, they prided themselves on cloaks formed of feathers and furs, on feathered head-dresses, and on necklaces and earrings wrought of shells, precious stones, or precious metals. They had fixed habitations and a settled form of government. A religion of nature—usually dominated by the worship of the sun—was well organized among them, and their ritual ceremonies were elaborate. They were familiar with an empiric system of medicine, and the profession of physician no less than that of priest was honoured among them.

Tribes who had reached such levels of social development were scattered over the eastern side of both the northern and southern continents of America from Labrador to Argentina. Their customs and institutions differed greatly in detail among themselves, but in broad outline they were of one pattern. Their languages, although greatly varying in vocabulary, were of the same agglutinative structure. All were innocent of inflexions—the characteristic feature of European speech. Although this aboriginal type fell far below the standard of culture which had been reached in Mexico and Peru, it ranged far above the disorganized savagery which was habitual under varied repellent shapes to the nomads of the far interior, and of lands lying about the extreme southern or the middle western coasts.

It was only this intermediate kind of American whom the sixteenth-century Englishman had the opportunity of observing or interrogating on English shores. To England came from the misty regions of Labrador, Canada, New England, Virginia, Florida, Guiana, and Brazil specimens of this widespread type of humanity. There was a uniformity of crude nurture among these distant travellers who were known to the Old World either as American Indian, or, from the prevailing colour of their complexion, as Red Indian or Redskin. The name of Indian, which they bore throughout Europe, was fruit of the old geographical misconception which represented the whole continent of America to be an outpost of the Indian continent of Asia. Owing to that colossal delusion, the inhabitants of the newly discovered Western hemisphere shared the appellation which was already appropriated by dwellers in the Orient.

Throughout Shakespeare's lifetime court and country repeatedly entertained in England this manner of Indian. The sovereigns Elizabeth and James I readily accorded them audience. In their honour noblemen and bishops gave banquets. With them scholars and ministers of religion sought converse, while enterprising speculators, zealous to turn to their own account the curiosity of the multitude, engaged some of them for purposes of public exhibition, charging pence for the privilege of inspecting them at close quarters.

No feature of this experience was peculiar to England. The courts of Spain and France also welcomed the American native of the normal type in the early or middle years of the century. In spite of the misgivings of his patroness, Queen Isabella, Columbus had set the example of bringing to Europe American aborigines of docile disposition. The step was justified by the Spanish pioneers on various pretexts, all of which found echo in Elizabethan England. Only thus could native interpreters be satisfactorily trained for the subsequent service of European explorers, whose advance was always impeded by the difficulty of conversing with the American native. In the second place, the American heathen was thereby given opportunities, which were otherwise impossible, of observing Christianity at work in her own citadels. Moreover, the native visitor was likely to impart to his kinsfolk, when he rejoined them in his own country, the knowledge of civilized custom which he was bound to acquire more or less effectually at the fountain-head. Finally, the boundless curiosity, which reports about the natives provoked in the old countries, invited practical endeavours to exhibit living examples to those who were unlikely to visit the aborigines in their own haunts. Navigators of Tudor England convoyed Americans across the ocean, mainly from a wish to satisfy the inquisitiveness of friends at home. When Englishmen at the close of the century formally embarked on their career of American colonists, this motive acquired increased efficacy, although its purport was at times disguised. Many Elizabethan promoters of colonial enterprise openly recommended the bringing into England of representatives of native races, so that home-dwellers of inquiring temper might learn at leisure from the uncouth strangers the full story of the unknown land. Eager pupils abounded.

The practical results of the visits of the Indians to Elizabethan England may be easily exaggerated, but the visitors did not depart without leaving a permanent trace of their coming. Their presence quickened English interest alike in theories of human progress and in colonial enterprise. The seed which the native visits sowed in Elizabethan England fructified in one direction to rare purpose. Shakespeare, the profoundest intelligence of the age, yielded more fully than his fellow dramatists to the prevalent curiosity, and offered in the creation of Caliban an illuminating conception of the native problem. The entrances and exits of American Indians to and from sixteenth-century England are in themselves, apart from higher considerations, curious byways of history. But their significance is impressively enhanced by their relation with Prospero's servant-monster. Such an imaginary portrait sheds a liberal flood of light not merely on contemporary speculation as to the place of the American native in human development, but on the ultimate or universal relationship of civilization to savagery.

III

Mariners of Bristol made in 1501 an attempt, which bore little fruit, to follow up John Cabot's shadowy clues in the North Atlantic. To these western Englishmen belongs the credit of first bringing to England natives of the 'New-found-land'. Unlike their Spanish contemporaries, English sailors of this period omitted to record their achievements. All that is quite certain about these Bristol sailors' adventure is that they returned to port with three strangers, three American Indians. The mysterious visitors, who were the first representatives of the American people to tread English soil, came from the arctic north. They were clothed, we are told, in beasts' skin. They ate raw flesh. They spoke such language as no man could understand. Quickly carried from Bristol to London, they enjoyed royal hospitality. Gentle usage recommended to them English modes of life. They adopted the clothing of their hosts, and after two years' experience of English society were indistinguishable from Englishmen. Their complexions, when freed of pigments, proved nearly white. Their resemblance to Europeans created general bewilderment.

There is little doubt that these first American strangers to reach England were Eskimos, living at home in underground dwellings, from which they rarely emerged except in the summer months. Skilful huntsmen and fishermen, and expert in the manufacture and use of canoes and sleighs, they were well acquainted with the value of warm clothing, and wore boots of walrus- and seal-skin, and gloves of deerskin. Such effective raiment won the admiration of Englishmen, with whom, in fact, Eskimos have always found favour. John Davis, the greatest arctic explorer of late Elizabethan days, described them as a 'people of good stature and tractable conditions'. None ventured to condemn them as 'rudely barbarous'. Englishmen who saw the American native in England for the first time were more startled by those characteristics in which the strangers resembled themselves than by those in which they differed.

Some three decades passed before the experience was repeated. Then homekeeping Londoners saw at their doors a typical representative from a southerly clime of the normal American race. It has been argued that the Eskimos, despite superficial resemblances, were of a human family altogether different from the other American peoples. At any rate, the Brazilian more strictly conforms to the normal aboriginal type which is disseminated through the great continent. To the wonder of the English nation, a chieftain or cacique of Brazil paid his respects in person to King Henry VIII at Whitehall.

Brazil, which was nominally ruled by Portugal and not by Spain, was less rigidly closed than the Spanish dominions in America to European merchants of non-Spanish nationality. The native Americans who most often found their way to France in the sixteenth century came from Brazil. It was on reports of aboriginal modes of Brazilian life which Sir Thomas More received from lips of sailors at Antwerp that he based much detail in his 'Utopia'; it was from conversations with Brazilian visitors to the French court that Montaigne, the French philosopher and essayist, deduced his half-ironical praises of the simple American Indian life. The Brazilian, who was of gentle disposition, was reputed to organize his social institutions with exceptional consistency and success on a communistic basis. He was generally acknowledged to be the ideal type of communist. Though the incompleteness of his attire and the abundance of his ornamental finery betokened a modest scale of culture, he won respect as the inventor of certain domestic appliances, which deeply impressed travellers and wrung from Europeans the flattery of imitation. The hanging couch or hammock (a Brazilian word), which was cleverly contrived of fibres of the palm-tree, was, as far as Europeans knew, a Brazilian invention. Hammocks were afterward met with in Guiana and other parts of South America; but they were long called in the Old World 'Brazil beds', and were constant reminders of the ingenuity of the aboriginal Brazilian.

It was a chieftain of Brazil with whom the second entry in the catalogue of native American visitors to England is concerned. William Hawkins, the slave-dealing captain of Plymouth, who sold many negroes from the west coast of Africa to the Portuguese in Brazil, brought home a native ruler of the Portuguese province. The Brazilian chief visited England on conditions. A hostage was left with his tribe during his absence. Hawkins's companion, Martin Cockeram, a citizen of Plymouth, readily undertook that role.

The Brazilian 'king', as he was called, reached Plymouth in safety, and won the hearts of his hosts by his amiable demeanour. But he caused them some anguish when he decked himself out in his ceremonial garb on occasions of state. In his cheeks, we are told, were holes wherein 'small bones were planted, standing an inch out', while in his lower lip was fixed a precious stone of the size of a pea. Such painful adornment was, he explained, 'reputed in his own country for a great bravery'. The Brazilian was in no hurry to regain his native land. He prolonged his stay in England for a year. But illness overtook him on his return voyage, and he unhappily died in mid-ocean. The friends of Martin Cockeram, who was left as his surety in Brazil, grew alarmed. But no hurt befell the English hostage. Within a few months he returned to Plymouth unharmed, a witness to the innate humanity of the Brazilian people.

It is worth pointing out that Cockeram was one of the earliest Englishmen to reside for any period of time on American soil. He did all he could to make the name of Englishmen respected. In spite of Portuguese precautions against foreign immigration, English merchants within two decades succeeded in settling their agents within Brazilian boundaries, and English ships often anchored off the coast. Cockeram's conduct and the pleasant experiences of the Brazilian cacique at Henry VIII's court bore good fruit. English shipmasters reported a few years later that Brazilian natives often offered to sail home with them. The midmost years of the sixteenth century form a stagnant period in the history of Anglo-American relations. The English trade in African negroes, whom Englishmen captured in Africa and sold in West Indian and Brazilian ports, was the chief mode of intercourse between the two countries. Popular curiosity temporarily turned from the ethnological puzzle of the American Indian to that of the black African. Five tall and strong negroes from the Guinea coast were brought to London early in Queen Mary's reign, along with elephants' teeth and gold dust. English meat and drink proved congenial to them, although the cold and moist climate caused them suffering. Successful efforts were made to teach them the English language, and most of them were repatriated, to the delight of their kindred, to spread a knowledge of the English tongue in their native places. Only one of them seems to have stayed behind and he married 'a fair Englishwoman'. The result of the union gave Englishmen's pride a fall. Consternation prevailed in the country when a son was born to the negro's English wife 'in all respects as black as his father'. The episode disconcerted public opinion, which resented that an English mother should compromise her racial superiority by giving birth on English soil to a 'coalblack Ethiopian'.

IV

A youth of nineteen, who was to play a great part in England's earliest colonial efforts, acted as one of the guardians of Queen Mary's negro immigrants on this voyage from the Guinea coast, and the experience stimulated his interest in native problems. The youthful observer was Martin Frobisher, whose endeavour to reach the fabled empire of Cathay through arctic America in the second decade of Queen Elizabeth's reign practically inaugurated the exploring and colonizing career of the

English nation. One of Frobisher's professed aims was to get into close touch with the natives of the New World and to bring eight or ten of them home. Like Queen Isabella of Spain, his patroness, Queen Elizabeth, while encouraging the enterprise, deprecated the forcible capture of natives. 'You shall not bring', she wrote to adventurous Captain Frobisher, 'above three or four persons of that country, the which shall be of divers ages, and shall be taken in such sort as you may best avoid offence of that people.'

Frobisher followed an extreme northerly course on each of the three expeditions which were seriously designed to bring all north-west avenues to Cathay under English sway. The natives whom he met were Eskimos, but, although they held intercourse with him without much demur, they showed unreadiness to take passage with him to his own country. He and his companions made zealous efforts to master the native language, and prepared elaborate vocabularies with reports on native habits. But the aborigines were indisposed to accept the explorer's invitation to accompany him home.

In his first expedition Frobisher succeeded in enticing only one native into his ship. Owing to the growth of English interest in American affairs, the arrival of the unhappy man at Harwich produced a sensation far greater than any which the preceding visits of Indians had caused. 'The like of this strange infidel was never seen, read, nor heard of before,' wrote one elated reporter. 'His arrival was a wonder never known to city or realm. Never like great matter happened to any man's knowledge.' The fellow was described as broad of face and fat of body, with little eyes and scanty beard. His long coal-black hair was tied in a knot above his forehead, and his dark sallow skin, of which the natural colour was hidden beneath dirt and paint, was likened to that of tawny Moors or Tartars. His expression was 'sullen and churlish, but sharp withal'. But the great public reception destined for him was frustrated by his death from cold. There seems to have been

just time, however, for a distinguished Flemish artist who
was at the time settled in England, Lucas de Heere, to
sketch his portrait. The drawing, which still survives in
the public library at Ghent, initiated a practice, which
subsequently became common in Elizabethan England,
of commissioning artists to transfer to canvas the features
of strange visitors from the New World.

On his second expedition Frobisher was more fortunate
in his hunt for human prey. He brought back two natives
—a man and a woman—and their presence in England
again caused an intense popular excitement. They curiously combined savage and civilized custom. Their leather
clothing was thoroughly well made, and they knew how
to roast meat. Yet occasionally they would eat raw flesh,
washed down with a draught of oxen's blood. There is
abundant testimony to the whiteness of their skin. There
can be little doubt that they were Eskimos, although
Richard Hakluyt, the great collector of American travellers' reports, detected in them close resemblances to the
inhabitants of unsettled and remote parts of Mexico, whom
Spanish explorers had already carefully described. Popular
tracts, which were soon thumbed out of existence, emphasized the singularities of this 'strange kind of people',
without apparently throwing sure light on ethnological
problems. Art was summoned by Queen Elizabeth to
provide her with permanent mementoes of the two
strangers. Life-like portraits of them from the brush of
fashionable painters long hung in Hampton Court Palace.
Unfortunately, the change of scene and climate proved,
after an interval, fatal to Frobisher's pair of Indians. At
the end of the year the man died at Bristol of inflam-
mation of the lungs, and the course of the illness was fully
narrated by a distinguished physician. The woman does
not seem to have survived her partner long. But a child
who was lately born to them—the first and probably the
last of his tribe to have England for his birthplace—
apparently survived his parents. The American infant
finally passed away at the Three Swans Tavern in the city

of London, and was accorded Christian burial in the Church of St. Olave's, Hart Street, which survived the Great Fire of London.

Frobisher's third expedition failed to bring back any native. Repugnance on the part of the aborigines to life in the Old World was not diminished by the fatalities attending the recent visits of their fellow countrymen. The Elizabethan populace had tasted blood. There was a widespread anxiety to see the newly discovered people at close quarters. The desire grew in intensity among both the educated and uneducated classes. Explorers made increasingly liberal offers of English hospitality to the Indians with whom they came into contact. Strenuous efforts were made to grasp their ideas and speech. In conformity with Frobisher's example, later Elizabethan chroniclers of American travel were generous in notices of native customs and in vocabularies of native words.

The expeditions which Sir Walter Raleigh fitted out to Terra Florida, with a view to colonizing that part of the region which he named Virginia, brought England into relations with one of the most important American races of the normal Indian type. Virginia and North Florida were occupied by numerous independent clans of the people called Algonquins, a race of agricultural warriors. In the early days of the projected English settlement this aboriginal people displayed a friendly feeling for the invaders. Captain Barlow, the leader of the first English expedition to Virginia, described the Indians there with attractive *naïveté* as 'a people most gentle, loving, and faithful, void of all guile and treason, and such as live after the manner of the golden age'. The native instincts of hospitality were highly developed. When some of the first adventurers insisted on spending the night on their ship instead of in the huts put at their disposal by the natives on shore, the wife of an absent chief sent down a well-cooked supper and a supply of mats to protect the Englishmen from the night dews. The Indian princes vied with one another in offers of food and menial services. Jealousies and domestic quarrels among the tribes disturbed this Arcadian harmony. The new-comers unwisely intervened in local feuds. There was inevitable growth of suspicion on the natives' part in regard to the invaders' ultimate intentions. But, before the situation on American soil grew critical, Virginians accepted the hospitality of their English visitors and were crossing the Atlantic.

In the first English ship that returned from Virginia in the autumn of 1584 there sailed two sturdy Virginians, who played very different parts in the early history of the English colony. Their names were Manteo and Wanchese. Close acquaintance with the English in their own homes made Manteo the fastest of friends with his hosts, while Wanchese developed an invincible distrust. Both returned, after a seven months' stay in England, with Raleigh's second Virginian expedition, of which the hopes ran very high. Then Wanchese encouraged his kindred to harry the English settlers, but Manteo sedulously preached to the natives the prudence of amity. His services as interpreter and adviser proved invaluable during a year of grave anxiety.

At the end of the twelvemonth Manteo repeated his visit to England under notable conditions. Sir Francis Drake, homeward bound from a raid on the West Indies and the Spanish main, found himself near the Virginian coast, and offered to rescue the English settlers from dire peril. Their native ally was reluctant to interrupt his pleasant intercourse with his English masters, and he came a second time to England under the auspices of Drake, the greatest English mariner of the age. For ten months Manteo lingered once more on English soil. At length he returned to his native land in the company of a third party of English colonists. To the new leader, John White, he attached himself with undiminished ardour.

The English, through the disasters of these early Virginian days, had no firmer friend than this kind-hearted and capable Redskin. His enthusiasm for the English cause never waned. He introduced English friends to his old mother, who lived on an island off the North Carolina coast, and his family eagerly offered them entertainment. Sir Walter Raleigh was always interested in his welfare. The last that we hear of him is that after much delay and hesitation he accepted the rite of baptism, and was granted by his English allies, in recognition of his tried fidelity, the high-sounding title of 'Lord of Roanoke and Dusamonquapek'.

Governor White came back to England after half a year's further futile struggle to set England's Virginian empire on a sure basis. Manteo did not accompany him. White contented himself with bringing home a fellow-countryman of Manteo, who soon, unhappily, found a burial-place at Bideford. The governor had devoted his leisure to depicting in water-colours the Virginian native in his own home. That valuable sketch-book, which is now preserved in the British Museum, sheds a brilliant light on the manners and customs of Manteo's kinsfolk, in whom Elizabethan interest, being once excited, never wholly died.

V

The earliest English endeavour to colonize Virginia proved a failure in spite of the energy of the pioneers. In the last decade of the sixteenth century the great scheme was languidly pursued. The active centre of American interest for England temporarily shifted to South America. Raleigh, although he was the virtual projector of Virginia, did not visit that country in person. To South America he went himself in order to seek a fabled Eldorado in that region of Guiana which is now better known as Venezuela. The new purpose brought English explorers the acquaintance of another American race, scions of which were soon familiar figures in the streets of London.

Near the banks of the river Orinoko, which Raleigh and his company ascended, there lived vagabond tribes who were falsely credited with fabulous distortion of the human shape. It was in that district that rumour placed the homes of

> . . . men whose heads
> Do grow beneath their shoulders,

—imaginary beings who are twice mentioned by Shakespeare among the world's newly revealed wonders. The Elizabethan travellers were truthful enough, while giving hearsay accounts of such human monstrosities, to disclaim having seen them for themselves.

The natives of Guiana, whose acquaintance Raleigh personally made, had no obvious association with the inferior human strata of wild America. Raleigh's aboriginal allies formed a branch of the widely spread people called Caribs—a race which always seems to have been of gentle disposition, in spite of Spanish imputations to the contrary. They had inhabited the West Indian islands before the Spanish invasion drove them in headlong flight to the mainland. The Caribs of Guiana were clearly of the highest Indian type, outside Peru or Mexico, and were more than qualified to confirm the favourable impressions which Virginians like Manteo had left upon the Elizabethan mind. Raleigh, who was prone to generous enthusiasm, was an indulgent student of native character and physiognomy. The men and women whom he met in Guiana lacked, in his eye, neither comeliness nor courtesy nor intelligence. At a place in Guiana on the Orinoko, which he calls Toparimaca, he writes of the wife of one of the chiefs, 'In all my life I have seldom seen a better favoured woman.' Her countenance, he proceeds, was excellent; her hair, almost as long as herself, was tied up in pretty knots, while her discourse was very pleasant. 'I have seen a lady in England', Raleigh concludes, 'so like to her, as but for the difference of colour, I would have sworn it might have been the same.'

With a king of Guiana called Topiawari, who ruled over a place called Aromaia, Raleigh formed something like close intimacy. The man was of patriarchal age. In one place Raleigh describes him as one hundred years old and in another as one hundred and ten. These were probably swollen figures; but in any case his physical strength was remarkable. He readily walked fourteen miles to meet his English visitor in hot weather, and returned the same day on foot in spite of Raleigh's polite remonstrances. Raleigh describes King Topiawari as a man of gravity, judgement, and good discourse, though he had no help of learning nor of breed. Proud of his independence, he was anxious to escape the Spanish yoke. He had been, at one time, their prisoner, and had paid as ransom one hundred plates of gold and divers chains of spleenstone. He was no sycophant. He regarded Christianity with suspicion, and resented the conversion of two members of his family, a nephew and a nephew's son, on whom the Spanish priests had conferred the baptismal names of Juan and Pedro respectively. He was a confirmed polygamist, and complained that in the recent wars with the Spaniards he had been robbed of many of his wives. In the old days a chieftain reckoned on the companionship of ten or twelve conjugal partners. Now he had to content himself with three or four.

At Raleigh's suggestion Topiawari cheerfully agreed to permit his son to return with the English explorer to England, there to learn the English language and to give Englishmen full information of native affairs. It was settled that by way of exchange Raleigh should leave with the old chief two Englishmen. Francis Sparrow, a servant of Captain Gifford, 'was desirous to tarry and could describe a country with his pen'. Consequently he, along with an English boy, Hugh Goodwin, remained with Topiawari when the old man's heir and some native attendants embarked with Raleigh for England.

Raleigh characteristically took two Indians of Guiana into his domestic service in London, and in the early days of his imprisonment in the Tower they waited on him there. On one of these men the vague records bestow no name, and it is just possible that he was the young prince of Guiana, Topiawari's son, whose fortunes in England are difficult to trace. Inquiries about him were often made by his relatives of English travellers in Guiana in the course of the next decade. His English visit was clearly prolonged. When he ultimately regained his native land, he found that the Spaniards had extended their dominion in his absence, and he had difficulty thenceforth in holding his own. Another of Raleigh's Indian attendants in the Tower of London was well known to Raleigh's friends as Leonard Regapo. He does not seem to have been of exalted rank. After giving ample proof of fidelity to his master, he finally made his way back to his native country, where he spread flattering reports of Raleigh's generosity. Raleigh, till near his death, showed affectionate interest in the man's fortunes. While still a prisoner in the Tower, he sent out clothing to him in one of the smaller English expeditions to Guiana, and, when he made his final and fatal voyage to that region, he sought out his faithful Indian servant Leonard, and exchanged with him affectionate greetings. The Caribbean's respect for Raleigh's memory was lasting, and he paid sedulous attention to every Englishman who in later days came his way.

All the adventurers who followed Raleigh's path in South America during the early years of the seventeenth century endeavoured to maintain among the aborigines the amiable tradition which he inaugurated. Captain Charles Leigh, when exploring Guiana, thought to improve on Raleigh's efforts by sending as many as four Indian chiefs to England. But, though the proposal was well received by the tribes, the arrangement fell through. Spanish raids were keeping the country in perpetual tumult. The protagonist of the English alliance, Topiawari, had been driven to the mountains by Spanish menace soon after Raleigh took leave of him. There his long life ended. His two English guests, the boy Goodwin and the man Sparrow, accompanied him in his fatal wanderings. The boy is said to have been 'eaten by a tiger', but the man Sparrow, after capture by the Spaniards, managed to escape to Mexico, and finally reached England in safety. There he published an account of his sufferings, and commended his Indian hosts to the favourable notice of his countrymen.

VI

With the accession of James I, in 1603, the question of colonizing North America entered on a new and finally successful phase. Resolute endeavours to form permanent settlements both in Virginia and New England were to bear fruit before the king's reign ended. Prospecting expeditions were equipped almost every year, and public curiosity about the natives of the northern continent of America grew more acute. Every endeavour was made to encourage and conciliate native guests in England, so that they might report favourably of the home country to their kindred across the seas.

A very interesting party of natives reached England in 1605 in the charge of Captain George Weymouth, whose exploration of North American shores enjoys the added interest of having been mainly subsidized by Shakespeare's patron, the Earl of Southampton. Captain Weymouth coasted round New England, where he rendered much service to geographical knowledge, but he went south before he sailed homeward. It is from Virginia that he claims to have brought back native guests. The men were five in number, and they carried with them two canoes and their bows and arrows. One of the strangers was described as 'young' and 'of a ready capacity'. Two others were brothers of a notable chief. All are reported to have received 'exceeding kind usage' at English hands. In the earliest days of the Jamestown settlement a leading colonist acknowledged that the colony owed much to one of these native visitors to England, who on his going back sedulously spread through his tribe praises of the virtues of the English king. Great was the importance attached to the experience of English hospitality, which was enjoyed by all these five men. It was the 'accident' of their

English entertainment, wrote their friend, Captain Weymouth, which 'must be acknowledged the means of putting on foot and giving life to our plantations'.

The Spanish ambassador in London was moved by this incursion of Virginians to complain of the progressive practice of welcoming natives to England. He denounced it as a menace to Spanish predominance in the New World. All the Indian visitors, the Spanish diplomatist pointed out, were taught English, and were not only entertained in London, but were sent about the country. Yet in spite of Spanish lamentation, for some dozen years following the actual settlement of Jamestown, in 1607, the chain of native visitors to England knew no interruption. Not all now came from Virginia. A few were brought from the territory of New England, which was at length undergoing more or less systematic study with a view to colonization.

The New England Indians, although they were of the normal semibarbarous type, belonged to a nationality different from that of the Virginians. They were of the historic race of the Iroquois, no representative of which visited England before the early years of the seventeenth century. The first New Englanders to reach England were a party, said to number ten or more, who arrived in London in 1611. Like recent Virginian visitors, they came under the auspices of the Earl of Southampton, who paid the expenses of their convoy. They easily learned English, and two of them, called respectively Tantum and Squanto, subsequently proved of great value as interpreters to English invaders of the northern provinces. Squanto was a native of Patuxet, the Indian name of the native settlement, which New Plymouth was to supersede. For some years he lived in Cornhill, London, in the house of an enterprising merchant and colonial projector, John Slaney. Squanto's devotion to his English hosts fits him to be linked in the memory of Englishmen with his Virginian predecessor, Manteo, or his Guianan predecessor, Leonard Regapo.

One New Englander achieved a more peculiar notoriety while visiting England in the same years as Squanto. Known by the name of Epenow, this American visitor was a man of unusually fine physique, and of a stature far above the average. His courage was declared to be no less than his strength, and he was credited with an authoritative mien and good understanding. But to the discredit of his hosts he was, after a while, 'showed up and down London for money as a wonder'. He is no doubt the 'strange Indian' of large proportions who is mentioned in the play of Henry VIII as fascinating a mob of London women. But Epenow got even with his captors. He represented that he had exclusive knowledge of a gold-mine in an island off the New England coast. On this representation a small syndicate was formed at Plymouth to equip an expedition. In the ship Epenow sailed as guide. But no sooner did he come within swimming distance of his native shores than he leaped overboard and abandoned his dupes to their devices. Efforts to recapture him proved vain, and the ship turned home without more treasure than she held at her setting forth.

More tragic disasters attended some contemporaneous designs to bring to England native dwellers from the new Virginian settlement. The overlord of the neighbouring region, Powhatan, readily allowed two of his followers to cross the seas soon after the foundation of the settlement. One of these, called Namontack, was described as a man of 'shrewd and subtle capacity', in whom both Powhatan and the English reposed great trust. Unluckily, his companion, Matchumps, was of an evil disposition. The two Indians sailed for England together by way of the Bermudas. But in that island they had a fierce quarrel, with the result that Namontack was slain and secretly buried by his companion. The murderer, Matchumps, ultimately made his way back to Virginia. The news of the murder did not come to Powhatan's ears for some years, during which he was constantly making plaintive inquiries after 'his man in England'.

Of a third subject of Powhatan, one Nanamack, who actually reached England in the first decade of the seventeenth century and remained till his death, a more curious account is given. For a year or two he lived in English houses where religion was little considered, and drinking and swearing and like evils prevailed, so that 'he ran, as he was, a mere pagan'. But he was ultimately taken in charge by a godly family, and, learning to read, delighted in the Scriptures. His newly acquired religious sentiment led him to bewail the ignorance of his own countrymen. At length arrangements were made for his baptism. But he died before the rite could be performed, 'leaving, however, behind such testimonies of his desire of God's favour that it moved such godly Christians as knew him to conceive well of his condition'. But Nanamack's checkered experience, no less than the murder of Namontack by his native companion, might well justify doubt whether the purposes of religion and humanity gained much by the voyage of American aborigines across the dividing ocean.

VII

Shakespeare was yet alive, and in more or less active work, while this strange procession, which I have described, of natives of Virginia, Guiana, and New England defiled through English ports. Of most of them the dramatist doubtless caught a glimpse. But it was just after his death that the most imposing of Virginian visitors reached London. Pocahontas, the young daughter of the chief Powhatan, had conceived as a child a romantic attachment for the English settlers, and had (it was alleged) protected more than one of them from the murderous designs of her kindred. At length she joined the newcomers as a willing hostage, and in 1613, when not more than eighteen years of age, she boldly defied all Indian and English conventions by marrying an English settler. Immediately afterward she accepted Christianity, and expressed anxiety to visit her husband's Christian country. Accordingly, in the summer of 1616, she arrived in the

English capital with her husband, an infant son, her brother Tamacomo, and some native women attendants.

A splendid reception was accorded the Virginian princess. State and Church combined to do her honour. James I received her and her brother at court. They attended a performance at Whitehall of a Twelfth Night masque by Ben Jonson (January 6, 1617), of which they spoke with approval. The Bishop of London entertained her 'with festival pomp'. The princess's portrait was painted and engraved by distinguished artists. Her dignified bearing was generally commended, although hints are given by Ben Jonson that the princess was occasionally seen, to the dismay of her hosts, to enter tavern doors. Her entertainment, at any rate, seems to have been thoroughly congenial to her, and she was reluctant to shorten her visit. At the end of ten months, however, she travelled to Gravesend with a view to embarkation for her native land. But while tarrying at the port, to the general grief, she fell ill and died. The parish register of Gravesend describes her as 'of Virginia, a lady born'.

The princess's English husband soon returned to Jamestown, leaving behind him his son and his wife's native companions, all of whom gave some trouble. The husband's brother, Henry Rolfe, who looked after their boy Thomas, complained of the expenses of maintenance to which he was unwillingly put. After some years the lad rejoined his father in Jamestown, where he married an Englishwoman and begot offspring. Pocahontas's brother, Tamacomo, was also long tolerated with some impatience in London society. Samuel Purchas, the voluminous compiler of records of travel, relates how he often conversed with him at the house of a leading London physician. On occasions the Virginian amused the company by singing native songs and dancing what his hearers characterized as 'his diabolical measures'. He discoursed of his country and religion. Unlike his sister, he declined to accept Christianity, and was prone to blaspheme all religious beliefs but his own. Nevertheless, England left a deep impression of wonder in his mind. He never ceased to marvel at the density of population and the abundance of cornfields and trees.

The Virginian girls who came with Pocahontas, or followed her to England, experienced singular fortunes. One became a domestic servant in the house of a mercer at Cheapside, but, falling ill of consumption, she was nursed in the household of a popular Puritan preacher, William Gouge, who paid her every attention. A subscription was opened in London to provide her with additional comforts. Other Virginian maidens, after being maintained for some years at the expense of the Virginian Company in England, were sent to the Bermudas, where husbands were found for them by the governor. One of their weddings was celebrated with great ceremony at the public expense, and as soon as the union proved fruitful the family was dispatched to Virginia to rejoin the girl's kindred. This experiment was reckoned a politic mode of encouraging aboriginal sympathy with civilized life.

By the wisest onlookers the plan of bringing natives to England to convert them into civilizing instruments among their own people was pronounced a mistake. In 1620 a serious proposal was ventilated to extend the practice by importing into England a large number of Indian lads to be educated on English lines. Good argument was then forthcoming to show that such native immigrants as were at the moment in England were assimilating the vices rather than the virtues of civilized life. Religious teaching benefited them little. The drinking habits of the Elizabethan or other vicious indulgences chiefly appealed to their idiosyncrasies. The hope of Anglicizing the aboriginal population of America by extending English hospitality to Indian visitors to England was recognized by the generation following Shakespeare's death to be a snare and a delusion.

VIII

Elizabethan drama faithfully reflected current aspiration and experience, but the American native left upon it a slighter impression than might have been expected. The wonders of the New World expanded tardily under Englishmen's gaze, while the Elizabethan dramatists were winging their highest flights. Yet America offered little effective suggestion to the playwrights. In the early days of Elizabethan drama America only figured on the stage as a vague fairyland, whence Spain gathered gold and precious stones, or as a shadowy paradise of Arcadian innocence. Through the middle years of Shakespeare's career the genuine significance of the great discovery was practically ignored in the theatre. It was only when Shakespeare's working days were nearing their close that the light of his genius illumined one aspect of the mighty theme—the mystery of the native dweller.

Christopher Marlowe, Shakespeare's tutor in tragedy, ended his short life before English colonists had established themselves on American soil. To Marlowe 'rich America' was alone familiar as a reservoir of Spanish treasure. All that Marlowe seems to have learned about the American natives was confined to the inaccurate suggestion that the frozen north of the continent was

> Inhabited with tall and sturdy men,
> Giants as big as hugy Polypheme.

No reference to the Eskimo natives, whose average stature was rather less than that of Europeans, could be more misleading.

To John Lyly, a pioneer of Elizabethan comedy, America presented itself as a Utopia, where men and nature still flourished 'in their first simplicity'. Lyly deemed the 'Nicotian herb' the most characteristic feature of the new continent, and he credited the plant with marvellous properties for healing human ills. Lyly's imagination, when it touched the New World at all, seemed to lack the guidance of precise knowledge as conspicuously as Marlowe's imagination.

The rapid spread of information about America after Queen Elizabeth's death still failed to inspire the playwrights with interest or enthusiasm. Theatrical references to the early Virginian expeditions of the seventeenth century were usually made in a light sarcastic vein. Virginia was a country where gold was to be had for the asking, or lay about the roads for the passer-by to pick up. The country was a fit asylum for ne'er-do-wells or spendthrifts. Sneers in this key came plentifully from the lips of Ben Jonson's dramatis personae. Contemporary leaders of literature, like Spenser and Bacon, Drayton and Chapman, showed a truer sense of the mysterious promise of an English colonial empire in America. But complete justice was only done to the marvels and resources of the New World in the flood of treatises or pamphlets which flowed from the prosaic pens of travellers or economic theorists.

There were some curious attempts to present scenically the visits to England of the Virginian natives. But these efforts took the form of masques, and scarcely fell within the category of drama. Twice in 1613 living pictures of Virginian life were presented by amateur companies of actors before distinguished London audiences. On each occasion the players were drawn from the ranks of London barristers. The earlier of these entertainments was given at Whitehall by a combined company of lawyers from the Middle Temple and Lincoln's Inn. The occasion was the celebration of the marriage of the King's daughter, Princess Elizabeth, to the Elector Palatine. The spoken words came from the pen of George Chapman, who showed in them less subtlety than was his wont, but the scenic devices and costumes proved the chief attraction, and they were designed by the eminent decorative artist and architect, Inigo Jones. Some of the London barristers paraded before their sovereign and his guests at this high festival in the dress of Virginian chiefs. High-sprigged feathers rose from their heads, while their brows were adorned by shining suns in gold plate sprinkled with pearls. Feathers were the prevailing characteristics of the costumes. The robes were trimmed with various coloured feathers. Actors representing Virginian priests wore ingeniously contrived hoods of feathers. The episodes included a scenical gold-mine and a dance of baboons. But it was the religious ritual of sun-worship which was the central feature of the performance. The priests made obeisance to the solar deity and sang a hymn in his honour. Finally, a character called Eunomia, typifying the civilization of Europe, was made by Chapman to address this challenge to the Virginian nation:

> Virginian princes, you must now renounce
> Your superstitious worship of these Suns,
> Subject to cloudy darkenings and descents;
> And of your fit devotions turn the events
> To this our Briton Phœbus, whose bright sky
> (Enlightened with a Christian piety)
> Is never subject to black Error's night,
> And hath already offer'd heaven's true light
> To your dark region, which acknowledge now;
> Descend, and to him all your homage vow.

The 'Briton Phœbus' was, of course, James I.

No less crude was a similar scenic presentment of Virginian customs, in which the gentlemen of Gray's Inn engaged on the celebration of another marriage, a few months later—that of the disreputable Earl of Somerset to the more disreputable Lady Frances Howard. This second effort, which bore the title of 'The Masque of Flowers', acquires additional interest from the fact that all the expenses of the performance were defrayed by Francis Bacon, who may be credited with interest in the subject-matter, if not with some share in the composition of the quaint speeches of the entertainment. Again the religious rites of the Virginians, who now bore the alternative appellation of 'Floridans,' filled the centre of the stage. The central scheme of the masque was a debate

between champions of drinking and of smoking, wine
being allegorically represented by a character called Sile-
nus, and tobacco by the Virginian idol, a minion of the
Sun-god, entitled Kawasha. The name of the idol is no
invention, but is literally drawn from contemporary accounts of Virginia. Kawasha is, moreover, addressed in
one place as 'a great potan', in mock honour of the Virginian chief Powhatan, father of Princess Pocahontas.
The burlesque figure of the idol, who filled a speaking
part, was carried on the stage by two lawyers of Gray's
Inn attired like Indians of Florida. In his hand he carried
an Indian bow and arrows, while his sergeant attended
him with a grotesque tobacco pipe as big as a caliver or
light musket. The idol proves himself a spirited contro-
versialist in behalf of the smokers, and sings with secular
hilarity:

> Nothing but fumigation
> Doth chase away ill sprites;
> Kawasha and his nation
> Found out these holy rites.

The Virginian or Floridan was pictured by the Gray's
Inn lawyers, under Bacon's auspices, for the most part in
a farcical light.

IX

Shakespeare alone of contemporary dramatists seems to
have realized the serious significance of the native problem
which America offered thinking men. In the character of
Caliban he brought to its consideration an insight which
richly atones for the frivolous treatment which it received
at other hands. Shakespeare had his own limitations, and
of the general potentialities of the New World he showed
little more consciousness than the other playwrights of his
day. In the majority of his direct allusions to America he
confines himself, like Marlowe, to vague hints of the continent's harvest of gold, which Spain was reaping. From

the New World came 'the Armadoes of Spanish caracks
ballasted with rubies, carbuncles, and sapphires', of which
mention is made in *The Comedy of Errors* (III. ii. 137–42).
In the same vein Sir John Falstaff compares Mistress Ford
to 'a region in Guiana, all gold and bounty' (*Merry Wives*,
I. iii. 66–9). Very rarely does Shakespeare suggest other
aspects of the Western hemisphere—of the great expanse
of land and sea, which Spain primarily brought within
European vision. There is in *As You Like It* a slight
allusion to the opportunity of maritime adventure, of
which Spain, throughout the dramatist's career, was avail-
ing herself in the South Pacific Ocean. The dramatist
knew something, too, of the 'new map', which embodied
the recent 'augmentation' of the world's surface and surprised unscientific observers by its endless series of rhumb-
lines; to these features of the 'new map' of the New
World Shakespeare likened the wrinkles on Malvolio's
smiling countenance. But there is no indication in Shakespeare's plays that he was deeply stirred either by the
geographical revelations, or by the colonial aspirations of
his fellow-countrymen which belatedly reflected Spanish
example. His alert intellect, as far as it touched the New
World, was mainly absorbed by the fascination of aboriginal man.

The dramatist squarely faced that mysterious topic at
the end of his career, but he shyly betrayed an interest
in it at earlier periods. Four times in the course of his
early work Shakespeare alludes to the dominant trait of
the American Indian religion—the worship of the sun—
and his allusions are none the less recognizable because he
followed the common habit of designating the Far West,
like the Far East, by the one word 'Ind'. In almost his
earliest play, *Love's Labour's Lost*, he describes in gorgeous
language how

> A rude and savage man of Ind
> At the first opening of the gorgeous East
> Bows low his vassal head, and strucken blind
> Kisses the base ground with obedient breast.

Some years later, in *All's Well That Ends Well*, Helena was made to remark

> Indian-like,
> Religious in mine error, I adore
> The sun.

Sun-worship was widely distributed among uncivilized peoples. But Elizabethans knew it almost exclusively as the distinguishing cult of the American Indians, who had invested its ritual with most elaborate ceremonies. Almost every hill in Mexico, Peru, and neighbouring countries was crowned by Temples of the Sun of varying solidity—from cyclopean edifices of stone to lightly jointed wooden scaffolds or platforms. The earliest histories of America include pictorial illustrations of these slighter structures. In many parts of America the native sun-worshippers could only account for the apparently miraculous advent of invaders from Europe, whom they credited with super-human attributes, by identifying them with children of the sun. Shakespeare's words about sun-worship echo with much literalness descriptions which Elizabethan travellers repeatedly gave of the American Indian's daily obeisances to the solar deity. The same descriptions were more prosaically reproduced in scenic action by the law-yer-masquers of 1613.

At the end of his working life, when his mental power had reached its highest stage of development, Shakespeare at length offered the world his final conception of the place the aboriginal American filled in human economy. In Caliban he propounded an answer to the greatest of American enigmas.

When it is traced to its sources the play of *The Tempest* is seen to form a veritable document of early Anglo-American history. The general scheme of the piece in which Caliban plays his part is an imaginative commentary on an episode of the foundation of the first lasting settlement in Virginia. There is no reasonable ground for disputing that the catastrophe on which the plot of the play hinges was suggested by the casting away, in a terrific storm, on the rocky coast of Bermuda, of a ship bound for the new settlement of Jamestown. Prospero's uninhabited island reflects most of the features which the shipwrecked sailors on this Virginian voyage assigned to their involuntary asylum in the Atlantic. Mysterious noises led the frightened men to the conviction that spirits and devils had made 'the still-vexed Bermoothes' their home, and that they were face to face with nature's elementary forces in energetic activity. Such a scene easily stirred in the dramatist's fertile imagination the ambition to portray aboriginal man in his own home, and to define his form and faculty.

From the philosophic point of view the native problem had received the most suggestive treatment that had yet been given it in Europe from the French essayist, Montaigne, whose work had spread far and wide among Englishmen in the classical translation of Florio. The Frenchman had supported with fine irony the paradoxical thesis that the Indians of America realized in their native paradises the 'simple life', and that the Utopian conditions of their being put to shame the conditions of European civilization. Parenthetically, in his romance of *The Tempest*, Shakespeare liberally and literally borrows, through Florio, Montaigne's naïve picture of the charming innocence of aboriginal America. The interpolation, although relevant to the main argument, has no bearing on the slender plot of the drama. Montaigne's conception of aboriginal society is set by Shakespeare on the lips of Gonzalo, the one honest counsellor of the King of Naples. The sanguine veteran lightly plays with the fancy that, had he the government of the desert isle in the Western ocean on which he and his companions were wrecked, he would prove loyal to the alleged ideals of primitive man; he would found his state on a communistic basis; he would exclude sovereignty, learning, labour, wealth, and war; he would rely solely for sustenance on the unimpeded operations of nature.

Gonzalo repeats without variation the words of Montaigne, but Shakespeare makes brief comments of his own on the specious theory in the speeches which follow Gonzalo's borrowed deliverance. 'Thou dost talk nothing to me,' ejaculates one of his hearers, and Gonzalo finally admits that he has been indulging in 'merry fooling'. Shakespeare cherished none of Montaigne's amiable dreams of the primitive state of man in America. He merely introduces the Frenchman's fancies in order to clear the ground. Their flimsiness serves to bring into bolder relief the satisfying substance of his own conception.

Caliban is no precise presentation of any identifiable native American. He is an imaginary composite portrait, an attempt to reduce the aboriginal types of whom the dramatist and his contemporaries knew anything to one common denominator. The higher standards of civilization, which were discovered on the American continent in Peru and Mexico, were excluded from Shakespeare's survey. Few English travellers had been suffered by Spain to come to close quarters with Incas or Aztecs, and in Caliban's personality there are only fused the characteristics of the aboriginal tribes with whom Elizabethans came face to face.

Yet Elizabethan experience enabled Shakespeare to cast his net over a wide field. The part that his patron, Lord Southampton, had played in bringing natives to London in the early days of the seventeenth century may well justify the belief that the dramatist enjoyed some personal intercourse with the strangers. Such opportunities were readily supplemented by talk with travellers, or by perusal of their published information.

Sufficiently varied for his main purpose were the phases of uncivilized humanity in America, over which Shakespeare threw his luminous intelligence. Traits of the normal tractable type of Indian to which the Virginian and Caribbean belonged freely mingled in the crucible of his mind with those of the irredeemable savages of Patagonia. At the same time it is obvious that Shakespeare was eclectic

in garnering his evidence, omitting some testimonies
which one would have expected him to include, and falling
elsewhere into error. But finally, from his imaginative
study of the 'idea' of aboriginal life, there emerges a moving
sentient figure which, in spite of some misrepresentations,
presents with convincing realism the psychological im-
port of the American Indian temperament. Shakespeare's
American is not the Arcadian innocent with whom Montaigne identifies him. He is a human being, endowed with
live senses and appetites, with aptitudes for mechanical
labour, with some knowledge and some control of the
resources of inanimate nature and of the animal world.
But his life is passed in that stage of evolutionary development which precedes the birth of moral sentiment, of
intellectual perception, and social culture. He is a creature
stumbling over the first stepping-stones which lead from
savagery to civilization.

Though Shakespeare in Caliban makes a large generaliza-
tion from the data of aboriginal habit which lay at his disposal, he at many points reproduces with literalness the
common experience of Europeans in their first encounters
with aboriginal inhabitants of newly discovered lands.
Caliban's relations with the invaders of his isle are facts
of history. The savage's insistent recognition in the bru-
tish Trinculo of divine attributes is a vivid and somewhat ironical picture of the welcome accorded to Spanish,
French, and English explorers on their landing in the New
World. Thus did Pizarro present himself to the native
imagination in Peru, Cortes in Mexico, Cartier in Canada,
and Sir Francis Drake on the western coast of California.

It is fully in accord with recorded practice of European
pioneers in America that Prospero should seek at the outset to win Caliban's love in the guise of a patient teacher.
Prospero warns him against his crude conceptions of sun,
moon, and stars, and explains to him their true functions.
Every explorer shared Prospero's pity for the aborigines'
inability to make themselves intelligible in their crabbed,
agglutinative dialects, and offered them instruction in

civilized speech. On many a native Indian's ear there had fallen Prospero's words:

> When thou didst not, savage,
> Know thine own meaning, but wouldst gabble like
> A thing most brutish, I endow'd thy purposes
> With words that made them known.

At the same time there was much instruction that the native could offer his uninvited guest. Like every colonist, Prospero depended on his savage host for his knowledge of 'all the qualities' of the undiscovered country. From the aboriginal inhabitant alone could come, as in the play, indications of fresh-water springs or of the places where edible berries grew and good fish could be caught. There is an historic echo in the promise 'I'll show thee every fertile inch o' th' island', with which Caliban seeks the favour of the stranger Trinculo.

The menial services which Caliban renders his civilized master, the cutting and stacking of firewood, the scraping of trenchers, the washing of dishes, specifically associate Prospero and his servant with early settlements of Englishmen in Virginia. The native Virginians rendered to the Elizabethan invaders indispensable aid as hewers of wood and drawers of water. But Shakespeare's very precise mention of Caliban's labours as fisherman is the most literal of all transcriptions in the play from records of Virginian native life. 'I'll fish for thee,' Caliban tells Trinculo, and as soon as he believes that he has shaken off Prospero's tyrannical yoke, he sings with exultant emphasis, 'No more dams I'll make for fish'. This line from the play has not hitherto received comment from any of the thousand and one editors of *The Tempest*, and it may be questioned whether any student has yet appreciated its significance. Caliban's apparently careless declaration that he will make in his harsh master's behoof 'no more dams . . . for fish' is a vivid and penetrating illustration of a peculiar English experience in Virginia.

The Virginian natives had brought to rare perfection

a method of catching fish which was almost exclusively known to America, although some trace of it has been found in Burmah and other regions of the Far East. In their wide rivers the Virginians were wont to construct dams or weirs, which were contrived with singular ingenuity. It was on the fish which was thus procured by the Virginian natives that the first English settlers mainly depended for their sustenance. The reports of Raleigh's early agents in Virginia are at one with those of the later founders of Jamestown in their expression of amazement at the mechanical skill which the natives brought to the construction of their fish-dams, whereby they secured an uninterrupted supply of fresh fish. A series of fences made of willow poles and bound to one another by intricate wicker-work, ran in a series of circular compartments from the bank into the river-bed, and a clever arrangement of baskets within the fenced enclosures placed great masses of fish every day at the disposal of the makers and owners of the dams. The secret of construction was well kept by the natives, and European visitors, to their embarrassment, never learned it. The system was widely spread over the continent, and is still occasionally practised by the natives in remote places in both North and South America. In Shakespeare's day Englishmen only knew of the Indian art of weir fishing from the accounts that were given by travellers in Florida and Virginia.

One of the chief anxieties of the early English settlers in Virginia was lest the natives should fail them in keeping the dams in good order. When Raleigh's first governor of Virginia, Ralph Lane, detected, in 1586, signs of hostility among the natives about his camp, his thoughts at once turned to the weirs. If they were once broken by the revolting aborigines, and none were willing to repair them, starvation was a certain fate of the colonists. For no Englishmen knew how to construct and work these fish-dams, on which the settlement relied for its chief food. The gloomy anticipation of the failure of the dams through native disaffection came true in those early days, and was a chief cause of the disastrous termination of the sixteenth-century efforts to found an English colony in Virginia. The narratives of the later Virginian explorers, Captain John Smith and William Strachey, whose energies were engaged in the foundation of Jamestown, bear similar testimony to the indispensable service rendered by the natives' fish-dams to English colonists. Caliban's threat to make 'no more dams for fish' consequently exposed Prospero to a very real and a familiar peril.

Definite as are the touches which link Caliban with Virginians or Floridans, there are plain indications also that Shakespeare, in sketching the outline of the portrait, had flung his gaze on Raleigh's visitors from Guiana. Caliban's name comes philologically from that of the widespread race of Caribbeans, who were the first of American aborigines to see the face of Europeans. It was on their homesteads in the West Indies that Columbus descended, and when the Spanish invaders drove them from their island abodes, they took refuge on the northern coast of the southern continent, where Raleigh met them. Their generic name is very variously given in the early reports of American exploration. The first syllable appears not only as Car-, but as Cal-. In one of its more or less corrupt shapes it is indistinguishable from Caliban, while in another it gave birth to the more familiar form of Cannibal. Some rapid study of the Carib race was clearly an ingredient in Shakespeare's composite conception of aboriginal America.

But Shakespeare also incorporated traits of other American races, who ranked far lower than Virginian or Caribbean in the scale of human development. The dramatist's mention of the god Setebos, the chief object of Caliban's worship, echoes accounts of the wild people of Patagonia, who lived in a state of unqualified savagery. Patagonia is bounded on the south by the Magellan Straits, and the mighty exploits of Magellan in first threading that tortuous waterway first brought the Patagonians within the cognizance of Europe. An Italian mariner who sailed in

Magellan's fleet first put into writing an account of their barbarous modes of life and their uncouth superstitions. His tract circulated widely in Shakespeare's day in English translations. During the dramatist's lifetime the mysterious people was more than once visited by adventurous English seamen, and curiosity about them spread. Sir Francis Drake and Thomas Cavendish, in their circumnavigations of the globe, both paused on Patagonian territory, and held intercourse with its strange inhabitants. One of Drake's companions was left behind on Patagonian shores, and lived among the savages for eight years, ultimately reaching England in safety, as if by a miracle, to narrate his startling experiences. Controversy arose among sixteenth-century visitors to Patagonia as to whether the wild dwellers there were giants or no. Drake denied them any excessive stature. It is certain that they belonged to the most rudimentary type of humanity with which Europeans had yet come into contact, and that in 'their great devil Setebos' centred the most primitive conceptions of religion which had come to the knowledge of civilized man. When Caliban acknowledges himself to be a votary of 'the Patagonian devil' he declares his affinity with an Indian type, which was very abhorrent to European sentiment.

In one respect Shakespeare departs from his authorities. Although untrustworthy rumours spread abroad that aboriginal tribes in unexplored forests about the river Amazon were hideously distorted dwarfs, the evidence is conclusive that the average Indian of America—even the Patagonian—was physically as well formed and of much the same stature as Englishmen. Yet Caliban is described as of 'disproportioned' body; he is likened to 'a tortoise' and is denounced as a 'freckled whelp', or a 'poor, credulous monster '. Such misrepresentation on Shakespeare's part is no doubt conscious and deliberate. Caliban's distorted form brings into bolder relief his moral shortcomings, and more clearly defines his psychological significance. It is an involuntary homage to the Platonic idea, which Elizabethan poetry completely assimilated, that the soul determines the form of the body. Shakespeare's seeing eye invested his 'rude and savage man of Ind' with a shape akin to his stunted intelligence and sentiment. The creation of Caliban is a plea, however fantastically phrased, for common sense interpretation of the native problem. In Caliban's personality Shakespeare refutes the amiable delusion that the aborigines conserved Utopian ideals which civilization had abandoned and would do well to recover. At the same time Shakespeare tacitly offers the more hopeful and the more fruitful suggestion that human development marches forward, and never backward, and that creatures like Caliban embody an embryonic manhood which European civilization had outgrown, and to which it could not revert. Shakespeare cherished no delusions about the imperfections of current civilization. He knew all the 'instruments of darkness' which threatened civilized human nature. Nevertheless, he could hold out no hope of salvation to Prospero's servant-monster unless he were ready in due time, without undue coercion, loyally to follow in civilized man's footsteps. This was the only substantial moral which the visits of American Indians to Elizabethan England helped to point for Shakespeare.

THE PATH TO JAMESTOWN

I

NEARLY eleven decades intervened between the first permanent settlement of Spaniards on the mainland of America and the first permanent settlement of Englishmen. The sixteenth century, with all its wealth of incident and idea, began and ended in the interval. The space of time was as large as that which divided the death of Washington from the first installation of Mr. Roosevelt as President of the United States. Very tardily did England join Spain and France in competition for the glory of peopling the New World.

It is common knowledge that in the spring of 1606 the English King and Government, overcoming obstinate scruples of the past, frankly proclaimed responsibility for colonial endeavour in America. Very familiar is the fact that a year later there were laid, under the auspices of King James I, the foundation of that colonial plantation of Englishmen—the first to survive infancy—of which the tercentenary was lately celebrated. The royal name of James distinguished that primal settlement as well as the river leading to it from the sea. Jamestown on James River, despite vicissitudes which threatened premature ruin, was the acorn whence sprang the mighty oak of an English North America. From the first Stuart monarch descends the American Republic. The line, if devious, is uninterrupted. Romance alone associates any genuine share of such parental honours with the more glorious name of Queen Elizabeth.

Uncertain and wayward were the processes which prepared the land for the sowing of the fruitful seed. Failure and disappointment darkened the colonial experiments of Queen Elizabeth's subjects in the New World. The patches of light are few and shifting. Tragic gloom shrouded those paths to Jamestown which the Elizabethans sought to tread. The strength of the barriers has often been underrated. Yet a fuller understanding of the Elizabethan repulse enhances the credit and interest of the Jacobean triumph. In these pages an endeavour will be made to set in the perspective of contemporary senti-ment the long series of skirmishes which failed to bring Elizabethan Englishmen to the goal of their colonial am-bition, and left the guerdon to be won by their Jacobean successors.

II

With miraculous ease did Spain absorb the Latin notion of a colonial empire across the seas, which should, despite the strain of distance, be securely welded to the mother country. Such a notion was assimilated with difficulty by the average Elizabethan mind. In the early days of Queen Elizabeth's reign, when the American empire of Spain was near half a century old, the English sovereign herself confessed a strangely complete ignorance of the colonial conception. In 1563 rumours of stirring adventures, which befell Spanish and French explorers in the newly discovered paradise of Florida, caused fluttering of heart among some English seamen. Thomas Stukeley, a bom-bastic buccaneer of Devonshire, organized, by permission of the English crown, an expedition to the seductive territory. Three ships were commissioned for the service, and before they sailed their blunt-spoken leader Stukeley had an interview with his sovereign. With engaging frank-ness he informed Queen Elizabeth that his aim was in-dependent sovereignty in America. The Queen showed no surprise, nor did she raise objection. 'Would he re-member her', she inquired, 'when he had settled in his kingdom?' 'Yes,' he replied, 'and write unto you also.' 'And what style wilt thou use?' continued the ruler of England. 'To my loving sister, as one prince writes to another,' was the answer. The adventurer left the royal presence with felicitations and without rebuke. Not yet had it dawned on the Queen that she was able to wield a

sceptre over subjects who should fix their domicile on the
farther shore of the Atlantic Ocean.

Stukeley did not push his declared design far; piratical
raids on shipping in the high seas were more in his sphere
than an experiment in empire. Yet his unrebuked avowal
of a resolve to create an English kingdom in America
not for his Queen and country, but for himself, carries
a significant moral—a moral, too, which may not be palatable to those of little faith in the beneficence of active
monarchical interposition in the world's affairs. Events
were to prove that genuine fruition could not come of the
colonial idea in England until the English crown plainly
acknowledged a title and an obligation to govern and
control subjects who left their homes for new and
distant lands. Queen Elizabeth's views of kingship never
developed in that direction; the attitude which she assumed
to Stukeley she maintained to the end. She rarely withheld
approval from colonial effort of private persons, but she
declined official responsibility for its conduct or maintenance. Hakluyt, the literary champion of the colonial
idea, vainly pointed to the examples of the sovereigns of
Spain and France, and appealed to her to accept the
leadership of a colonial movement. Her ears were closed
to his 'soul-animating strains'. The problem of linking
oversea colonies with a mother country fell outside her
political horizon. Her successor's notion of colonial sovereignty in America was foreign to her political ambitions.

The average home-keeping Elizabethan was as slow as
his sovereign to perceive advantage in a sustained attempt
to colonize America. It was not as a colonizing field that
the New World swam into his ken. News of guerilla
assaults by Hawkins or Drake on Spanish shipping and
Spanish trade warmed his blood. Spoil of gold and pearl
exerted on him its allurement. But geographical discovery
with the practical view to colonization had for him a
visionary savour. It was the Utopian fancy of romantic
idealists. Long before and long after Queen Elizabeth
reached the throne, the typical Englishman's desultory

hope of discovering in the new hemisphere unknown lands and seas was confined within narrow bounds. His trading instinct limited his American aspiration to 'increase of traffic', to the finding of new markets for home manufactures, or of new reservoirs of precious metal and other raw material for home consumption. Little notion of settlement in distant America coloured the normal mercantile aspiration of Tudor England. A representative Elizabethan merchant-captain frankly deprecated colonial designs, and warned the men in his employ that should they attempt to settle in any new country which they visited with a view to trade, they would, if captured, be treated as deserters, and suffer condign punishment. The argument that the ranks of labour at home were overfull and that some outlet was needed for the surplus population made small appeal to Elizabethan capitalists. Not till the next century was opening did the dominant trading spirit of the nation countenance a national policy of oversea colonization. Then only did the colonial plea, which men of letters and knight-errants had already urged with imaginative enthusiasm, begin to sway the rank and file of men of business and politicians.

III

The conservative temper of the average Elizabethan merchant was reinforced by the reluctance of the average Elizabethan mariner to sail in latitudes which were not clearly traced on the charts. There was, too, the natural tendency of average public opinion to contrast, with some declamatory vehemence, the insecurity of life in unknown countries with the certain safety on one's own hearthstone. But apart from these discouragements, there was a substantial political obstacle to the early colonial ambition of the Elizabethan. The niceties of diplomacy checked English advance on America and even descents on the islands off the coast. From the outset of the Spanish Discovery in the fifteenth century and through most part of the century that followed, Spain stiffly held by the

R r

doctrine that international law practically closed America
—islands and mainland alike—to English colonial effort.
That churlish doctrine was only formally challenged in
England after much delay.

Despite the impatience of papal doctrine, which conquered the English mind during the sixteenth century,
there attached to papal authority a specious sanction of
which Tudor England never wholly rid herself. Englishmen, while chafing against the contention, hesitated to
deny point-blank the validity of Rome's formal gift at the
end of the fifteenth century to Spain or Portugal of all
land in the new hemisphere which lay south of the forty-
fourth degree of latitude. Probably none in England knew
at the outset what territory was situated either north
or south of that line. There existed an impression that
it marked (as was doubtless intended) the furthermost
northern limit of habitable land in the New World.
Very gradually was that misapprehension dissipated. Very
slowly the conception dawned on England of an habitable
area to the north of the pretended sphere of Spanish and
Portuguese influence. Only by very gradual degrees did
Englishmen realize that, even if the papal decree had
binding force, there lay beyond Spanish dominion the
spacious regions of Canada, with its ample northern and
western provinces as well as that broad band of the earth's
surface which ultimately harboured six expansive northerly states of the American Union. Ultimately it was
recognized that the papal donation to Spain overlooked a
generous half of the northern continent and that, save for
the great empire of Mexico in the extreme south, and
some sparse outlying settlements in mid-Florida and
California, the Spanish hold on North America lacked
substance. But it cost England near a century to take this
all-important lesson to heart. Meanwhile the English
Government was fertile in warnings against encroachment
on the Spanish claims. Even when colonial hopes were
acquiring more or less formal shape in the later days of
Elizabethan England, the Government admonished ad-

venturers that 'only remote heathen and barbarous lands, countries, and territories *not actually possessed of any Christian prince or people*' were open to their incursions. On their first expeditions to the New World, Englishmen as a consequence ventured mainly to the inhospitable extremities of the North so as to avoid the possible menace of Spanish pretensions. Yet even through these desolate regions, which lent colonial aspiration small encouragement, it was sometimes feared that Spain might question the right of way. When a scheme for an English expedition to the fabled empire of Cathay on the other side of the Arctic regions temporarily attracted in the middle of the century some mercantile and maritime enterprise of London, it was deemed safer, in view of the papal donation, to seek a north-east rather than a north-west passage through the Arctic Ocean.

It was no conscious pressure of colonial zeal which led Elizabethans to demand of Spain some abatement of her extravagant claim. On another ground was objection based. The maritime adventurers who raided Spanish ships and ports with an eye to plundering Spanish trade, found the risks of their activity greatly multiplied by Spain's grotesque theory that the entrance of any foreign ship within the western hemisphere amounted to a trespass, if not to an act of war. The Elizabethan sea-rover, despite his indifference to colonizing ambition, resented Spain's pretension to exclude altogether his semi-piratical energy from the Atlantic and Pacific oceans. At the urgent entreaty of Sir Francis Drake, the boldest of Elizabethan seamen, Queen Elizabeth's Government took a diplomatic step which, although it fell short of disputing the validity of Spain's title, usefully limited its application. English lawyers were induced by the buccaneers to enunciate the axiomatic but new principle that occupation was a condition of possession, and that occupation was something more than 'descents on the coasts and the building of cottages and the giving of names to the country'. The law of nations offered no hindrance to 'foreign princes from freely navigating those seas' and even visiting and occupying, if they so wished it, 'those parts *where the Spaniards did not inhabit*'.

Thus in 1580 was evolved the legal maxim: 'Prescription without possession availeth nothing.' It was a two-edged weapon, for it left all sparsely settled territory at the mercy of every fresh invader. But as a specific challenge in legal terminology of Spain's claim to the whole continent of America, it swept out of the road a real preliminary obstacle to England's imperial advance. So long as the papal division of the New World's surface went unquestioned, those who were neither Spanish nor Portuguese were presumably guilty of a breach of international comity by engaging in maritime, mercantile, or colonial enterprise within the American area. The territory of Virginia, where the colonial flag of England was first unfurled to any purpose, fell well within the prohibited bounds of Spain. It had been traversed by Spanish pilgrims; nearly eighty years before Englishmen arrived there the Christian faith had been preached on the site of Jamestown by Spanish monks; Elizabethans first learned of Chesapeake Bay from the maps of contemporary explorers of Spain. Though no Spaniard had made a permanent home in Virginia, the English title was incapable of legal definition until virtual occupation by the Spaniard became an acknowledged condition of his legal possession, and his mere prescriptive right was repudiated.

IV

Out of the way of Spain, in the extreme north, far above the Spanish papal border, Elizabethans made their first poor colonial experiment in the New World. By slow gradations and at substantial intervals of time the questionable limit of Spanish dominion was approached from the north and then was crossed by the colonial pioneers. The opening chapter of English colonial effort is the story of a descent by intermittent stages from the Arctic to the temperate zone.

Shadows of the papal donation darkened the horizon of Sir Humphrey Gilbert, the earliest prophet of North American colonization. He never ventured actively to dispute Spain's monopoly of southerly latitudes. His attention was absorbed by regions of the north. It was by a somewhat circuitous process of thought that Sir Humphrey came to recommend, in speeches and writings, a first English settlement on the American continent. At the outset he confined his energies to preaching discovery of the fabulous treasury of Cathay, by way of a north-west passage through the Arctic Ocean. It was a second and subsidiary thought of his to plant an English colony on that north-west road of snow. The main condition of Gilbert's original plan was that England should command the Arctic approaches to the gold and pearl of Cathay. The scheme gives its framer no small title to fame, although it was traced on melting ice.

The hopeless design was pursued in all seriousness. Three expeditions at Gilbert's instance set out for untracked latitudes of the Arctic Sea. The command was borne by Gilbert's disciple, Martin Frobisher, whose colonial failure was fully atoned by his heroic invasion of unknown Arctic regions. With equal earnestness he sought to discover the north-west waterway to the East, and to plant an English colony on the land bordering the ice-bound passage. The revelation of the frozen shores and seas of Labrabor was the main reward of his energy. Appropriately he named the new country Meta Incognita.

It was on Frobisher's second voyage that the colonial hope for the first time challenged active support in England. A hundred Englishmen, 'well minded and forward young gentlemen', volunteered to go out and test for twelve months life on American earth. Forty were soldiers, thirty were 'bakers, carpenters, and necessary persons', and thirty were men willing to work, if opportunity arose, in mines. With ignorant complacence they talked of the cold climate and hostile natives that awaited them, and of the sure protection that would be afforded them by 'a strong fort or house of timber', which was a chief part of their empirical equipment. But the rigours of the Arctic sky quickly froze the adventurers' blood, and after a few weeks' suffering they acknowledged defeat and sailed home. The colonial design had gone altogether astray; it had involved itself in ridicule. It is a curious comment on this first misconceived plan of Englishmen to inhabit American territory that, in spite of all the exploring activity of the intervening period, the site of Frobisher's colony was not revisited by men of European blood for two hundred and eighty-four years. Then in 1862 Captain C. F. Hall, an American searcher after the North Pole, discovered remains of Frobisher's settlement. Frobisher's experiment made plain that a colonial home must be sought farther south, if colonial hope of America were to live.

In the second act of the Elizabethan colonial drama, Sir Humphrey Gilbert, Frobisher's patron, played the master-role in person. His colonial ideas developed in the light of the warnings of Frobisher's experience. The old tradition of Cathay was shedding a false light on the colonial path. Colonial aspiration asked a freer area of exercise. And something more was required. Gilbert foresaw that, if colonial projects were to win respect and were to promise results of substance instead of shadows, the English Government must lend openly its help and prestige. Spain and France had treated colonial experiments as imperial undertakings. Was England to do less?

The future was on Gilbert's side, but for the present Queen Elizabeth and her advisers hesitated. Not yet would the rulers of England identify themselves with the design of a colonial occupation of America. But Gilbert was at the moment strongly backed. His importunity admitted of no unqualified negative. But he had to rest content with an innocent formula, in the shape of letters-patent, authorizing him to discover and occupy unknown lands. The document had ancient warrant, and committed the authorities to little or nothing. Sir Humphrey Gilbert was granted 'free liberty and license from time

to time and at all times for ever hereafter, to discover,
find, search out and view such remote heathen and barbarous lands, countries, and territories not actually possessed of any Christian prince or people, as to him, his
heirs and assigns, and to every or any of them shall seem
good, and the same to have, hold, occupy, and enjoy'. As
far as the official instrument went, Gilbert was free to
discover and occupy any unclaimed part of Europe, Asia,
or Africa. No mention of America figured in his letters-
patent. Spanish susceptibilities were not to be ruffled.
The English Government declined to avow responsibility
for what its subjects might be minded to do across the
Atlantic. The existence of the New World was officially
ignored.

Embarrassing contradictions weakened the framework
of Gilbert's vague charter. In the preamble Gilbert's
rights were declared to be perpetual, but the main clauses
of the document limited the grant to a period of six years,
and nothing was said of a renewal. Although the topic
was lightly indicated in shadowy outline, none of the
crucial questions touching the constitutional relation of a
colony to a mother-country received attention. Gilbert's
colonists, in whatever quarter of the unoccupied globe
they might plant themselves, were to enjoy the privileges
of free denizens and natives of England, and were to
maintain allegiance to the crown of England and to the
established Church. The Queen and her Government
claimed of them no other services or duties than the pay-
ment into the royal exchequer of a fifth part of all gold and
silver ore which might be discovered in the new country.
This was a tentative assertion of the feudal right over
mines of precious metal, which was claimed by monarchs
of their subjects all the world over, and had been of late
loudly asserted in the New World by the kings of Spain
and Portugal. For the rest, independent sovereignty was
made over to Gilbert. For six years at any rate he was
authorized to make his own statutes, laws, and ordinances;
save with his permission none might approach within two

hundred leagues of his settlement. If an English colony were to come into being across the ocean, Queen Elizabeth wished it made clear that she was indisposed to accept the active anxieties of rule.

It was not until that term of six years, which was stipulated in the helpless formula, was nearly ended that Gilbert found serious opportunity of making the colonial experiment on which he had set his heart. An earlier preliminary effort brought him no nearer North America than the Cape Verde Islands. Five years intervened before any genuine advance was essayed. Then Gilbert sailed for the 'New Found Land', by which was vaguely meant a territory somewhere to the south of Frobisher's Meta Incognita, and somewhere to the north of any known Spanish settlement.

V

Honest enthusiasm was Gilbert's strongest credential. Of the shape and extent of North America he, like his contemporaries, had learned little, and he cherished many misconceptions. Of the French explorations in the Canadian region, which was already christened Nova Francia, he knew much less than he might. Reports had reached him of a flourishing semi-civilized native kingdom off the north Atlantic, called Norumbega, but that realm was a geographical fiction. French, Spanish, and English fleets had long fished for cod in the summer months off Greenland and the Newfoundland banks. But whether the adjoining shores belonged to scattered islands of the Atlantic or to the American mainland was mere food for conjecture among Elizabethan sailors. Spanish and French reports had revealed, on the continent farther south, the smiling territory of Florida, the coast of which had been lightly surveyed by Drake and Hawkins. Of the precise relations of Florida to the northern country no study had yet been made.

Small heed was paid to the story of the men who, abandoned in 1568 by Sir John Hawkins on the Mexican

coast, claimed to have measured on foot some 2,000 miles
before they reached the confines of Nova Francia, where
they took passage for England in a French vessel. Useful
hints lurked in the neglected allegation, which may well
have been true.

Gilbert had endeavoured, with as much pertinacity as
any Elizabethan, to ascertain the geography of North
America. But the truth for the most part eluded him.
He had devised a map of the world, but his strange sketch
of North America presented Labrador and Canada as
islands adjoining the extreme north of a shapeless continent, on which he set two labels, the upper one bearing the
words 'New France', and the lower one the word 'Florida'.
Nor did greater success attend another English effort in
North American cartography which, just before Gilbert
set sail, was published under the auspices of so ardent a
seeker after knowledge as Sir Philip Sidney. There North
America figures as two crude rectangles with the lower
corner of one intruding into a top corner of the other.
The upper irregular rectangle, which is small, is called
Canada and the lower rectangle, which is large, is designated Florida, while the northern boundary of sea is thickly
studded with islands large and small. It was by the aid of
the vaguest guesswork and of the untutored imagination
that Gilbert proceeded to fulfil his great design of a North
American colony.

On all sides ignorance encompassed Gilbert. That
manual labour was a first essential to the success of colonial
effort was ill-appreciated by those who offered him their
company. It was a lesson their English successors were
slow to learn. The result of Gilbert's venture is sufficiently familiar. His companions deemed their task completed when, with some pomp and pageantry, they had
planted the standard of England in the harbour of St.
John on the east coast of the island of Newfoundland—the
nearest point to England in the New World.

Ignorance finally claimed the toll of Gilbert's life on the
voyage homewards. Conservative English mariners still

adhered to the medieval habit of hugging the land as far
as was practicable even in ocean travel. Neither on the
outward nor on the homeward journey was Gilbert suffered to keep a direct course across the waters of the North
Atlantic. Confidence was sought by endeavours to coast
round the islands of the South Atlantic. On a shoal near
the Azores the ship that was bearing Gilbert to England
foundered. Thus was the earliest colonial ambition of an
Elizabethan prematurely quenched. The recently devised
maxim 'prescription without possession availeth nothing'
rendered it doubtful whether Gilbert had conveyed to
English ownership any rood of American land. At best
he had asserted a claim to an island. The mainland was
still untouched.

VI

Without alteration of its helpless terms, Gilbert's
passport to unknown coasts was transferred on his death
to his half-brother and fellow-enthusiast, Sir Walter
Raleigh. With the transference of the passport the scene
of ineptitude shifts.

Before Gilbert reached Newfoundland some better-
informed Englishmen suggested that Spain had so sparsely
settled the spacious territory of Florida as to leave room
for new-comers. In view of Gilbert's and Frobisher's fruitless ventures in the northern region of North America,
it was prudent for Gilbert's heir to canvass the colonial
possibilities of the South. Raleigh, on succeeding to Gilbert's privileges, set to work to test the suggestion. The
resolve marked an important advance in colonizing effort.
Yet the new chapter in its main drift merely played, after
a misleadingly auspicious prelude, variation on the old
note of tragic ignorance.

Within little more than six months of the tragic ending
of Gilbert's career, two small ships sailed at Raleigh's
expense for North America. They followed the customary
route of the Canaries and West Indies. After thirteen
weeks they landed on what was judged to be the northerly

limit of Florida. It was the island of Roanoke, off
what is now North Carolina. It is on that island, not
yet on the mainland, that the next act in the colonial
drama was played. The sailors returned to spread
exultant impressions of their brief experience of life in
America. Raleigh and his friends were blindly confident
that their hour had struck, and, in their first enthusiasm,
they sought to invest their scheme with an imposing
sanction. Raleigh improved on Gilbert's appeal for the
sovereign's support. He requested the legislature to confirm and define Gilbert's intangible privileges, which had
been made over to himself. He invited the nation assembled in Parliament to lend its countenance to a definite
plan for the Elizabethan colonization of America.

As a result, nearly ninety years after the discovery of
America, the English Parliament took cognizance of the
New World's existence. A Bill was quickly passed through
the House of Commons to purge Gilbert's letters-patent
of a part of their incertitude. A region of Florida was to be
granted by statute to Sir Walter. Following the reports
of Raleigh's first agents, the House of Commons called the
land by the unfamiliar appellation of Wyngandacoia, after
its alleged native owner. The English nation soon re-
christened the territory Virginia, after their virgin Queen,
but the parliamentary journals ignore that familiar appellation. Only a bare official note survives of the first, second,
and third readings of the American Bill in the Commons
and of the first reading in the Lords. A full report of these
earliest colonial debates in the English Parliament is wanting, but there is no doubt that the Bill became law, and
that, in spite of much prejudice against pledging the
nation's credit to unknown risks, Parliament blessed a
limited enterprise of 'Wyngandacoian' colonization. Parliament only forbade prisoners for debt, persons under arrest,
married women, wards, and apprentices from enlisting in
this colonial service. The more important question of how
the Home Government should exert authority over the
distant colonial settlements lay as yet outside official

consideration. But it was something, although less than might appear, that for the first time with the sanction of Parliament a colonial experiment was set on foot.

The Parliament's benediction dates from December 1584. Four months later as many as six score Englishmen eagerly emigrated to the Virginian region which lay near the indeterminate bounds of Florida. The island of Roanoke off the North Carolina coast, which had already been surveyed, was reoccupied. But victory was still far off. Elizabethan gentlemen viewed with impatience the humble toil of colonial pioneers. Supplies failed; labour was scarce; quarrels multiplied; home-sickness wore out energy. A year dragged its tedious length, without communications from the old country. Then Sir Francis Drake, while bent on maritime raiding, by chance descried from the sea the settlement of despair. He carried the whole company back to their native land. With no compunction did Drake cut short the colonial adventure. The seaman only recognized the colonists' impotence and helplessness. For him the New World meant opportunity of naval war and a treasury to be despoiled. No conception of a possible home attached to America in the restless and aspiring minds of the men whose ambition lay in gathering Spanish spoil, and in wounding Spanish pride.

But Drake was justified on more material ground in scorning the proferred aspirations of Queen Elizabeth's first Virginian colonists. They were merest sciolists in colonial lore. In the smiling plains and fruitful forests of the Virginian solitude many of them had yearned for 'fair houses and dainty food or soft beds of down and feathers', and they avenged their foolish misapprehensions by speaking ill at home of the new country. Yet the truth did not elude all. One of the experimental settlers, Thomas Hariot, then a youth of twenty-five, who in maturer years was to acquire world-wide fame as mathematician and free-thinking man of science, sought, in a practical treatise on the natural products of Virginia, to stem the tide of ignorance and prejudice which was threatening colonial zeal. His work chiefly relieves the first invasion of Virginia from the reproach of barrenness.

Blind chance was for twenty years yet to govern the tide of England's colonial effort. Wanton challenges of disaster were now to be requited by the death of English colonists not at sea alone, but on American soil. An ominous incident which followed Drake's rescue of Hariot and his friends preludes the most dismal of historic tragedies. A relief expedition arrived just after the colonists' departure, and fifteen men were left behind to solve the mystery of the temporary disappearance of their fellow-countrymen whom Drake was conveying home. The fifteen lives were flung away in the tangle of cross-purposes.

Within two years Virginia was to take eight times as large a toll of English flesh and blood. When for a second time the Virginian trail was deliberately pursued by Elizabethan pioneers, there was design of abandoning the island site, and of gaining at length the mainland of the new continent. It was a departure of significance. The Spaniards had lately explored Chesapeake Bay, and had marked it for the first time on maps. Hopeful reports of the neighbouring country were wandering through Europe. There were warnings in the air that the English project would not go uncontested by other nations of the Old World. Raleigh's agents undertook to anticipate rivalry by hoisting the English flag on the inner shore of the far-spreading bay, of founding there a city to be known by their master's surname. But a careless or treacherous pilot, of foreign race, annulled the English hope of reaching the main territory. He carried the new settlers to the old island of doubtful omen. The mainland still lay outside the colonial sphere of Elizabethan England.

In one regard, organization of Elizabethan colonial venture now underwent a change, which seemed of fresh and fertile promise. English women and English children were to accompany husbands, brothers, and sons. Virginia was to become a veritable English home. The second Virginian colony, which was led by the artist-explorer,

John White, one of the settlers of Hariot's year, comprised
ten married couples along with eighty-four men, seven
spinsters, and nine boys. There were 120 souls in all. It
was the first time that English women trod American
ground. But it was to be the only time in Elizabethan or
even in early Jacobean days. Yet all was at present delusive. The women's presence, so far from bringing any
turn of colonial luck to Elizabethan England, carried a
worse fate than any that marked preceding colonial
endeavours. Hardly was the foundation of Raleigh's
second Virginian colony laid than doubts arose, and
Governor White was sent home for counsel and supplies.
Calamity straightway struck down the men, women, and
children to whom he bade farewell. There is small ground
for imagining that any survived his departure beyond a
few weeks. For nearly twenty years after, Queen Elizabeth's subjects, when they turned their gaze towards
North America, were lost in tearful surmise as to the fate
of their lost kindred in Virginia.

VII

This catastrophe of 1587 damped the ardour of Elizabethan advocates of colonization for nearly two decades.
Virginia fell in English eyes into ominous disrepute, from
which recovery could only be gradual. Raleigh and White
recognized it to be a point of honour to relieve any colonist who might perchance survive. But it was a futile search
in the way of which perverse fortune interposed delay.
The ill-starred devious course across the Atlantic by way
of the Azores, the Canaries, and the West Indies often
wasted on the passage fifteen or twenty precious weeks.
Spanish gunships, too, were never far from this circuitous
path. The year of the Armada followed that of the Virginian tragedy. Spain and England were at open war, and
the avenue to Virginia was wellnigh closed.

Three years passed before the fatal soil of Virginia was
retrodden by English feet. At length, in 1590, a relief
expedition under White's command spent five weary

months on the outward voyage, and a disproportionately
brief fortnight on the spot where leave was taken of the
colonists. Nothing was revealed beyond some footprints
on a sandy bank, and a carving on a tree-trunk of three
capital letters, which gave no certain sign. Plans of further
inquiry were discussed in despair.

The grim disaster of 1587 drove Virginia beyond immediate range of colonial hope. It was elsewhere that
colonial champions thought to make experiment, if their
aspirations were to live. Raleigh accepted the situation
and turned to the southern continent. He set out in
person to find Eldorado in Guiana—in that part of Guiana
which is now known as Venezuela. Half-heartedly he
promised to divert his course to the Virginian shore when
either going or returning. But he never steered for the
fatal settlement, and came home with his resolution confirmed to persuade his fellow-countrymen to acknowledge
failure in their northern quest and to concentrate all
energy on richer regions nearer the equator.

In the Northern continent, too, there were regions
forbidden, outside the range of Virginia, which absorbed
some thought and energy of champions of colonization.
Colonial aspiration was not large enough to be distributed
widely with impunity, and was now to be imperilled by
diversity of aim. Very soon after Raleigh's venture to
Guiana, three London merchants, two of whom, of Dutch
nationality, were filled with their countrymen's growing
zeal for maritime exploration, revived Gilbert's design
on Newfoundland. A small expedition under Charles
Leigh's guidance, was dispatched to test the possibility of
colonizing an island in 'the great river of Canada', the
Gulf of St. Lawrence. But Gilbert's failure was not retrieved, and the effort swelled the volume of deluded
hopes.

Only in the very last year of Elizabeth's reign were there
slender signs of returning zeal for the Virginian quest.
Samuel Mace of Weymouth, 'a very sufficient mariner,
and an honest sober man', crossed thither in a small

barque, once more under Raleigh's wavering auspices, and he wandered for a month about the scene of the forsaken settlement. Of the puny endeavour a modest cargo of sassafras was the only fruit. But the fallen Virginian breezes were rising. Within a month of Mace's return, a mariner cast in a larger mould, Bartholomew Gosnold, thought to repeat his experiment. His design was on a slightly larger scale and even included a vague notion of planting a Virginian colony anew. The venture linked itself very closely with one heroic episode of the past; for among Gosnold's colleagues was Bartholomew, son of Sir Humphrey Gilbert. The issue differed from aught that was intended. By significant accident Gosnold missed his route, and his miscalculation shed unintentionally a gleam of light prophetic on the dark close of Elizabethan colonial endeavour in North America. After touching the Azores Gosnold sailed for the west, and landed on what he took to be a northern stretch of the Virginian coast. Neither he nor his companions clearly realized that they had reached a country which maps hitherto ignored or misapprehended. The point of debarkation was midway between the old Virginian settlement and the scene of Sir Humphrey Gilbert's achievement. It proved to be Cape Cod on the Massachusetts coast. In that neighbourhood the last of the Elizabethan colonial adventurers lingered for a month, christening new headlands and islands, and bestowing on one the name of Queen Elizabeth, whose days were now numbered. On his setting out choice had been made of a score of his two-and-thirty companions to make a new colonial trial of Virginia. But when the moment came for farewell the chosen crew proved recalcitrant, and this colonial project, which had been involuntarily diverted to the district of Massachusetts, ended before it began.

Gosnold crudely named his newly discovered territory North Virginia. The time was at hand when North Virginia, under its more lasting cognomen of New England, was to prove a formidable competitor with 'South'

Virginia for colonial honours. But Gosnold was himself an inheritor of unfulfilled renown. Returning to England with his mind set on revisiting the region of Cape Cod, he was denied the opportunity of which others availed themselves. Circumstances led him to resume the quest of the older Virginia of the South. There he proved a foremost contriver of the permanent settlement in 1607, but he was cut off by death as soon as the foundation-stone was laid. The fruit of all his labours escaped his hand. A better fate was merited by the only Elizabethans who brought to Queen Elizabeth's subjects the knowledge, bare though it was, that the land which was to become New England existed on the world's surface.

VIII

The most sanguine of Englishmen, who advocated the colonial advance on America, could not resist a sense of depression when, at the date of Queen Elizabeth's death, he surveyed the results of his fellow-countrymen's efforts to settle in America. With more or less confident hope there had been planned, in the last quarter of a century, English colonial settlements in five different regions of America, regions for the most part distant from one another, and amply representative of the varied natural capacities of the New World. In the northern continent, Labrador, Newfoundland, North Carolina, Massachusetts, —in the southern continent, Venezuela (to give the places their modern names), had all been more or less tested from the colonizing point of view. But from all the same helpless response of negation had come back in monotonous sequence. No living English colonist occupied a foot of land in America when Queen Elizabeth died.

Sea-power had failed to minister to the realization of the colonial ideal. The maritime adventures of Elizabeth's reign had singed the beard of the King of Spain but had done little in the process to cherish the colonial hope. The exploits of Drake and Cavendish were fertile in exhilarating romance, and made the name of Englishman a word of fear on the Spanish main. But they had not diminished by conquest the area of Spanish dominion in America. Nor had the wide range of their sea travel revealed for certain any hitherto unknown habitable land which was open to English colonists and was free from the active menace of Spain. It was only in the inhospitable Arctic zone that Elizabethan mariners had made geographical discoveries for which the credit goes unquestioned. In Southern latitudes Drake came nearer the Pacific shores of Cape Horn than any before him, and he invaded a region of California into which it is doubtful if the Spaniard had penetrated. John Davis, the Elizabethan seaman, whose fame was made in Arctic seas, was probably the first European to catch a glimpse of the Falkland Islands in the South Atlantic. But neither Drake nor Davis widened the practicable outlook of the Elizabethan seeker after colonizing fields.

These Elizabethan buccaneers sought their abiding place on sea rather than on land, and little of their experience encouraged the conception of America as a home of safety for Englishmen. Tragic was the penalty too often paid by the heroic sea-rovers for the spoil of Spanish treasure and of Spanish prestige in the waters of the New World. Elizabethan fighting ships, which were usually of the tonnage of small yachts, wandered in the track of Spanish fleets for weeks or even months together. Very far from friendly ports, they could reckon on no peaceful refuge from the tempests of Mid or South Atlantic. If they weathered the storm they were driven out of their course, and their stores were in danger of exhaustion. Many times it happened that the greater part of the crew who escaped drowning died of hunger or thirst, and that the poor remnant reached a haven with hardly strength enough left 'to take in or heave a sail'. In the last years of the great Queen's reign death was especially active among Elizabethan adventurers in American seas, and their tragic fate deepened the gloom which hung over the colonial prospect. Cavendish had perished in the South Atlantic while making for 'the South Sea and the Philippines and the coast of China'. Drake himself died of dysentery off the coast of Panama, on which he had made an attack that failed. His body, enclosed in its leaded coffin, was laid to rest off the Isthmus, and with his ocean's funeral the hearts of colonial aspirants, who had dimly foretold England's sway of America, sank low.

IX

Unpromising as was the colonial outlook when James I ascended the English throne, yet forces which had lacked effective voice were at work to convert with strange celerity the failures of the past into triumphs of the future. No help came from a quarter in which it might presumably have been looked for. Of small moment was the turn of the political wheel which brought about peace between England and Spain in 1604. Whether the King of Spain was at peace or at war with the King of England, it was no intention of his to admit Englishmen to share with him the glories of American empire. The peace of 1604 stipulated for the exclusion of Englishmen from the Spanish Indies, and Spain's back was stiffened. With greater sternness than amid the distractions of war did she assert her ancient papal claim to North as well as to South America. The whole of Florida, in her view, spread northward beyond known limits, and it embraced the North and the South Virginia of English interlopers. Those regions no less than Mexico, Peru, and Brazil were to be protected from the invasion of English colonists. When the attempt on Virginia was renewed by the subjects of James I, protests from Madrid fell on London statesmen's ears with greater fury and frequency than at any earlier epoch. It was after Spain had become England's nominal ally in the Old World that England pressed onward to her colonial destiny in the New in the teeth of Spain's sharpened opposition.

It was religious and social problems rather than political questions or greed of treasure or love of adventure which finally gave the colonial aspirations of England the impetus required for a lasting issue. Religious and economic considerations had provided fuel for the Elizabethan champions. But their pleas had been heard with impatience or indifference by men of practical bent. The conception of the New World as a refuge for the surplus population of the Old remained unconvincing until, on the one hand, an industrial crisis was plainly reached in England, and on the other American soil gave clear proof of the capacity to yield familiar necessaries of life. The Elizabethan advocate had confined the religious justification of colonial settlements in America to the hope of spreading the Christian faith among the Pagan aborigines, a pious aspiration which has always looked visionary to the hard-headed. But when James I was firmly settled on the throne, both religious and economic diseases developed acuter phases than in the old century. In the seasons of crisis, anxious men began to look in earnest to America for means of cure.

In the middle of the sixteenth century French Huguenots first suggested to Protestant reformers of Europe that the solitudes of America might offer them that liberty and repose which Catholic rulers denied them at home. In England the religious conditions of France were reversed. After the Reformation of Henry VIII, Protestantism was the dominant power, and Catholics by sure stages fell into the position of the persecuted minority. The coercive enforcement of uniformity in religion was the life-blood of Queen Elizabeth's ecclesiastical policy. But in the later years of the sixteenth century the situation assumed a new complexity. The Protestant majority took to warfare within its own ranks, and the government of the country, while it continued to pursue with increasing vigour recusant Papists, extended the policy of persecution to aggressive Puritans. In the closing decade of the Queen's reign, the difficulties of reducing dissentient Protestants to obedience defied solution, and the views of the ecclesiastical governors of England underwent a corresponding qualification. They reached the conclusion that the banishment of nonconformists was a surer means than penal legislation of promoting religious unity. On this point the dissentients, although their affection for their country was strong, were not disposed to quarrel with their oppressors. The teaching of the Huguenots enjoyed authority amongst them. Through the closing years of the sixteenth century and the opening years of the seventeenth, Puritans, following the example set by their French brethren, were earnestly considering emigration to a country which should offer them religious freedom and peace.

The decision in favour of America was not taken hastily, but it was entertained at an early stage. The Calvinistic martyr, John Penry, before his execution in 1593, recommended his followers to settle in a new country, but he mentioned no place. Holland, where Protestantism prevailed, was nearer England than the New World and lay within the sphere of European civilization. There the first foreign refuge was sought by English nonconformists. But, before and after they migrated thither, their gaze turned to America. In 1597 four Puritan leaders sailed with official approval in Charles Leigh's disastrous expedition to the Gulf of St. Lawrence, which Dutch merchants, in London, in part financed. The misfortunes of that venture had the effect of darkening the American outlook, but it failed to extinguish it. The English Puritans, who emigrated to Holland, were unwilling to surrender their nationality, or their language. Their hold on both was imperilled by life under foreign rule. A settlement in hitherto unoccupied territory, where the English flag might yet fly above religious institutions of their own devising, was the ideal to which their hearts were wedded. It was the development of such a sentiment which helped to invest the American aspirations of Jacobean England with irresistible force.

The conception of America as an asylum from religious persecution was not only cherished by Puritan minds. The spread of the notion among Englishmen is curiously illustrated by proposals, secretly made in the first year of James I's reign, to form in the New World an English settlement of oppressed Catholics, to whom the Anglican establishment was repugnant from quite other than Puritan points of view. Catholic victims of the penal legislation of Elizabethan England were, when under the obligation of seeking a foreign refuge, more happily placed than their Puritan compatriots. All Europe, save Holland and parts of Germany, was open to them. The Pope and the Catholic kings of Spain and France encouraged the settlement within their dominions of English Romanists, for whom life in their own country was unendurable. But even among English Catholics, who found a welcome on the Continent, the sense of nationality was powerful enough to suggest the advantage of colonizing unpeopled solitudes where the English language and English modes of life might flourish at the side of their religious ceremonies. To Father Parsons, then rector of the English College at Rome, the strenuous leader of the English Catholics throughout Europe, there was submitted, in the first year of James I's reign, a scheme for a Catholic colony in the New World. The scale was far larger than had characterized any earlier colonial plan. Rich and poor were to join together in unprecedented numbers. Skilled craftsmen and agricultural labourers were to reach a total of four figures. Land-owners were to sell their property to provide substantial capital. Father Parsons detected difficulties in fulfilment of the design. But he did not reject it hastily. He believed in the mission of English Catholics to share in the work of bringing North America under the sway of Catholic orthodoxy, but he deemed the moment inopportune, on political and social grounds, for a vast migration of English Catholics from Europe. Yet this Catholic project remains a beacon of the times; it marked progress in the growth of the idea that the quest of religious liberty gave colonial enterprise its surest warrant.

The pressure on England of economic problems during

the opening years of James I's reign contributed hardly less than the religious problem to the colonial advance. The Poor Law legislation of Queen Elizabeth's reign, which bore witness to the urgency of industrial difficulties, had not lessened the evils of unemployment. Industrial distress soon threatened rebellion in the Midland counties of Jacobean England. The population seemed to be growing out of proportion to the means of sustenance. The limits of industrial endurance appeared to be well-nigh reached. The argument that those who had been driven by want into beggary and crime might find profitable labour in the New World, acquired for the first time a driving power. All, it was widely urged, would be well, if it were generally acknowledged that there was a spacious land, the way to which was through the sea, where everybody might find work and adequate reward.

With such sentiments abroad, interest in the colonial schemes renewed itself with unexampled strength. Men of influence in all walks of life—statesmen, courtiers, judges, clergymen, merchants—soon vied with each other in discussing colonial schemes and in offering contributions to the expenses of exploring expeditions. That colonial settlements were justifiable was no longer in dispute. That they were practicable it was an imperative duty to prove. It remained to determine where the first experiment was to be made, and whether or no private enterprise stood in need of State control. Such complicated questions required time for answer, but it was of good omen that they should be asked.

X

Gosnold's discovery of Massachusetts gave the leading cue to the maritime enterprise of the early years of James I's reign. But the Elizabethan tide of failure was not to turn immediately. Disaster was still to alternate with success. Much energy was still to be dissipated by lack of a single purpose or a single guide.

The earliest Jacobean venture carried on in full measure

the tragic tradition of Elizabethan disaster. Gosnold's companion, Captain Bartholomew Gilbert, Sir Humphrey's son, ventured on a trading expedition in the West Indies, whence a generous impulse carried him to the Virginian Coast in a last despairing hope of renewing the search for the lost Virginian colony. The fate of those victims of colonial effort had never ceased to depress the spirit of Sir Humphrey Gilbert's son. Like Gosnold he went farther north than he intended, but not quite so far as that noteworthy commander. Bartholomew Gilbert landed off Chesapeake Bay, at which Elizabethan ambition had vainly glanced, well to the north of the old Virginian settlement. But, falling in with a tribe of hostile natives, he was fatally wounded by their arrows. Four companions forfeited their lives with him, and unwillingly rejoined the lost colony in death. The first year of the new reign had lengthened the roll of American martyrs, and the cloud that hung over Elizabethan Virginia looked darker than of old.

Happily the gloom of this tragedy was relieved by the success of a Devonshire seaman, Martin Pring. With the aid of Bristol merchants he sailed of set purpose in Gosnold's tracks. For the second time an English ship surveyed the Massachusetts coast-line, and the birth of New England was brought a stage nearer. But the rising colonial enthusiasm was still menaced by divided counsels. The claim of South America on Englishmen's colonial energy was not yet rejected altogether. It was still possible to question the fitness of the North American continent for England's colonial expansion. Pring, who followed Gosnold northward, did not commit himself to the northern trail hastily. In the year following his return from Massachusetts he lent his influence and his maritime skill to a revived endeavour to settle Englishmen in the rival South. The moving spirit of this unblessed digression was Captain Leigh, whose misfortunes in a late Elizabethan assault on the Gulf of St. Lawrence, had alienated his sympathies from northern enterprise. Now, resolved to establish the superiority of a golden haven in the Southern continent, he sailed for Raleigh's Eldorado in Guiana, and founded a settlement there. But despair and disaffection spread rapidly among his followers, and death adversely decided the issue for him and most of his companions. In all directions tragedy assailed the unlucky experiment. The narrative of an attempt to relieve Leigh sounded a very ghastly note. The crew of the relief ship, dissatisfied with her equipment, landed on the outward voyage off the West Indian island of Santa Lucia; there nearly all were slain by savages in the cruellest massacre that had yet marked the path of English visitors to the western hemisphere. Pring escaped before the fatal close of this southern venture, and returned to England to prepare for more searching study of northern possibilities. The South had not advanced its title to preferential consideration.

Accident and miscalculation of the kind that gave Gosnold his chief title of honour were still crucial factors in the solution of the colonial problem. A momentous advance northwards in 1605 was another fortuitous outcome of a design to revisit Elizabethan Virginia. Untrustworthy charts led a new actor in the drama, one George Weymouth, to make on the Virginian voyage so liberal a bend to the north as to bring the State of Maine well within the colonial range. He clung to the fancy that he was surveying a new expanse of old Virginia while he was really exploring the northern river Kennebec. Weymouth's voyage is notable for something beyond an extended view of New England. One of its financial supporters was Shakespeare's patron, the Earl of Southampton, who was quickly to play a leading part on the colonial stage. The Earl first comes on the American scene as promoter of Weymouth's expedition, which sensibly widened the Northern horizon.

Weymouth's reports of the fertility of these northern stretches of so-called Virginia redoubled in James I's subjects the interest which Gosnold and Pring had inaugurated. New stimulus came from a foiled effort at fresh

progress. An adventurous gentleman of Plymouth, Henry
Challons, soon engaged Weymouth's pilot in order to
trace with him Weymouth's promising steps. In a ship
of twenty-five tons burden, manned by one and twenty
men, Challons resolved on 'a farther discovery of these
coasts'. But fickle fortune decided otherwise. The little
vessel, which sailed the traditional West Indian route, was
captured off Porto Rico by a galleon of Spain. Despite the
peace, Challons and most of his companions were carried
prisoners to Seville. Ultimately they escaped to England,
but for the time they were given up for lost. Now that
colonial zeal was alert in circles of influence, anxiety respecting the fate of Challons and his men grew acute. The
Lord Chief Justice of England (Sir John Popham) was
fired to engage in an effort at rescue. At his bidding Pring,
just home from Guiana, voyaged to North Virginia to
ascertain Challons's fortune. Details of Pring's experience
are wanting. But it is plain that he brought back descriptions more alluring than any who had preceded him of
'coasts, havens and harbours' about Maine and Massachusetts. The Northern curtain was lifted higher than before.

Thus, through the three opening years of the new reign,
was the hope of colonizing North Virginia steadily nearing
fulfilment. The burden of an ill-starred history had
stemmed the advance of Elizabethan Virginia in public
favour. North Virginia had inherited from the old reign
none of the discouraging memories of the South. The
experiences of that trio of New England pioneers, Gosnold, Pring, and Weymouth, whose names have received
smaller meed of fame than is their due, seemed in the
third year of James I's reign to have substituted the
Northern region for the Southern as the chief magnet of
colonial aspiration. At any rate, before Anglo-American
history well began, North and South on the northern
continent had each its English champions. But it was only
for the moment that the balance swayed in the direction
of the North. In the fifth year of the new reign the scale
slightly turned. By a hair's breadth the advocates of the

Southern region prevailed, and Virginia of the South was endowed with the honours of a narrow priority in the permanent settlement of America by Englishmen.

XI

Even in 1605, when victory was unexpectedly at hand, the colonial situation seemed to crave in vain a unifying or centralizing impulse. Enterprise, which was born of merely private spasmodic and isolated effort, was clearly unequal to the task it had set itself. A typical agreement, which Weymouth drafted with a private capitalist after his triumph in North Virginia, illustrates the narrow conception which continued to blight the outlook. Weymouth accepted a private capitalist's offer to finance a second voyage to the district of Maine in order to secure independent possession of the country. Two tracts of land of unlimited area were to be mapped out, of which one was to be seized in perpetual and unconditional ownership by the capitalist, and the other by the exploring captain. The English Crown's proprietorship of American soil seemed still an undiscovered principle.

But no sooner was Weymouth's agreement drawn up than the national conception of colonial endeavour suddenly took concrete shape. James I intervened to claim as his own the whole of the vaguely defined territory of Virginia whether in northern or southern latitudes. Abstract right had no obvious place in the royal declaration, and those who study it in solely the light of after-events may denounce it. But a close survey of contemporary conditions and experience justifies no adverse criticism. Not otherwise could the need of the time be met.

In the year 1606 the course which English colonial enterprise had hitherto pursued was justly summed up in these matter-of-fact contemporary words: 'Private purses are cold comforts to adventurers and have ever been found fatal to all enterprises hitherto undertaken, by reason of delays, jealousies, and unwillingness to back that project which succeeded not at the first attempt.' Unless in reasonable conditions public authority pledged public credit, the colonial future looked in 1606 no brighter than in the old century. Without change of method the Atlantic voyagers were likely to labour on bootless errands till the day of doom. By royal intervention the path to Jamestown was finally won, and as a corollary the future of New England was assured. National responsibility was proclaimed for colonial endeavour, which, for lack of such nourishment, had wellnigh perished.

James I's assertion of sovereignty over North America was not made precipitately. The first suggestion of practical definition and reform of colonizing method came to Jacobean England from Holland, which now, after long delay, was cherishing to effective purpose colonial ambitions. The Dutch Government had created a stock or fund to be applied to colonial experiments. The English Parliament was petitioned to institute, after the Dutch model, a guaranteed American stock. The proposal was coldly received; it did not go far enough. Steady supplies of capital were one essential to colonial expansion. But it was not the only, nor indeed the primary, need. A central control under authoritative influence was the more imperative requirement. No mere manipulations of finance could build a road to salvation.

Financial devices other than a Government stock were, too, more familiar to English merchants, aimed at the same ends, and had a better chance of adoption. The system of private joint-stock companies for purposes of foreign trade was already known to England. Joint-stock experiments had been made for the promotion of private trade with Russia and various populous regions of the East. But in spite of the recent growth of colonial aspirations among men of wealth and position in London and the chief centres of southern England, the joint-stock principle of trade seemed in the shifting light of past experience inapplicable on any adequate scale to unsettled America. Definite security for a permanent occupation and colonization of unpeopled lands in America under English law must be forthcoming first. Two associations of knights, gentlemen, merchants, and others, one at London and the other at Plymouth, examined the possibilities of the situation, and were willing to face risks in the American cause, provided that the state identified itself with their effort, and assumed supreme control of and responsibility for American colonization.

The problem was solved on the 10th of April 1606, by James I's formal announcement that the King of England had annexed a tract of territory six hundred and sixty miles long and one hundred miles broad, stretching along the American coast, with all adjacent islands, between the latitudes of 34 and 45 degrees. The sea-board of America from the bay of Fundy off the State of Maine to a southern point of the State of North Carolina was declared to be an English province under the perpetual rule of the English monarch. There was irony in the declaration as well as something like lawless usurpation. A long expanse of the stated line of coast was still veiled from English vision. English seamen had hitherto evaded the barrier-strip between 'south' and 'north' Virginia, the heart of which was pierced by the Hudson river. The land destined by history for the empire State of the American Republic fell within the boundaries of James I's asserted sovereignty when the king formally attached mid-North-America to the dominions of England and Scotland; but no Englishman was yet conscious that such territory existed. Some years later Robert Hudson, an Englishman in the Dutch service, first brought to the knowledge of his fellow-countrymen that their Virginian realm was cut asunder by an unsuspected central region. Fate reserved that intervening land for dominion by Dutch colonial competitors through more than half a century.

James I's royal scheme, which owed much to the example of Spain, at once came into operation. A central body, vested with supreme authority over all American affairs, was instituted in London under the title of the

King's Council of Virginia. It was a pale reflection of the Council of the Indies at Madrid.

The main obstacle to the application of joint-stock enterprise to American affairs was now removed, and that mercantile machinery was tentatively applied to the royal colonial scheme. Under the royal council's auspices, two joint-stock companies, formed respectively of London and Plymouth capitalists, were brought to birth, and definite colonial functions were devised for them. To each company was allotted the duty of planting at its own expense a separate colony in the New World. The two settlements were to be cut off from one another by a border measuring 100 miles. The London company was to plant its colony in the southern region of Virginia, which so many clouds had darkened. The Plymouth company was appointed for the northern region, where the sky of late looked bright.

Far as the colonial idea had progressed, it was unequal to the task of contriving an organization that would work easily. The fortuitous methods of the past were replaced by new codes of cut-and-dried instruction. The regulations formed a blended mosaic of both home and foreign experience, but the pattern was lacking in adaptability to circumstance. The central council of London was to appoint in each colony a local council to fulfil its instructions and orders. No strokes of the royal pen could prevent friction among the wheels within the new engine. The local council was free to elect and depose its own president, to coin money, to repel intruders, and to administer criminal law. But safeguards abounded against any assertion of independence of the dictates of London. Orders from home left little to the discretion of the men on the spot. Directions were framed how to choose sites for settlements and on what plan to raise buildings. For five years colonists were to hold all property and produce, not individually, but in common. The introduction of a principle of communism, however novel and suggestive, was a sure invitation to embittered controversy.

The relations of the colony to the outside world were also over-elaborately defined. High tariffs were imposed to discourage attempts of foreigners to trade with the new settlements. For seven years necessaries might be imported from the home country free of duty. In his claim to personal profit from the colony the King kept well within the bounds of legal tradition. He merely asserted conventional royal rights to a proportional produce of mines. To him were due one-fifth of all the gold and silver ore and one-fifteenth of all the copper ore that might be discovered.

The immediate sequel to King James's pompous entry on the American stage is more exhilarating when surveyed from a distance than when examined close at hand. The London Company, to whom old or South Virginia had been assigned for colonial experiment, was first in the field to make trial of the new system.

The slate had been cleaned, and there was a prejudice against raising the English flag anew on the site of the old Elizabethan settlement. Many miles to the north of that island scene of tragedy were the Jacobean foundations of Jamestown laid on the mainland. The spirit of disaster was not at once exorcised. At the outset most of the old difficulties revived. Insubordination and antipathy to hard work exposed the new settlement to the ancient perils. Notes of despair were sounded, and within a year plans of abandonment were entertained. But there were now protecting bulwarks which proved equal to the strain of impatience and discontent. The home communication was no longer uncertain. Intercourse with England was maintained with regularity. Both in London and in Jamestown there were men who constituted themselves champions of the nation's colonial prestige, and they preached to the colonists the doctrine of endurance and the gospel of hard work. Among the first Jamestown settlers none worked harder in the colonial cause than the invincible Captain John Smith. Under such inspiration the early storms were weathered, and Virginia passed permanently from the dark Elizabethan shadows of blighted hopes into the sunshine of strength and prosperity.

Progress of the new system in the North faced, despite recent prohibitous portents, a greater initial peril. In North Virginia the first step in the Jacobean advance proved false. A year after the London Company initiated its work at Jamestown, the Plymouth company set out to fulfil its task in the North. A settlement was formed at Sagahadoc on the river Kennebec in Maine, the scene of Gosnold's and of Pring's exploits. The trials of winter, which tried to the uttermost the Jamestown planters, wholly conquered the energies of Sagahadoc. That colony re-enacted the Elizabethan story of failure. Four years later Captain John Smith, who had infected Jamestown in its first days with his self-assertive confidence, once more sailed to North Virginia and resurveyed colonial chances. A great triumph was scored when he formally christened the region New England. By word and pen he taught the obligation of giving as full effect to James I's proclamation of American sovereignty in New England as in the land that centred in Jamestown. The two spheres of occupation were lawfully knit together, and the great scheme of 1606 was shapeless without a northern colony as equipoise to a southern settlement.

It was the yearning for religious freedom that put into Smith's plea for the North the breath of life. The Puritan exiles in Holland, while resolute to safeguard liberty of conscience, longed to renew their allegiance to their king and country. Many of them had from of old believed America to be the fated goal of their wanderings, but the precise region was long in question. Some of them had debated whether scope for their ideals might not be found in untenanted districts of the South American continent, in spite of the proximity to Spain. It was only after much deliberation and hesitation that they chose migration to New England. They were conscious there of the risk to their faith from the dominant religious establishment in

England. But patriotic sentiment turned the scale in favour of a land that the English King now formally claimed as his own. The patriotic Puritan's surest hope in 1620 of the untried solitudes of North Virginia or New England came from the knowledge that the tangled path to Jamestown in South Virginia had been won in 1607, in spite of all the disquieting Elizabethan memories, and was at length open and secure.

INDEX

Alexander the Great, 46, 57.
Alphonse, Jean, 236–7.
Amyot, Jacques, 34, 46.
Angellier, A., 24.
Angelo, Michael, 144, 166.
Ariosto, 36, 62, 152, 154–5, 170, 173;
  Orlando Furioso, 178.
Aristotle, 106, 142.
Asquith, H. H. (Lord Oxford), on
  Biography in *Occasional Addresses*,
  58–9.
Avila, Don Pedro Menendez de, 253.

Bacon, Francis, 3, 19, 28–30, 43, 106–7,
  148, 155–6, 186, 242, 287–8, 289;
  Advancement of Learning, 29, 107;
  History of Henry VII, 186.
Bandello, 111, 162–5.
Barlow, Captain, 274.
Barrow, Isaac, 14 n.
Beaumont, Francis, 176.
Bembo, Cardinal, 116, 145, 150, 157,
  161–2.
Bercuire, Pierre, 116.
Berger, P., 24.
Berreo, Antonio de, 228.
Blake, William, 24, 173.
Boccaccio, 48, 111, 143, 162–3, 165,
  168.
Boileau, 175.
Boscan, 177.
Boswell, James, 52–5, 62–3, 66, 69,
  73–4, 81, 91; *Life of Johnson*, 52–5,
  64, 80.
Bowes, Sir Martin, 256.
Bradley, A. C., 31 n.; *Oxford Lectures
  on Poetry*, 95 n.
Brandes, George, 92.
Browning, Elizabeth Barrett, 168.
Browning, Robert, 32, 87, 89, 90, 115,
  168; *At the Mermaid*, 93–4.
Bruno, Giordano, 137, 152–4, 157,
  167; *Gli Eroici Furori*, 153; *Spaccio
  de la Bestia Trionfante*, 153.
Burke, Edmund, 91.
Burns, Robert, 24.
Byron, Lord, 41, 168, 174–5.

Cabot, John, 147, 197, 201–2, 268.
Cabot, Sebastian, 212–15, 219.
Caesar, Julius, 35, 43, 46, 125.
Calderon, 188.
Calvin, John, 242, 244–5, 247.
Campanella, Tommaso, 160.
Campbell, Lord, 42.
Canaletto, 63.
Carew, Richard, 180.
Carlyle, Jane Welsh, 69, 70.
Carlyle, Thomas, 32, 45, 63–6, 69, 70,
  73, 79, 81, 87, 93; *Life of Sterling*, 64.
Cartier, Jacques, 234–40, 258.
Castiglione, Baldassare, *Il Cortegiano*,
  150.
Catullus, 125, 141.
Cavendish, Thomas, 223, 298, 319–20.
Caxton, William, 117.
Celestina, 187.
Cervantes, 188.
Challeux, Nicholas le, 257.
Challons, Henry, 328.
Champlain, Samuel de, 237–8, 255.
Chapman, George, 287, 288.
Charles I, King of England, 180.
Charles II, King of England, 251.
Charles IX, King of France, 250.
Chartier, Guillaume, 245, 247.
Chaucer, Geoffrey, 87, 170.
Chaucer Society, 21, 168.
Cicero, 47, 91, 141.
Cinthio, Giraldo, 111–12, 163, 165–6.
Cobbett, William, *Advice to Young
  Men*, 17 n.
Cockeram, Martin, 270.
Coleridge, S. T., 40, 93, 107, 152.
Colet, John, 149.
Coligny, Admiral, 244–5, 249–51.
Collins, William, 175, 181.
Columbus, Christopher, 147, 197,
  200–1, 205, 211, 219, 225, 230, 266,
  297.
Columbus, Diego, 200.
Cortes, Hernando, 197, 216, 225.
Cortes, Martin, 216, 221.
Courthope, W. J., 22, 26.
Cowper, William, 173.

Daniel, Samuel, 155, 176.
Dante, 22, 48, 142, 152, 168, 170; *De Vulgari Eloquentia*, 116; *Inferno*, 125.
Darwin, Charles, 32.
Davis, John, 221–3, 268, 320.
De Bry, 257.
Dekker, Thomas, 182.
Demosthenes, 47.
D'Este, Alfonso, 172.
D'Este, Leonora, 172.
Dickens, Charles, 87.
Dictionary of National Biography, 22, 29, 45–6, 61.
Disraeli, Benjamin, 43.
Dolce, Ludovico, 116.
Doumic, René, 107.
Dowden, Edward, 92.
Drake, Sir Francis, 207, 223, 227, 259, 275, 298, 302, 305, 310, 314–15, 319–21.
Drayton, Michael, 287.
Dryden, John, 11, 117, 175, 181.
Du Bartas, 177.
Durand, Nicholas, Seigneur de Ville-gagnon, 244–9, 254, 258.

Eden, Richard, 215, 218–19, 221, 257.
Edward VI, King of England, 213–15.
Eliot, George, 60, 87.
Elizabeth, Queen of England, 20, 45, 75, 103, 117, 172, 180, 182, 185, 220, 238, 243, 264, 266, 271–3, 287, 299, 302, 305, 308, 310, 314, 318–19.
Ellis, A. J., 26.
Elstob, Elizabeth, 21.
Emerson, R. W., 92–4, 97, 100–1, 115.
Encyclopaedia Britannica, 39.
Epenow, a Redskin, 282.
Ercilla, Alonzo de, 218.

Fairfax, Edward, 180–1.
Feuillerat, A., 24.
Ficino, 137.
Fitzgerald, Edward, 32.
Fletcher, John, 193; *The Faithful Shepherdess*, 176–7.
Francis I, King of France, 117, 234–5.
Franklin, Benjamin, 59.
Frobisher, Sir Martin, 221, 223, 271–4, 307–8, 310, 312.

Froissart, *Chronicles*, 186.
Froude, Anthony, 32, 66, 79, 81; *Life of Carlyle*, 64, 79.
Fuller, Thomas, 34, 60.
Furnivall, F. J., 21, 26.

Galileo, 146.
Galton, Sir Francis, 45.
Gamboa, Sarmiento de, 226–8.
Garcilaso, 177.
Gayangos, Señor, 190.
Gentili, Alberico, 152.
Gibbon, Edmund, 26.
Gifford, Captain, 278.
Gilbert, Captain Bartholomew, 326.
Gilbert, Sir Humphrey, 221, 223, 258, 307–13, 317–18, 326.
Gladstone, William Ewart, 43, 50.
Godfrey, of Bouillon, 169, 171, 181.
Goethe, J. W., 87, 182.
Golding, Arthur, translation of *Metamorphoses*, 117–21, 124, 128–37.
Gomara, 219, 221.
Gondomar, Count de, 189–90.
Gonneville, Captain de, 239–40.
Goodwin, Hugh, 278.
Gosnold, Bartholomew, 318–19, 325–8, 334.
Gouge, William, 285.
Gourgues, Le Sieur Dominique de, 254, 258.
Gray, Thomas, 175.
Grenville, Sir Richard, 226–7.
Grimm, Jacob, 21.
Grocyn, William, 149.
Guarini, *Pastor Fido*, 176–7.

Hakluyt, Richard, 219, 222, 224, 258–9, 273, 302; *Virginia rightly valued*, 225.
Haldane, Lord, 13.
Hall, Captain C. F., 308.
Hare, Archdeacon, 69.
Hariot, Thomas, 314–16.
Harvey, William, 156.
Hawkins, Sir John, 223, 252–3, 259, 302, 310.
Hawkins, William, 202, 270.
Heere, Lucas de, 273.
Henry VII, King of England, 200, 264.

Henry VIII, King of England, 212, 264, 269–70, 322.
Henry II, King of France, 241.
Heywood, Thomas, 81, 181.
Hoby, Sir Edward, 150.
Holinshed, Ralph, *Chronicles*, 110–12.
Homer, 125, 171, 177–8.
Hoole, John, 181.
Horace, 123.
Howard, Lady Frances, 288.
Howell, James, 187.
Hudson, Robert, 331.

Inquisition the, as censor of books, 186–8; its expurgation of a Shakespeare second folio, 184, 188–94; in the New World, 209–10.
Isabella, Queen of Spain, 266, 272.

James I, King of England, 103, 172, 180, 266, 280, 284, 288, 321–5, 328–35.
Johnson, Samuel, 35, 52–5, 59, 63–6, 69, 73, 78, 80–1; *Life of Savage*, 79; *Lives of the Poets*, 63, 74.
Jones, Inigo, 287.
Jonson, Ben, 89, 176, 284, 287; *The Faithful Sheperd* (*sic*) apparently for *The Sad Shepherd*, 177.
Julius II, Pope, 239.
Jusserand, J. J., 24.

Keats, John, 167, 175, 181.
Keymis, Laurence, 228.
Kitchin, Dean, 107.
Knivet, Anthony, 249.

Lamb, Charles, 181.
Lancaster, Sir James, 259.
Landor, W. S., 175.
Lane, Ralph, 296.
Las Casas, Bartolomeo, 209–10, 221.
Laudonnière, René de, 251–3.
Legouis, Emile, 24.
Leigh, Captain Charles, 279, 317, 323, 326–7.
Le Moyne, 251, 253, 257.
Leonardo da Vinci, 146.
Linacre, Thomas, 149.
Lockhart, John Gibson, *Life of Scott*, 54–5, 64, 66, 80.
Lodge, Thomas, 164.

Lok, Michael, 219.
Lope de Vega, 188.
Louis XII, King of France, 239.
Louis XIV, King of France, 194.
Lowell, James Russell, 32.
Lucretius, 138.
Luther, Martin, 242.
Lyly, John, 24; *Euphues*, 171.

Macaulay, T. B., 26, 87, 198.
Mace, Samuel, 317–18.
Mackail, J. W., *Henry Birkhead and the Foundation of the Oxford Chair of Poetry*, 14 n.
Magellan, 215.
Mandeville, Sir John, 261.
Manso, 175.
Manteo, a Redskin, 275–7.
Marcus Aurelius, 127.
Marlowe, Christopher, 286–7, 289.
Marot, Clément, 116, 246, 252.
Martyr, Peter, 208; *Decades of the Ocean*, 219.
Mary, Queen of England, 216–20, 243, 264, 271.
Mary, Queen of Scots, 44, 75.
Masson, David, *Life of John Milton*, 45.
Matchumps, a Redskin, 282.
May, Phil, 50–1.
Medici, Catherine de, 241.
Mendel, Gregor, 39.
Meredith, George, 32.
Meres, Francis, *Palladis Tamia*, 124–5.
Milton, John, 3, 13, 45, 61, 159, 168, 175; *Apology for Smectymnus*, 12 n.; *Lycidas*, 13 n.
Mirandola, Pico della, 146, 149, 150, 156–7.
Molière, 103.
Montaigne, 173, 241–2, 269, 292–3; *Essays*, 117–18.
Moore, Thomas, *Life of Byron*, 65.
More, Hannah, 53, 73.
More, Henry, 185–6.
More, Sir Thomas, 150, 185, 211; *The Utopia*, 149, 211, 241, 269; *Works*, 186.
Morley, Lord, *Life of Gladstone*, 50, 80.

Namoutack, a Redskin, 282–3.
Nanamack, a Redskin, 283.

Napoleon I, 35, 40.
Napoleon III, 40.
Nelson, Lord, 38, 41.
Newbolt, Sir Henry, *Minora Sidera*, 61.
New English Dictionary, 21, 29.
Nicholas, Thomas, 217.
North, Sir T., translation of Plutarch's *Lives*, 111–12, 171.
Noyer, Captain, 259.

Ovid, 140; *Amores*, 124; *Fasti*, 125; *Metamorphoses*, 116–18; translations of, 117; Shakespeare's familiarity with, 118–23; influence on the *Sonnets*, 123–39; *Tristia*, 123.

Paolo Veronese, 152.
Paris, Mathew, *Chronica Majora*, 186.
Parker, Archbishop, 186.
Parnell, C. S., 41.
Parsons, Father, 184, 324.
Pater, Walter, 7, 93.
Peend, Thomas, 117.
Penry, John, 323.
Pepys, Samuel, 59.
Petrarch, 116, 143, 151, 155, 166, 170.
Philip II, King of Spain, 184–5, 188, 217–20.
Pindar, 123.
Pizarro, 197, 225.
Plato, 19, 106, 137, 143–4, 149, 166.
Pliny, 261.
Plotinus, 137.
Plutarch, 34, 46–9, 53, 72, 110–12, 114, 171.
Pocahontas, daughter of Powhatan, 283–5, 289.
Politian, 116.
Popham, Sir John, 328.
Porson, Samuel, 41.
Powhatan, a Redskin, 282–3, 289.
Priestley, Joseph, 55.
Primaticcio, 117.
Pring, Martin, 326–8, 334.
Purchas, Samuel, 284.
Pythagoras, 126, 128–9, 134.

Quevedo, 188.

Rabelais, 116, 236–7, 241, 258.
Raleigh, Professor, Sir Walter, 92–3.

Raleigh, Sir Walter, 178, 223–9, 257–9, 274–9, 296–7, 312–18; *History of the World*, 186.
Raphael, 161–2.
Regapo, Leonard, 279.
Ribaut, Jean, 250–4, 256–7.
Richardson, Samuel, 87.
Richer, Pierre, 245–6.
Roberval, Le Sieur de, 236–7.
Rolfe, Henry, 284.
Romano, Julio, 160, 161.
Ronsard, 123, 174, 241.
Roosevelt, Theodore, 300.
Rossa, 117.
Rousseau, Jean Jacques, 59; *Confessions*, 91.
Ruskin, John, 32, 64.

St. Gelais, Mellin de, 237.
Saintsbury, George, 22.
Sanazzaro, 151–2.
Sanchez, Guillén, 188–90.
Sandys, George, 117.
Savage, Richard, 78.
Savile, Sir Henry, *Rerum Anglicanarum post Bedam scriptores praecipui*, 186.
Scott, Sir Walter, 80, 87, 93, 109, 115.
Seneca, 127.
Shakespeare, Judith, 113.
Shakespeare, William, 4, 10, 12, 20, 37–8, 49, 50, 52, 72, 81, 140–6, 148, 150–2, 154–5, 170–1, 173–5, 181–3, 197–8, 200, 221, 280, 283, 285–6, 327; as a Renaissance humanist, 156–8; expurgation of second folio at Valladolid, 184, 188–94; familiarity with Ovid in Golding's version, 117–39; Italian influence on, 158–68; the American Indians in his plays, 289–99; the impersonal aspect of his art, 85–115.
All's Well that Ends Well, 97 n., 163, 191, 291.
Antony and Cleopatra, 101, 110–12, 190.
As You Like It, 101, 119, 121, 163–4, 191, 290.
Comedy of Errors, 190–1, 290.
Coriolanus, 97 n., 101, 104–5, 110–12, 188, 190.

Cymbeline, 102, 104, 163, 190.
Hamlet, 85, 101–4, 156, 182, 193–4.
King Henry IV, Part I, 95, 191.
King Henry IV, Part II, 95, 131, 190.
King Henry V, 97, 104.
King Henry VI, Part I, 191.
King Henry VI, Part II, 191.
King Henry VI, Part III, 190.
King Henry VIII, 12 n., 104, 192–3.
King John, 104, 119, 192.
King Lear, 101–2, 104, 111–12, 193.
Julius Caesar, 97 n., 190.
Love's Labour's Lost, 118, 159, 176, 191, 290.
Lucrece, 122–4.
Macbeth, 85, 101, 103, 107, 111–12, 120, 193.
Measure for Measure, 111, 163, 165.
Merchant of Venice, 98, 104, 159, 191.
Merry Wives of Windsor, 95, 121, 190–1, 290.
Midsummer Night's Dream, 190.
Much Ado about Nothing, 101, 104, 121, 163, 191.
Othello, 101–2, 105, 107, 111, 159, 164, 190.
Pericles, 114.
Richard II, 13 n., 104, 190.
Richard III, 104, 190.
Romeo and Juliet, 97 n., 104, 163, 165, 190, 194.
Sonnets, 88, 172; Ovid's influence on, 123–39.
Taming of the Shrew, 95, 120, 190.
Tempest, 102, 113–14, 120, 191, 291–9.
Timon of Athens, 114, 161, 190.
Titus Andronicus, 119–20, 190.
Troilus and Cressida, 97 n., 193.
Twelfth Night, 101, 104, 129, 165, 190.
Two Gentlemen of Verona, 97 n., 176, 190.
Venus and Adonis, 122–4, 138, 159 n.
Winter's Tale, 102, 104, 114, 160, 163, 190.
Shelley, Percy Bysshe, 41, 91, 168, 172, 175.
Sidgwick, Henry, 32.

Sidney, Sir Philip, 151–4, 171, 177, 257, 311; *Apology for Poetry*, 152, 171; *Arcadia*, 151.
Slaney, John, 281.
Smith, Captain John, 297, 333–4.
Somerset, Earl of, 288.
Southampton, Earl of, 280–1, 293, 327.
Sparrow, Francis, 278–9.
Speed, John, *History of England*, 189.
Spencer, Herbert, 59, 87.
Spenser Edmund, 155, 159, 170, 175, 177; *Faerie Queene*, 137–8, 154, 174, 178–80; *Shepherd's Calendar*, 171.
Squanto, a Redskin, 281.
Stephanus, 116.
Stephen, Leslie, 26, 31–4, 49, 55, 61 n.
Sterling, John, 68–70.
Stevenson, R. L., 10, 34; *Memories and Portraits*, 11 n.
Strachey, William, 297.
Stukeley, Thomas, 301, 302.
Suetonius, 34, 40.
Swift, Jonathan, 74.
Swinburne, A. C., 168.

Tacitus, 34, 141.
Talma, 108.
Tamacomo, a Redskin, 284.
Tantum, a Redskin, 281.
Tasso, Torquato, 154–5, 169–83; *Aminta*, 172, 175–7; *Gerusalemme Liberata*, 171–2, 174, 178; translations of, 180–1; dramatic versions of, 181–2; *Il Padre di Famiglia*, 178; translation of, 178; *Rinaldo*, 171; *Tasso's Melancholy*, 182.
Telesio, 155.
Tennyson, Alfred, Lord, 32, 41, 72–3, 87.
Thevet, André, 258.
Thorne, Robert, 212.
Thorpe, Benjamin, 26.
Tintoretto, 116, 144, 152.
Tirso de Molina, 188.
Titian, 116, 144.
Topiawari, a Redskin, 277–9.
Torquemada, 188.
Toynbee, Paget, 22.

Valdivia, General, 217.

Vasari, 161.
Verrazano, Giovanni de, 234.
Vespucci, Amerigo, 211–12.
Virgil, 125, 141–2, 175, 177–8.
Virgilio, Giovanni del, 116.
Voltaire, 148.

Waller, Edmund, 180–1.
Walton, Izaak, 40.
Wanchese, a Redskin, 275.
Warton, Thomas, *History of English Poetry*, 22.

Webbe, William, *A Discourse of English Poetry*, 127.
Wellington, Duke of, 37.
Wesley, John, 59.
Weymouth, George, 280, 327–9.
White, John, 275–6, 316.
Wordsworth, William, 24, 42, 175, 181.
Wright, Edward, 221.
Wyclif Society, 21.

Zarate, Augustine de, 216–17, 221.